T0339747

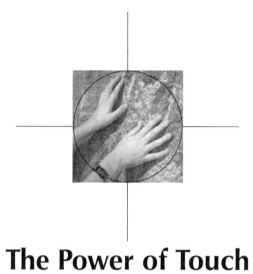

The Power of Touch

Publications of the
INSTITUTE OF ARCHAEOLOGY, UNIVERSITY COLLEGE LONDON
Director of the Institute, Stephen Shennan
Founding Series Editor, Peter J. Ucko

The Institute of Archaeology of University College London is one of the oldest, largest and most prestigious archaeology research facilities in the world. Its extensive publications programme includes the best theory, research, pedagogy, and reference materials in archaeology and cognate disciplines, through publishing exemplary work of scholars worldwide. Through its publications, the Institute brings together key areas of theoretical and substantive knowledge, improves archaeological practice and brings archaeological findings to the general public, researchers, and practitioners. It also publishes staff research projects, site and survey reports, and conference proceedings. The publications programme, formerly developed in-house or in conjunction with UCL Press, is now produced in partnership with Left Coast Press, Inc. The Institute can be accessed online at http://www.ucl.ac.uk/archaeology.

ENCOUNTERS WITH ANCIENT EGYPT *Subseries, Peter J. Ucko, editor*

Jean-Marcel Humbert and Clifford Price (eds.), *Imhotep Today*
David Jeffreys (ed.), *Views of Ancient Egypt since Napoleon Bonaparte*
Sally MacDonald and Michael Rice (eds.), *Consuming Ancient Egypt*
Roger Matthews and Cornelia Roemer (eds.), *Ancient Perspectives on Egypt*
David O'Connor and Andrew Reid (eds.), *Ancient Egypt in Africa*
John Tait (ed.), *"Never Had the Like Occurred"*
David O'Connor and Stephen Quirke (eds.), *Mysterious Lands*
Peter Ucko and Timothy Champion (eds.), *The Wisdom of Egypt*

CRITICAL PERSPECTIVES ON CULTURAL HERITAGE *Subseries, Beverley Butler, editor*

Beverley Butler, *Return to Alexandria*
Ferdinand de Jong and Michael Rowlands (eds.), *Reclaiming Heritage*
Dean Sully (ed.), *Decolonising Conservation*

OTHER TITLES

Andrew Gardner (ed.), *Agency Uncovered*
Okasha El-Daly, *Egyptology, The Missing Millennium*
Ruth Mace, Clare J. Holden, and Stephen Shennan (eds.), *Evolution of Cultural Diversity*
Arkadiusz Marciniak, *Placing Animals in the Neolithic*
Robert Layton, Stephen Shennan, and Peter Stone (eds.), *A Future for Archaeology*
Joost Fontein, *The Silence of Great Zimbabwe*
Gabriele Puschnigg, *Ceramics of the Merv Oasis*
James Graham-Campbell and Gareth Williams (eds.), *Silver Economy in the Viking Age*
Barbara Bender, Sue Hamilton, and Chris Tilley, *Stone Worlds*
Andrew Gardner, *An Archaeology of Identity*
Sue Hamilton, Ruth Whitehouse, and Katherine I. Wright (eds.) *Archaeology and Women*
Gustavo Politis, *Nukak*
Sue Colledge and James Conolly (eds.), *The Origins and Spread of Domestic Plants in Southwest Asia and Europe*
Timothy Clack and Marcus Brittain (eds), *Archaeology and the Media*
Janet Picton, Stephen Quirke, and Paul C. Roberts (eds.), *Living Images*
Tony Waldron, *Paleoepidemiology*
Eleni Asouti and Dorian Q. Fuller, *Trees and Woodlands of South India*
Russell McDougall and Iain Davidson (eds.), *The Roth Family, Anthropology, and Colonial Administration*
Elizabeth Pye (ed.), *The Power of Touch*
John Tait, *Why the Egyptians Wrote Books*

The Power of Touch
Handling Objects in Museum and Heritage Contexts

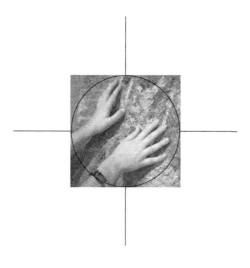

Elizabeth Pye
Editor

Routledge
Taylor & Francis Group
LONDON AND NEW YORK

First published 2007 by Left Coast Press, Inc.

Published 2016 by Routledge
4 Park Square, Milton Park, Abingdon, Oxon OX14 4RN
605 Third Avenue, New York, NY 10017

Routledge is an imprint of the Taylor & Francis Group, an informa business

Library of Congress Cataloging-in-Publication Data:

The power of touch: handling objects in museum and heritage contexts/Elizabeth Pye, editor.
    p. cm. — (Publications of the Institute of Archaeology, University College London)
    ISBN 978-1-59874-303-6 (hardback : alk. paper)
    ISBN 978-1-59874-304-3 (pbk. : alk. paper)

1. Antiquities—Collection and preservation—Social aspects. 2. Antiquities—Collection and preservation—Psychological aspects. 3. Cultural property—Protection—Social aspects. 4. Cultural property—Protection—Psychological aspects. 5. Touch—Social aspects. 6. Touch—Psychological aspects. 7. Museums—Social aspects. 8. Museums—Psychological aspects. I. Pye, Elizabeth.
    CC175.P69 2007   363.6'9—dc22

ISBN 978-1-59874-303-6 (hbk)
ISBN 978-1-59874-304-3 (pbk)

For Peter Ucko (1938–2007)

CONTENTS

LIST OF ILLUSTRATIONS

PREFACE

This volume arose from a very successful one-day conference entitled 'Magic Touch' held at the Institute of Archaeology, University College London, in December 2004. The conference was organised by Sally MacDonald, with help from Beverley Butler and from me. The intention was to publish the papers, and these form a large part of the book. The aim of both the conference and the book is to encourage discussion and re-evaluation of the use of touch in museums and other heritage contexts. As editor, I elicited a number of additional papers from colleagues in order to widen the coverage of the volume, and to present, as far as possible, a picture of current issues and activities focused on touch and handling in these contexts.

I have dedicated the book to Peter Ucko in affectionate gratitude for his encouragement. At the time of the conference Peter was both Director of the Institute of Archaeology and Chair of our Publications Committee. At the end of the conference, in typical fashion, he issued me with a challenge by saying 'I don't know how you're going to get a book out of that!' Despite this comment he supported the planned publication, but sadly he died in June 2007, and I will not discover what he might have thought of the final product.

I am very grateful to all the contributors for their forbearance in the face of numerous editorial requests. I am also grateful to the unknown referees for their comments, and to the Institute of Archaeology's Publications Committee for its support. I would like to acknowledge Sage Publications Ltd for permission to reproduce a slightly shortened version of Fiona Candlin's paper "Don't Touch! Hands Off! Art, Blindness, and the Conservation of Expertise" as Chapter 5 in this volume. The paper was originally published in 2004, under the same title, in *Body & Society*, volume 10 (© Sage Publications, 2004). I am also grateful to the individuals who gave permission for use of their illustrations. The book's contributors own copyright for nearly all the illustrations in the book; captions indicate where this is not the case.

Finally, I would like to thank very warmly my immediate colleagues at UCL Institute of Archaeology, James Hales, Renata Peters and Dean Sully, as well as my family, especially Nick and Fran Balaam. All have given me useful ideas and much appreciated encouragement, and have nobly tolerated my preoccupation with this volume, particularly during the past year.

Magdalen, Norfolk
July 2007

INTRODUCTION:
THE POWER OF TOUCH

Elizabeth Pye

For many people, visiting museums is associated with the injunction 'Do Not Touch'. This book is about the touching and handling of objects, particularly museum objects. It aims to look at what we know (or do not know) about touch, to examine some of our preconceptions and prejudices about touch, to explore why touch may be forbidden to the visitor, and to provide examples of current practice involving touch in museums. For both museum professionals and the more general reader this book encourages a re-evaluation of the role of touch in the study and appreciation of objects.

Ashley Montagu produced his important book, *Touching: The Human Significance of the Skin,* in 1971 but few other publications on the topic followed; recently, however, there has been a resurgence of interest in the senses generally, including the sense of touch (see Classen 1993, 2005a; Harvey 2003; Howes 2003). Pressures on museums to widen audiences and provide increased access to their collections (Hooper-Greenhill 1997; DCMS 1999) have underlined the importance of touch and handling as a form of access to museum collections.

We handle things all the time in our daily lives. Some handling is for everyday purposes (positioning objects in our work spaces, repairing bicycles) some is involved with assessing quality (the weight and texture of fabric in a shop) some is involved with learning (using books, playing musical instruments), some is pure enjoyment (playing board games). Similar kinds of handling take place in museums. Some is professional, some is by volunteers, some is by visitors. However, despite this frequency, the role of touch in museums is seldom debated. The way touch happens and who does it is controlled by the culture of museums so that some handling is taken for granted, some of it is hedged round with precautions, and some of it is hard-won.

The Fascination of Objects

Our own possessions may be comfortably familiar, and we may handle them without much thought. By contrast, unfamiliar objects can be intriguing. Our interest in trying them out, or discovering more about them, is what leads us to touch them. As Lubar and Kingery (1993, 3) put it:

> Artifacts constitute the only class of historical events that occurred in the past but survive into the present.

For this reason alone, many people are fascinated by old objects and seek them out through metal detecting or combing antique shops, and they preserve family heirlooms or join pressure groups to safeguard local historic monuments. Furthermore, objects may have as many different meanings, and provide as many different sources of pleasure or inspiration, as there are viewers:

> The object is inexhaustible ... the potential object is richer than any of its realizations. (Pearce 1994, 26)

The Senses

In Western thought touch is considered to be one of the five senses, and there was traditionally a hierarchy; the higher senses being sight and hearing and the lower senses taste, smell, and touch. While sight and hearing were considered masculine, dispassionate and intellectual, the lower senses were seen as feminine, sensual, and suspect (Classen 2005b). But human touch is bound up with emotional welfare, so, for example, the touch of the mother is known to be essential for the child to thrive (Montagu 1971; Synnott 1993). Touching things is an instinctive way in which we all test our surroundings; it is the way we learn as babies, and most of us retain this impulse into adult life. Our sense of touch gives us a sense of reality. For blind people it is an important way to sense the surrounding world.

Presumably because it was suspect, touch has been suppressed; Synnott (1993) describes early twentieth-century childcare guides that implied a mother's instinct to kiss and cuddle her baby was dangerous because babies should be treated as adults. In contrast, sight has been considered "our noblest sense" which "coincides with our noblest faculty, reason" (Synnott 1993, 209). Hence the primacy of the visual arts, set above even music, and the primacy of visual appreciation of our surroundings (Hall 1999).

There is more to discover about what creates and affects the sensations we receive through touch. While the functioning of nerves and muscles is well understood, other factors affect what we perceive about the object we are handling. Wing (Chapter 1) discusses experimental work which indicates that the ways we position our arms and use our hands (one hand or both hands) affect our appreciation of the weight of something we may be lifting. Spence (Chapter 2) shows that our senses do not operate in isolation; our perceptions of the qualities of what we are touching are affected both by sound and smell, as well as by what we see. These factors may well affect how museum specialists perceive objects; furthermore, this understanding may help us to design more satisfying and multisensory handling experiences in museums.

History of Touch

Touch has acquired some ambiguous, even contradictory, connotations: 'touchy-feely' may be used to describe someone who is considered to be over-emotional or who trespasses on our private space; a 'touchy' person is quick to feel slighted, but to be touched by something or someone is to be affected by deep emotion; and so on. There are plenty of terms to indicate both pleasant (stroking) and unpleasant (jabbing) touch. Montagu (1971, 10–11) devotes more than a page to different connotations of touch and related terms.

When did these contradictory notions first emerge? It appears that touch may have 'always' had ambiguous associations. There is evidence from many early archaeological contexts, such as the Neolithic site of Çatalhöyük in Anatolia, that small objects like clay or stone figures had a significant role in the life of the community, but these are difficult to interpret—they may have been made, handled, and positioned to ensure good luck, or to curse (Hodder 2006). However, Geller (Chapter 3) gives us some insight into ancient attitudes to touch in his discussion of ancient Babylonian texts, which reveal that touch was associated with both harm and healing.

The concept of endowing objects with power, and transmitting the power through touch, can be seen in the use of religious relics, or of rosary beads, 'worry' beads, good luck charms, or lockets containing a photograph (or a lock of hair) of a loved person (which may be held or touched at times of stress). In the Catholic Christian tradition, relics contain what may be claimed to be fragments of the bodies of saints and the relic is touched or venerated during prayer or other religious activity. This may be meaningless, or possibly repugnant, to non-believers but powerful to some practising Catholics. Geisbusch (Chapter 4) discusses the status of relics today, the way in which they are circulated and used, and the uneasy views of the church authorities. He also examines the position of reliquaries now in museum collections, no longer 'in use' and often lacking the relic itself, they appear to have become works of art.

It is important for museum professionals to realise what a powerful, almost magical, experience touch can provide when handling something venerated. This does not have to be an obviously ritual object—it could be a Palaeolithic hand-axe awesome for its extraordinary age, or a slave yoke redolent of misery, to give two of many possible examples.

Touch: The Museum Taboo

The earliest collections in the Western world were created by elites (by royalty, the Church, and later by learned societies) and consisted of valued rare objects and curiosities. These collections were accessible to polite society, and visitors could look at and often handle the objects, rather as books may be in a library. The first public museums controlled access by their visitors (applications for tickets were required in advance for the British Museum—Wilson 1989), and the smaller portable objects were placed in glass cases, for security as much as for fear of damage. During the nineteenth century there was considerable reservation about letting the working classes into museums, and much discussion of the dangers of disorderliness (Bennett 1995).

The ban on touch has been rationalised as a measure to protect the collections from harm. Fear of theft was certainly an issue—and of damage to objects—but the position was strongly influenced by social factors. The hierarchy of the senses also applied to the hierarchy of class. The upper classes were linked to the higher senses but "according to the sensory classification of society a low social status translated into a bad smell" (Howes 2005b, 10). As smell is perceived to relate to cleanliness, the lower classes were seen as dirty. There was thus a perceived danger that objects in museums might be touched and defiled by the hands of the working classes, or be stolen by the light-fingered; hence, touch was banned, and as far as possible prevented, by glass cases or rope barriers. Candlin (Chapter 5) discusses similar suspicions of the blind, who were long seen as inferior in some way (or even as being afflicted with blindness as punishment for their sins), a view that changed only slowly (see Barasch 2001). The blind, therefore, were even more affected by the taboo on touch, given that this might be their only way to perceive the collections.

Museums are not neutral places; they can transmit powerful messages. Many early public museums were intended to have an educational role, so objects were arranged in groups or sequences to illustrate current theories about, for example, geology, or cultural practices in other parts of the world, or to display industrial production methods. Other messages were less overt. Museums have sometimes been likened to temples in which objects are venerated, enshrined in their glass cases, or to marketplaces in which objects are commodities (and many of the early nineteenth-century purpose-built public museums were constructed on a similar pattern to the large shopping emporia of the day). They have also been seen as colonising institutions where the objects were used to define people and their social and cultural roles (Bennett 1995; Marstine 2006).

Another way in which museums have exerted control is to distance the objects from visitors. Museums are full of objects, but most of these objects have been and are still inaccessible to the normal visitor; some museums have very large stored collections, but relatively few objects on display (Keene 2005). Museum objects are inaccessible in other ways: they are protected from the visitor by being displayed behind barriers, or in glass cases, or in low light levels. Some museum collections, or parts of collections, now exist as digital images which anyone with a computer can access through the Internet, but these are not 'flesh and blood' objects, and represent a tiny proportion of total museum holdings (24hourmuseum, Keene 1998).

If protecting objects from damage is not the only reason for this caution about touch, is it time to examine our prejudices and re-evaluate the ban on touch, particularly as the emphasis on *viewing* objects has made museum collections inaccessible to blind and partially sighted people, and robbed nearly everyone of the pleasure and magic of contact with objects?

Professional Touch

Despite the taboo on touching by the public, objects are being handled all the time behind the scenes in museums, though this is not generally evident to the casual visitor. It is accepted that handling is potentially damaging; most museums provide training for their staff and issue guidelines for safe handling (e.g. Miles 1992). Objects are touched or handled when they are assessed by curators, treated by conservators, positioned for photography or drawing, measured for storage boxes or display mounts, or placed on display. They are taken off shelves or out of cabinets then replaced again, they are loaded onto and unloaded from trolleys. If they are on open display, they are routinely cleaned.

One important area of activity focuses on identifying and researching objects. Research can take many forms (e.g. identifying the work of a single maker or artist, dating ceramics, tracing early ethnographic collections back to their source communities). Normally these activities involve examining the objects and mentally, or actually, comparing them with other possibly similar objects. This kind of intimate examination and appraisal is used to write detailed entries in exhibition catalogues, to distinguish between real and fake, and sometimes to re-attribute objects such as paintings, and it is often referred to as *connoisseurship* (Kirby Talley 1989; Phillips 1997). MacDonald (Chapter 6) interviewed a number of connoisseurs and curators and provides a vivid picture of the way they developed and practised their skills and how they examine an object. The impression is of a multisensory approach, in which touch plays an important part, and of an almost instinctive reaction to the object.

Unfortunately, connoisseurship has acquired a slightly suspect reputation because of this apparently instinctive reaction, because its basis is difficult to define, and because it is often linked to authentication and assignment of a monetary value. But connoisseurship is based on extensive knowledge and "is a powerful scholarly tool, permitting rapid distinction between what is true and what is false" (Prown 1993, 4). Conservators develop a similar intimacy with objects and are highly skilled at recognising materials, technology, and condition (Pye 2001). This focus on material evidence aids them in deciding on appropriate remedial or preventive measures to deal with existing damage or to prevent future change. They may also be involved in restoring objects (cleaning obscured surfaces, reconstructing areas of loss) in order to make objects more understandable when on display. It is often the partnership of connoisseur and conservator, working together to investigate and reveal a painting, that leads to attribution or re-attribution (Phillips 1997); each bringing a particular knowledge to bear on the study of the object.

For conservators, highly developed practical (tactile) skills are essential and many see these skills as defining their profession. Pye (Chapter 7) discusses the many ways in which touch enhances understanding of objects, the 'signature' that conservators may leave in the objects they treat, and the limits to conservation practice. Increasingly, however, conservation is becoming recognised as a social process (Munos Viñas 2005; Pye & Sully 2007). Since conservation inevitably changes objects, but objects may have great significance for some people, it is important that conservators seek the views of those who have an interest before deciding whether, or how, to touch them. Conservators are increasingly collaborating with interest groups such as source communities in order to develop agreed practice (Sully 2007, and see Johnson, Chapter 14).

Objects do get accidentally damaged when being handled in museums, even by comparatively experienced staff, but damage is more likely to happen when objects are being moved from one part of the museum to another or transported between institutions. Some conservators spend a high proportion of their time assessing objects in order to decide whether they are in suitable condition to be lent to other institutions. They or a colleague will prepare and pack objects for transport, and unpack and check them at each destination to monitor any signs of damage.

Curators and conservators accept the privilege of intimacy and daily contact with objects but have the professional responsibility for the collections in their care, so they may be hesitant to make the privilege of touch more freely available to others. Is the ban on touch perpetuated purely out of care for the collections? Candlin (Chapter 5) argues that originally the ban was linked not just to suspicion of the blind and other possibly undesirable visitors, but to the curators' desire to protect their status, as represented by their expertise. This suggestion reinforces the argument in favour of re-evaluating our attitudes to touch and to who is allowed to touch.

Benefits of Touch

Current theory emphasises the importance of both children and adults' making their own meanings by being given the freedom to explore objects in their own way (Hein 1998; Pearce 1998). One of the ways in which museums have sought to widen their appeal, and their audiences, is through hands-on activities in the museum and increased access to the objects themselves, sometimes by taking them out into the community.

Touch: Evoking Memories

We all know how evocative sounds, smells, and objects can be, transporting us to some earlier event or remembered place. Sadly, just as cuddling babies had been discouraged, so was the reliving of memories by elderly people: "The 1960s had little truck with old men talking about their war wounds and trench experiences, and women remembering a lifetime of hardship" (Kavanagh 2000, 36). More recently it has been realised that reliving experiences and making sense of them is beneficial for some people. This has given rise to reminiscence activities with elderly people, using museum objects familiar from their youth to help them remember their early lives and encourage them to talk. This may be simply a pleasurable social activity, or it may have the therapeutic goal of encouraging isolated people to communicate, or helping elderly and confused people to keep hold of some of their personal memories (see Age Exchange; Age Concern; Kavanagh 2000; Golding 2006).

Familiar surroundings are also important for well-being; displacement from a known and safe environment surrounded by familiar objects, sounds, and smells can be disorienting, as for example for refugees who have fled their home countries with nothing, or for elderly people who are leaving their homes to enter some form of care. Rowlands (Chapter 8) discusses research into the reactions of elderly people now in sheltered accommodation. He suggests they maintain an intimacy with their surroundings through touch, and they construct and sum up their past through caring for objects and images linked to their memories. Jacques (Chapter 9) describes the work she does, using museum objects with elderly people who have dementia. Objects are chosen to help coax their memories from them so they not only reconstruct their life histories, step by step, and regain some of their own identity, but also become more interesting and 'rounded' individuals to the people caring for them.

These chapters show how important the familiar feel of objects can be in recreating memories, and that reminiscence can provide a stimulating and satisfying experience for the participants. Museums are also using reminiscence sessions as a valuable way for the elderly to pass their knowledge and experience to younger people (Golding 2006), and perhaps in doing so to regain a sense of self-worth.

Touch: Opening a New World

Blind and partially sighted people rely on touch and other non-visual senses to understand objects. The first major touch exhibition of sculpture in the UK was held at the Tate Gallery more than thirty years ago, in 1976 (Pearson 1991). Blind and visually impaired people have also been able to handle objects in some museums, but often only by making special arrangements in advance. With recent disability legislation (DDA 1995; MLA 2006) and political pressures for access, facilities for people with all kinds of disabilities have begun to improve in museums, starting with better access to the buildings themselves (Rayner 1998 Bone et al. 1993). Many national organisations for the blind, such as RNIB (formerly the Royal National Institute for the Blind) in the UK, or

AFB (American Foundations for the Blind), and specialist organisations such as Art through Touch, or Art Education for the Blind, promote inclusion and disseminate information on exhibitions and museums to their members (Weisen 1991, and see websites listed below).

Since 1976 many more exhibitions have been held, a current development being touch exhibitions for a general audience—for example, 'Touch me' at the Victoria and Albert Museum in 2005 (Durrant 2005). Large museums have appointed specialist staff to promote access, and many museums now provide for blind and visually impaired visitors through audio tours, touch exhibitions or touch tours, and tactile images or Braille descriptions to accompany visual displays (see, for example, the whole section on tactile diagrams in Axel and Levent 2003. Cassim (Chapter 10) reviews the recent history of access for blind audiences and discusses a project that she ran in Japan with a group of blind people. She provides insight into the different skills and needs of those born blind and those who become blind later in life, and explores the design and use of tactile images to aid the appreciation of two-dimensional art.

In contrast, Khayami (Chapter 11) describes a new project involving both sighted and visually impaired artists producing art intended to be appreciated through all the senses, including touch. Many exhibits have varied contours and surface textures and paintings have heavy impasto. It is an interesting and surprising experience, as a sighted visitor, to be invited to run your hands over the surface of paintings, and appreciate the image through touch! This project challenges both the museum taboo and the normal expectations of artists, critics, and the public, and extends the concept of 'handleable' objects.

Touch: Enriching Learning

Public museums were intended to have an educational role in that they were set up to inform the visitor; the Victoria and Albert Museum, for example, was established with the explicit aim of displaying the best examples of applied arts in order to improve the standard of design (Bennett 1995; Hein 1998). However, the focus on public education shifted in the 1920s to an emphasis on collection for study and research (Hooper-Greenhill 1991). The ultimate result was an accumulation of cultural capital in our museums consisting of stored collections that were under-used (Keene 2005). Some museums had continued to have a strong involvement in education, but it has been the relatively recent political and social pressures on museums to justify their role (and their funding) and to widen their audiences that have revived the emphasis on education.

The concept that children should be encouraged to make their own meaning has led to children's museums (discovery centres in the UK) where children explore and learn, using all their senses, by interacting with responsive exhibits (Pearce 1998; Hein 1998). This concept has also contributed to renewed interest in using 'real' museum objects, and many of the educational activities now organised by museums focus on encouraging learning through direct contact with museum objects. For school pupils, these may involve either educational visits to museums or loans of museum objects to the schools (Hall and Swain 2000). Trewinnard-Boyle and Tabassi (Chapter 12) describe the practicalities involved in the resuscitation of the loans collection at Nottingham Museums. They have worked with enthusiastic local teachers to devise loan boxes containing objects that can be used in the context of the National Curriculum; they are also working with local communities to devise boxes suitable for adults. Participants in handling sessions seem to enjoy them, and many teachers are convinced that encounters with real objects enrich learning. Nevertheless, the difficulties of evaluating this form of learning are widely discussed (e.g. Hein 1998; Binks and Uzzell 1999; Sachatello-Sawyer et al. 2002). Reading Museum, however, has been lending objects to schools for almost a century, and in 2000 undertook a ten-month evaluation in local schools which indicated that seeing and handling real objects is indeed an effective aid both to learning and to retaining the ideas and information associated with the objects (McAlpine 2002).

Touch: Conjuring Sound and Motion

In museums the processes of study, identification, cataloguing, and display all relate to the different ways in which objects are used to demonstrate their significance. There is a dilemma with objects that have moving parts, either mechanised or motorised (clocks, early motor-cars). How can they demonstrate their significance if they are sitting passively in store or on display (Mann 1994; Newey & Meehan 1999)? The argument against making them function is that this will inevitably lead to wear and tear, and may require extensive repair and even replacement of moving parts. A counter-argument is that during their working lives they would have been subject to maintenance and replacement of parts, so conservation/restoration could be seen as a continuation of this normal process. What is more important, the physical integrity of the object or the ability to demonstrate its characteristic movement and sound when in motion?

This is a particularly difficult question where musical instruments are concerned. In many cases, putting them into playable condition (e.g.

stringing a violin) and playing them puts them under considerable structural stress. One school of thought urges preservation of their original materials and technological detail, so they should not be played. The opposing view is that the essence of these instruments is the sound they make (Barclay 2005). How can we know what a serpent sounded like other than by playing it? Lamb (Chapter 13) describes the way in which the Bate Collection of musical instruments at Oxford approaches this dilemma. Essentially a playing collection (thus, effectively, a *handling* collection), nevertheless the instruments are graded according to their rarity and condition, and the risks attached to playing them. Some are regularly played, some are seldom played, and some not at all. The instruments are also used in other ways; for example, many of them can be studied, measured, and used as models for construction of playable replicas.

This approach is used on a limited scale when objects are selected for handling exhibitions, but it could be more widely applied to collections of other types. It is interesting to note that the Bate collection definitely benefits from providing this level of access, in that its specialist users make valuable comments on the playing qualities or provide detailed documentation of the instruments.

Touch: Regaining Cultural Identity

Ethnographic collections house objects that may continue to be of deep significance to the communities from which they came. Many of these objects were bought or appropriated by a then-dominant (often colonial) group. Now the source communities are increasingly eager to gain access to their ancestral objects held in museums (e.g. Ucko 2001; Clavir 2002; Peers & Brown 2003).

Handling these objects often provides opportunities for reminiscence and sharing of information (Feinup-Riordan 2003) and enables communities to study techniques and materials in order to regain traditional craft skills and cultural practices (Peers 1999). In some cases, objects are returned to the care of the communities themselves (Coote 1998), or are lent for use in ceremony. The National Museum of the American Indian (Washington, D.C.) has focused both its new building and its practices on the concept that its collections belong to the native communities and are simply cared for by the museum. Though it is not formally a handling collection, community representatives share in selecting objects for exhibitions and in preparing them for display. Curators and conservators also provide access to objects for ceremonies (Drumheller & Kaminitz 1994; Ogden 2004). Johnson (Chapter 14) outlines the processes involved in preparing for a recent exhibition. Collaboration included selecting the objects, and the shared conservation and restoration of an ancestor figure. This kind of collaboration breaks down the museum taboo and enables Native Americans to handle objects of deep meaning to their communities. It can be seen as a contribution to a 'healing' process; at the same time, the museum benefits enormously from the information provided by community leaders and artists about the collections and the significance and uses of individual objects.

Touch: Where Next?

Having recognised the power of touch, where should future development be focused? It appears there are two main avenues for research: one is in the new area of virtual touch; the other is in the possibilities of extending sensate touch.

Development of Virtual Touch

Touching objects with the hands not only contributes to wear and damage but also requires that the person touching be in the same location as the object. Now that many museums provide Internet access to digital images of their collections, it is possible to view these virtual collections at any time from the comfort of your own home (Keene 1998; MacDonald 2006). The ability to create 3D images already exists, and the possibilities of virtual touch are already being explored in the field of haptics. At some point in the future it may be possible to touch and handle selected objects remotely using the Internet. Prytherch (Chapter 15) reviews the present state of development, concluding that the currently available tools are not yet sensitive enough for this to be a satisfactory substitute for the direct contact of hand on object. But the technology is developing fast and may offer possibilities in the future for handling and exploring objects that are too fragile to be touched, or for enhancing the experience of investigating an object, perhaps by reaching otherwise inaccessible parts.

Digital imaging is already widely used in the art and design fields. For conservation it offers the opportunity to restore an object digitally without touching or altering the object itself (for example, to restore a missing feature, or reconstruct a now worn and fragmentary painted scheme – Geary 2004). One type of haptic tool, a form of stylus, can render satisfactory sensations of texture and hardness. This is apparently already being tested in the medical field to provide training for surgeons. Geary (Chapter 16) discusses two promising applications: the first is to develop the precision needed for engraving on metal plates. The second is to practice the skills needed to remove the backing from works of art on paper; this process involves paring away the old backing, and the amount of force must be carefully judged to avoid damaging the art itself. This latter application may be very helpful in training conservators, who otherwise start their learning on simulated or even real objects.

The potential of virtual touch has not yet been realised, and it may be that this technique will offer the possibilities of extending and enriching our contact with objects as well as protecting vulnerable examples from handling.

A Future For 'Real' Touch

Taken together, the chapters in this book provide many pointers towards possible future work with active touch, particularly research into what constitutes a satisfying touch experience and into the nature and extent of consequent damage to objects (and how this could be limited).

To provide a satisfactory experience, we need more guidance from both sighted and blind people about what they want to touch and handle, and we need to identify the characteristics of objects that yield information and pleasure when touched. Just because sculpture is three-dimensional does not necessarily make it satisfying to explore through touch. A sighted person's concept of what might be interesting is often driven by the visual attractions of the object, whereas different qualities may make an object interesting for a blind person.

We also need to know more about the effects of context. Simply handling for handling's sake may not be satisfying. Objects are 'passive' so, without some background information or some form of focus for handling sessions, the preconceptions people bring with them may go unchallenged and little discovery or learning take place (Owen 1999). Similarly, reminiscence sessions may not be fruitful without carefully considered prompting questions. For blind or partially sighted people, the design and use of tactile diagrams and other aids are also crucially important. Further, the environment in which the session takes place is likely to affect the success of a handling session; questions to consider might include whether participants are sitting or standing, what the lighting is like, and whether there is scope for using other senses (e.g. through the provision of sounds or smells that might be linked to the theme of the session).

Investigating the effects of touch on objects, and researching ways to limit damage, could focus on three things: causes of damage; analysis of what constitutes safe and skilled handling; and methods for selecting suitable objects. Where handling does take place, it is often focused on a 'handling collection' or a collection that is considered secondary and possibly expendable. A fruitful area of research would be issues related to handling 'mainstream' collections.

Should visitors be given guidance on how to handle objects? Visitors are not trained in how to *look*, but popular museum gallery talks help people learn more from their visual examination. Guidance on appreciation through *touch* could include not only historical and artistic context but also how to touch and handle objects. Through inclination, training, and experience, conservators generally handle objects skillfully and sensitively, but there seems to have been little or no research into how they do this and how their tacit knowledge of materials and structures translates into effective handling (and perhaps one of the most contentious issues that requires research is whether or not gloves are necessary).

Conclusion: Acceptance of Touch

A renewed appreciation of the senses and emotions can be seen in, for example, the acceptance of the concept of body language, the recognition of emotional intelligence, and the view that dyslexia is often linked with particular visual awareness (it appears that a high proportion of people working in the design field are dyslexic, and this may be so for connoisseurs; see MacDonald, Chapter 6). The expression *differently abled*, although not widely used, provides a pertinent reminder that a disability such as blindness does not mean lack of aesthetic or intellectual interests and abilities. The papers in this book indicate that our appreciation of our surroundings is multisensory, and that touch makes an important contribution to our well-being as well as our ability to understand and relate to the material world.

It is entirely reasonable to protect valuable and fragile objects in museums; both curators and conservators have a professional obligation to preserve museum collections because they represent the cultural heritage of us all. Is it appropriate, though, to put so much emphasis on preserving *for the future*? We do not know what future generations will think of these collections (they may have other preoccupations) and sometimes it seems that the obligation to preserve is so future-oriented that it is preventing access to collections now. Most people would probably agree that we should hand our collections on to our descendants so that they can study and enjoy them in their own ways; thus, using them now should not mean *using them up*, and access must be carefully considered.

The taboo on touch is gradually changing. Museums are exploring ways of extending access and, in the process, becoming more aware of the importance of their collections and of the many ways in which they can be used (Keene 2005). It is hoped that this book will encourage increased acceptance of touch alongside sight as a means of studying and enjoying objects in museums.

References

24hourmuseum. 2007. (http://www.24hourmuseum.org.uk) (Accessed 01.03.07)

AFB (American Foundation for the Blind). (http://www.afb.org) (Accessed 07.05.07)

Age Concern. (http://www.ageconcern.org.uk) (Accessed 07.05.07)

Age Exchange. (http://www.age-exchange.org.uk) (Accessed 07.05.07)

Art Education for the Blind. (http://www.artbeyondsight.org) (Accessed 13.04.07)

Art Through Touch. (http://www.art-through-touch.co.uk) (Accessed 07.05.07)

Axel, E., Levent, N. (eds.). 2003. *Art Beyond Sight: A Resource Guide to Art, Creativity, and Visual Impairment*. New York: Art Education for the Blind, AFB Press.

Barasch, M. 2001. *Blindness: The History of a Mental Image in Western Thought*. London and New York: Routledge.

Barclay, R.L. 2005. *The Preservation and Use of Musical Instruments: Display Case and Concert Hall*. London: Earthscan.

Bennett, T. 1995. *The Birth of the Museum: History, Theory, Politics*. London and New York: Routledge.

Binks, G., Uzzell, D. 1999. Monitoring and evaluation. In E. Hooper-Greenhill, (ed.), *The Educational Role of the Museum*, 2nd edn. London and New York: Routledge, 298–301.

Bone, W., McGinnis, B., Weisen, M. 1993. *Discovering Museums: A Guide to Museums in the United Kingdom for Blind and Partially Sighted People*. London: HMSO.

Classen, C. (ed.). 2005a. *The Book of Touch*. Oxford and New York: Berg.

——— 2005b. The witch's senses. In D. Howes (ed.), *The Empire of the Senses*. Oxford: Berg, 70–84.

——— 1993. *Worlds of Sense: Exploring the Senses in History and Across Cultures*. London and New York: Routledge.

Clavir, M. 2002. *Preserving What Is Valued: Museums, Conservation, and First Nations*. Vancouver and Toronto: UBC Press.

Coote, K. (ed.). 1998. *Care of Collections*. Committee for the Aboriginal and Torres Straits Islander Keeping Places and Cultural Centres. Sydney: Australian Museum.

DCMS (Department of Culture Media and Sport) 1999. *Museums for the Many: Standards for Museums and Galleries to use when developing Access Policies*. (http://www.culture.gov.uk/Reference_library/Publications/archive_1999) (Accessed 10.06.07)

DDA. 1995. Disability Discrimination Act. (http://www.opsi.gov.uk/acts/acts1995) (Accessed 13.04.07)

Drumheller, A., Kaminitz, M. 1994. Traditional care and conservation, the merging of two disciplines at the National Museum of the American Indian. In A. Roy and P. Smith (eds.), *Preventive Conservation: Practice, Theory and Research*. Preprints of the Contributions to the Ottawa Congress, September 1994. London: International Institute for Conservation, 58–60.

Durrant, N. 2005. Let's Get Physical. *The Times*. 11 June 2005.

Feinup-Riordan, A. 2003. Yup'ik elders in museums: Fieldwork turned on its head. In L. Peers and A. Brown (eds.), *Museums and Source Communities*. London and New York: Routledge, 28–41.

Geary, A. 2004. Three-dimensional virtual restoration applied to polychrome sculpture. *The Conservator* 28: 20–35.

Golding, V. 2006. Recollection, and the UK Museum: Object, image, word. Paper given at the ICME conference, *Connections, Communities, and Collections*. International Committee for Museums and Collections of Ethnography. Available at http://museumsnett.no/icme/.

Hall, J. 1999. *The World as Sculpture*. London: Chatto & Windus.

Hall, J., Swain, H. 2000. Roman boxes for London's schools: An outreach service by the Museum of London. In P. McManus (ed.), *Archaeological Displays and the Public*, 2nd edn. London: Archetype, 87–96.

Harvey, E. (ed.). 2003. *Sensible Flesh: On Touch in Early Modern Culture*. Philadelphia: University of Pennsylvania Press.

Hein, G. 1998. *Learning in the Museum*. London and New York: Routledge.

Hodder I. 2006. Çatalhöyük: *The Leopard's Tale*. London: Thames & Hudson.

Hooper-Greenhill, E. (ed.). 1997. *Cultural Diversity: Developing Museum Audiences in Britain*. London: Leicester University Press.

——— 1991. *Museum and Gallery Education*. Leicester: Leicester University Press.

Howes, D. (ed.). 2005a. *The Empire of the Senses*. Oxford: Berg.

——— 2005b. Introduction. In D. Howes (ed.), *The Empire of the Senses*. Oxford: Berg, 1–17.

——— 2003. *Sensual Relations: Engaging the Senses in Culture and Social Theory*. Ann Arbor: University of Michigan Press.

Kavanagh, G. 2000. *Dream Spaces: Memory and the Museum*. London and New York: Leicester University Press.

Kirby Talley, M. 1989. Connoisseurship and the methodology of the Rembrandt research project. *International Journal of Museum Management and Curatorship* 8: 175–214.

Keene, S. 2005. *Fragments of the World: Uses of Museum Collections*. Oxford: Elsevier Butterworth-Heinemann.

——— 1998. *Digital Collections: Museums and the Information Age*. Oxford: Butterworth-Heinemann.

Lubar, S., Kingery, W.D. (eds.) 1993. *History from Things: Essays on Material Culture*. Washington and London: Smithsonian Institution Press.

MacDonald, L. (ed.). 2006. *Digital Heritage: Applying Digital Imaging to Cultural Heritage.* Oxford: Butterworth-Heinemann.

Mann, P. 1994. The restoration of vehicles for use in research, exhibition, and demonstration. In A. Oddy (ed.), *Restoration: Is it Acceptable?* London: British Museum, 131–38.

Marstine, J. (ed.). 2006. *New Museum Theory and Practice.* Malden MA and Oxford: Blackwell.

McAlpine, J. 2002. Loan star. *Museums Journal* 102(1): 26–27.

Miles, G., 1992. Object handling. In J. Thompson (ed.), *Manual of Curatorship: A Guide to Museum Practice,* 2nd ed. London: Butterworth Heinemann, 455–58.

MLA (Museums, Libraries and Archives Council) 2006. *Website Policies: Disability.* (www.mla.gov.uk/website/policy/Diversity/People_With_Disabilities/) (Accessed 12.10.06)

Montagu, A. 1971 (3rd edn, 1986), *Touching: The Human Significance of the Skin.* New York: Harper & Row.

Munos Viñas, S. 2005. *Contemporary Theory of Conservation.* Oxford: Elsevier Butterworth-Heinemann.

Newey, H., Meehan, P. 1999. The conservation of an 1895 Panhard et Levassor and a 1922 prototype Austin Seven motorcar: New approaches in the preservation of vehicles. *The Conservator* 23:11–21.

Ogden, S. (ed.). 2004. *Caring for American Indian Objects: A Practical and Cultural Guide.* St Paul: Minnesota Historical Society Press.

Owen, J. 1999. Interaction or tokenism? The role of 'hands-on activities' in museum archaeological displays. In N. Merriman (ed.), *Making Early Histories in Museums.* London: Leicester University Press, 173–89.

Pearce, J. 1998. *Centres for Curiosity and Imagination.* London: Calouste Gulbenkian Foundation.

Pearce, S. 1994. Objects as meaning, or narrating the past. In S. Pearce (ed.), *Interpreting Objects and Collections.* London and New York: Routledge, 19–29.

Pearson, A . 1991. Touch exhibitions in the United Kingdom. In Fondation de France/ICOM, *Museums Without Barriers: A New Deal for Disabled People.* London and New York: ICOM in conjunction with Routledge, 122–26.

Peers, L. 1999. Curating Native American art. *British Museum Magazine, The Journal of the British Museum Society* 34:24–27.

Peers, L., Brown, A.K. (eds.). 2003. *Museums and Source Communities.* London: Routledge.

Phillips, D. 1997. *Exhibiting Authenticity.* Manchester: Manchester University Press.

Prown, J.D. 1993. The truth of material culture: History or fiction? In S. Lubar and W.D. Kingery (eds.), *History from Things: Essays on Material Culture.* Washington and London: Smithsonian Institution Press 1–19.

Pye, E., 2001. *Caring for the Past: Issues in Conservation for Archaeology and Museums.* London: James and James.

Pye, E., Sully, D. 2007. Evolving challenges, developing skills. *The Conservator* 30:25–43.

Rayner, A. 1998. *Access in Mind: Towards the Inclusive Museum*. Edinburgh: INTACT, the Intellectual Access Trust.

RNIB (formerly Royal National Institute for the Blind). (http://www.rnib.org.uk) (Accessed 12.04.07) (There are many links to other relevant websites.)

Sachatello-Sawyer, B., et al. 2002. *Adult Museum Programs: Designing Meaningful Experiences*. Walnut Creek: Altamira Press.

Synnott, A. 1993. *The Body Social*. London and New York: Routledge.

Sully, D. (ed.). (2007). *Decolonising Conservation: Caring for Maori Meeting Houses outside New Zealand*. Walnut Creek, CA: Left Coast Press.

Ucko, P. 2001. 'Heritage' and 'Indigenous Peoples' in the 21st Century. *Public Archaeology* 1(4):227–38.

Weisen, M. 1991. Art and the visual handicap. A role for the associations for the blind, the museums, and art associations and the official cultural authorities. In Fondation de France/ICOM, *Museums without Barriers: A New Deal for Disabled People*. London and New York: ICOM in conjunction with Routledge, 107–13.

Wilson, D.M. 1989. *The British Museum: Purpose and Politics*. London: British Museum Publications.

PART 1 SCIENCE OF TOUCH

1

WEIGHING UP THE VALUE OF TOUCH

Alan Wing, Christos Giachritsis and Roberta Roberts

Introduction

Vision often appears to determine the way we perceive the world. However, touch is the sensory modality that verifies the reality of what we see by allowing us to confirm the physical presence of objects and people around us. Vision may prompt us to make contact with an object or person but, by touching, we reinforce the subjective impact of that object or person. For example, we may decide to touch an object on the basis of its appearance (looks interesting) but the final sense of the object will also be based on its feel (feels good).

Touch provides us with knowledge about the location, geometry, and weight of an object by integrating information from the cutaneous receptors in the skin and proprioceptive receptors in the muscles. These receptors convert the mechanical effects of contact forces into electrical impulses in the nerves and are termed *mechanoreceptors*. The muscle mechanoreceptors provide cues to large- and medium-scale geometric features of an object, which allow us to perceive its size and shape as well as its weight and hardness. The skin mechanoreceptors provide us with information about small-scale geometry, which allows us to perceive texture. The skin also has receptors that allow us to detect thermal conductivity, or temperature, relative to the body.

Temperature is a very useful sensory cue, for example in discriminating metal (high thermal conductivity, so it feels cold) from wood (low thermal conductivity, so it feels warm), and also provides an important protective function. However, the sensing principles and information processing by the nervous system for temperature are quite different from those for the mechanoreceptors and it is the latter that we focus on in this chapter.

Size and shape inform us about the type of object we are handling (and thus its use, given we are familiar with the object, say, a garment). However, texture and weight indicate its quality (cotton, wool, fur). In a cultural heritage context, perceiving the geometric and material properties of an ancient artefact through touching and handling may be expected to provide us with clues about the way people used to live; for example, we might better appreciate the technologies they used.

Later in this chapter, we discuss human sensitivity to weight and how this sensitivity may vary depending on the way we grasp, handle, and manipulate an object. However, we begin by reviewing the neurophysiology of touch. We describe the nature of sensory coding in general, focus on the neural receptors that respond to mechanical events underlying touch, and outline the processes in the brain that take the incoming sensory signals and interpret them or use them for controlling actions. Finally, we provide a brief overview of the motor system of the brain, which is responsible for the control of movement and is critically dependent on touch sensory input.

Sensory Coding of Environmental Events

How do our senses tell us about the environment? Information from the environment is available in various forms of energy including mechanical, thermal, and electromagnetic. Using specialised receptors, our senses respond to such sources of energy and transform them into electrical signals, a series of millivolt electrical pulses, whose timing is related to the strength of the source. Different properties of an object may be uniquely signalled by different senses, for example, temperature by touch and wavelength of reflected light (colour) by vision. However, generally a given attribute of an object may serve as input to several senses because a common energy source leads to correlated physical effects on receptors in different sensory systems. Thus, as the water in a kettle starts to boil, the turbulence produces a pattern of stimulation that affects hearing, touch (through vibration of the kettle handle), and vision.

Once the sensory receptors have encoded the stimulus into a stream of electrical pulses, the pulses are transmitted via the nerves to different regions of the brain (Figure 1.1). Since different sensory inputs are all transmitted electrically, with nothing in the signal to indicate its

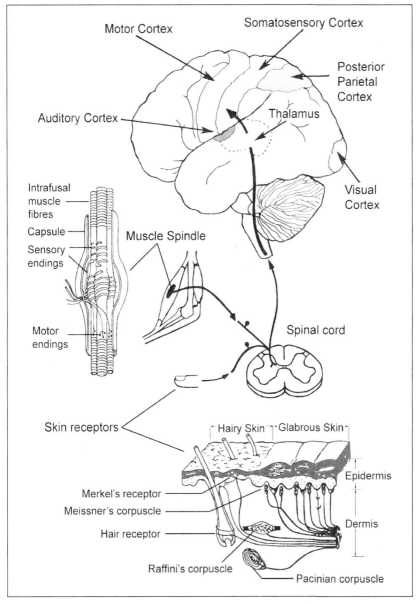

Figure 1.1: Cortical processing of touch. The somatosensory cortex receives sensory input via the thalamus from mechanoreceptors in the skin and muscles. Somatosensory inputs may affect motor actions directly via the motor cortex or indirectly via the posterior parietal cortex, which is important in the integration of touch and visual information.

origin, the target brain areas have to be specialised in order to utilise the incoming sensory information according to its particular sensory source (e.g. eyes, hands, ears, nose). For instance, processing of the sensory input in brain areas responsible for touch differs from processing by those areas underlying vision. Moreover, for each sense, the relevant brain area reflects the distribution of effects across the sensory receptors. Thus, in the case of touch, different body regions are represented in separate but neighbouring areas of the brain, effectively creating a map representing the body surface.

What Is Touch?

Information about an object's size, surface texture, shape, or orientation is gained by making contact with its surfaces. When contact is made, there is a deformation of the mechanoreceptors in the epidermal layer just below the outer surface of the skin. Although these tactile sensors are small (a fraction of a millimetre across), depending on how deep they lie some of them signal deformation of the overlying skin over a distance of several millimetres. Contact with any part of the body generally provides us with at least a vague sensation, that is, we know we have been touched and roughly where the touch occurred. However, our ability to make fine discriminations about the information varies depending on which part of the body comes into contact with the surfaces. This is because the tactile mechanoreceptors are not evenly distributed over all parts of the body but are concentrated in certain areas with special functional significance, such as the hands, and particularly the tips of the fingers (Johansson & Vallbo 1983). We are therefore better able to localise where we have been touched, or, for example, to discriminate between one and two closely spaced contacts on our hands, than if the touch contact is made, say, on the back of the arm.

The mechanoreceptors in the skin respond in two different ways when subject to deformation, either maintaining a steady series of electrical pulses while the deformation continues or responding only to changes in deformation due to pressure increases or decreases. Tactile receptors that respond preferentially to change are very sensitive to stimuli vibrating around 200 times per second, or to brief events that set up such vibrations in the skin. The functional significance is most likely to be in detecting initial contact when grasping an object and in sudden changes in skin stresses when a grasped object starts to slip or someone taps you on the shoulder to attract your attention. For example, researchers examined the responses of mechanoreceptors in the skin (using fine-wire electrodes inserted into volunteers' arms) when lifting an object from a table (Macefield et al. 1996). They showed that the sudden change in skin stresses associated with successful lift was marked by a burst of activity from the skin mechanoreceptors. They argued that, since lifting is normally associated with such sensory input, the absence of such activity from the mechanoreceptors could form the basis for triggering feedback correction to the lifting action if the object fails to lift, perhaps because it is heavier than expected.

The combination of static and dynamic sensing exhibited by the skin mechanoreceptors has parallels in the mechanoreceptors embedded within the muscles. Termed *muscle spindles*, these receptors convey information about muscle length (static) and change in length (dynamic) associated with movement of the joint about which the muscle acts. Muscles act in pairs about joints, and opposing pairs flex, stabilise, or extend joints depending on the balance of the tension exerted by the muscles. In signalling muscle length, the spindles provide the brain with an indication of joint angle. Such information may relate to the consequences of muscle action or to forces imposed on the limb as a result of contact with external objects. For example, the degree of flexion of the fingers in holding an object in the hand indicates whether the object is small or large. Combining information from shoulder, elbow, and wrist joints with information about the length of the upper arm and forearm provides a basis for determining hand position relative to the body. This class of sensory information is termed *proprioceptive* to reflect the body sensing its own internal state.

The Sensory Brain: Processing of Touch Information

Cutaneous and proprioceptive information from the skin and muscle mechanoreceptors is transmitted to the brain via the spinal cord and the thalamus, the latter being an important relay structure deep in the brain (see Figure 1.1). From the thalamus the information is transmitted to the primary somatosensory receiving area, (S-I), in the parietal lobe of the cerebral cortex, on the opposite side (contralateral) to the site of stimulation. (For a detailed review of these and other neuroanatomical topics, see Kandel et al. 2000). Thus, touch inputs from the left side of the body terminate in S-I in the right hemisphere of the brain and those from the right terminate in left S-I.

An individual neuron in S-I is responsive to stimulation over a limited region of the body surface, called the receptive field of the neuron. If a stimulus moves across the skin, it may cross the receptive fields of several neurons in S-I. Neurons with adjacent receptive fields tend to lie adjacent to one another in S-I and spatial relations between receptive fields correspond approximately to the spatial arrangement of neurons in the cortex. However, as already noted, the number of somatosensory neurons representing an area of skin is determined by the density of sensory receptors in that area. It is as though the scale of the S-I map is adjusted to the function of the body part, with a larger scale for those parts of the body whose sensory function is more important (Figure 1.2). Thus, for example, the cortical sensory map has relatively more space devoted to representing the face than the torso. Note also how much space is devoted to the hand and fingers. Thus the two areas with the most complex sensory and motor capabilities of the body are supported by the greatest amount of cortical tissue.

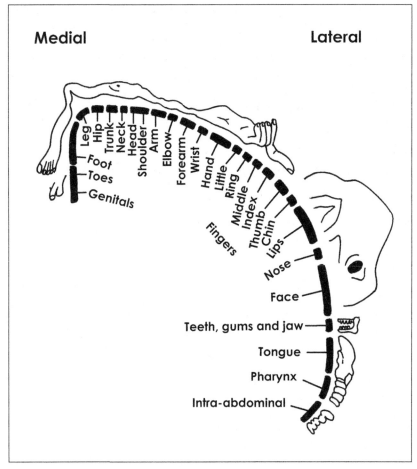

Figure 1.2 Somatosensory homunculus showing the distribution of the tactile inputs to the brain. (adapted from Penfield & Rasmussen 1950, taking account of Servos et al. 1999)

A number of distinct regions has been identified within S-I (Brodman's areas 3a, 3b, 1, 2). If different patterns of stimulation are applied to the skin, recordings of the activity of single neurons in these different areas show that processing of touch information undergoes a series of progressive transformations. In area 3b, which is early in the progression, the neurons respond to simple skin contact. Neurons in areas 1 and 2 signal more complex relational properties, which depend on integration of information across a number of neurons that subserve simple contact in area 3b. In this way, successive stages in cortical processing allow progressive elaboration of the nature of the touch stimulus. Neurons in area 3a (adjacent to area 3b) receive proprioceptive input from muscle receptors. They have important connections with neurons in area 2. Thus the latter area affords an opportunity for integration of cutaneous and proprioceptive information. This supports, for example, interpretation of cutaneous input from adjacent fingers in relation to information about the relative position of the fingers, a key component in recognising objects from their three-dimensional shape (stereognosis). An important target for touch information from S-I is posterior parietal cortex (PPC) (see Figure 1.1). In addition to receiving information from S-I, PPC also receives inputs from the visual and auditory systems. This brain area is important for integrating information from the different sensory modalities to build up a single integrated perception of an object.

The Motor Brain: Controlling the Muscles

Movements result from muscle action driven by activity in primary motor cortex (M-I) which lies in the frontal region of the brain just forward of S-I. Just as S-I provides a map-like representation of touch input, so adjacent areas of M-I drive activity in groups of muscles occupying adjacent areas of the body. Moreover, the amount of cortical tissue in M-I devoted to different areas of the body reflects the complexity of movement that can be achieved. This means that the face and hand have much larger representation (relative to their surface area on the body) than, for example, the torso.

Functioning of the neurons in the brain depends on the blood supply to support the metabolic needs of the cells. Loss of blood supply can lead to cell death, and the resulting impairment provides an index of the function of the part of the brain involved. Loss of blood supply to M-I results in weakness or complete loss of muscle control on the contralateral side of the body (the motor pathways cross from one side of the body to the other on the way from M-I to the spinal cord and on to the muscles). Although it is quite common to have weakness of movement affecting all of one side of the body (hemiparesis), sometimes the impairment of function can be localised, for example just affecting the hand and arm.

The ability to move our limbs plays a key role in allowing us to gauge the weight of objects. Skilled weight judgements are an important part of everyday life. An obvious application is in making purchasing decisions about quantity. However, sensing weight not only shapes what we think about an object but also how we handle it. A heavier object, for instance, requires more force to move than a light object and requires greater care to avoid an uncontrolled collision when setting it down. The weight of an object placed on the palm of the hand can be inferred from the pressure it exerts when the hand rests palm up on a table. But for many years it has been known that weight judgements are more accurate if muscle action is involved (Flanagan 1996). In active lifting, a 'sense of effort' appears to operate that is attributed to monitoring the level of muscle commands used to support the object. In lifting an object, the level of muscle activity changes with posture; for example, less shoulder muscle activity is required to lift an object close to the body than one held away from the body. This is because muscles have to overcome torque due to the weight of the object multiplied by its distance from the shoulder (you expend less energy if you lift the object close to the body). An interesting question, to which we return later, is whether, when asked to judge object weight, we can factor out the effects of torque. Or, does the same object lifted at a greater distance from the body feel heavier?

Despite the direct cortical connections, it takes time for feedback action to have an effect through the muscles. Instead of relying on such feedback, it is better if we anticipate the weight of an object, and pre-set lift forces to what we expect will be needed (Gordon et al. 1993). If we anticipate correctly, the result is a faster and more efficient lifting action that does not require correction. Object size judgements, which usually come from vision, but can equally involve touch, provide an important basis for predicting weight. Prediction of the weight of an object from perceived size cues, coming from vision or from the span of the hand required to grasp the object, can sometimes be misleading. Thus a small object, such as a full jar, will be heavier than a pack of crackers even though the latter may be physically larger. Curiously, perceived size can induce a weight illusion; if two objects are the same weight but one is larger than the other, the larger one actually feels lighter. The reason for this, it is suggested, is that we are very sensitive to discrepancies between predicted and observed sensory feedback. In the case of the large object, when it is lifted it feels lighter than we expect and this biases our judgements.

Returning to the anatomy of the motor system, the major influences on M-I are from the adjacent premotor cortex (PMC) and supplementary motor area (SMA) just to the front of M-I. These additional motor areas take input from PPC, but also from subcortical structures including the cerebellum. Supplementary motor area and PMC are important in the preparation of coordinated movement and, for example, damage to SMA can result in impaired bilateral coordination of the kind needed, for instance, in picking up a tray and keeping it level. The cerebellum is a key area in control of movement. It receives direct cutaneous and proprioceptive inputs but also inputs from parietal cortex, and its primary output is to motor and premotor areas of the cortex. It is thought that the cerebellum contributes to the coordination of movement through the use of networks (internal forward models) that provide rapid prediction of the outcome of muscle commands (Kawato 1999). Such prediction can be used to update muscle commands that may have been selected on inaccurate or incomplete information. However, it is also thought that prediction is used to condition cortical processing of sensory information arising from movement.

Judging the Weight of Hand-Held Objects

In the previous section we noted that weight judgement is more accurate with active movements of the hand holding the object. We observed that people appear to monitor the effort used to hold an object and that differences in the effort required to hold two separate objects can improve the subjects' ability to discriminate differences in weight. However, in some situations muscle effort may change (for example, with body posture) and hence indirectly affect the effort used to hold each object whose weight is being judged. Does this cause difficulties in the judgement of weight? This section describes two studies that we are carrying out in our laboratory to explore how postural changes can affect weight judgements. The first study examines the effect of changes in gravitational torque caused by raising and lowering the arm about the shoulder joint, changing the effort required to maintain arm posture. The second study investigates whether taking an object in two hands, and thus sharing the effort between the two sides of the body, results in altered perception of weight.

Study I: The Effects of Arm Position on Weight Judgement

The arm is capable of a wide range of movement. When fully extended, it can trace a complete hemisphere as it is rotated about the shoulder joint. Within this range of movement the weight of the arm produces gravitational torque about the shoulder that depends on shoulder angle. If the arm hangs vertically at the side of the body directly below the shoulder, the torque is negligible but if the arm forms a right angle with the body, the torque exerted at the shoulder is at a maximum. When we hold an object with the arm at the side in a relaxed position, cues to weight might be expected to come more from the grip force that is used to hold the object, than from the arm muscles, since there is no arm torque to be overcome. On the other hand, when we hold an object with the arm at an angle of 90 degrees to the body, when the gravitational torque is at maximum, cues to weight are likely to come from two sources: the grip force that is used to hold the object and the muscular force that is used to overcome gravitational torques acting on the arm. The muscular force used to maintain arm posture in the second case requires extra effort. Given that the heaviness of an object is generally related to the sense of effort used to hold or lift it (Flanagan et al. 1995), we hypothesized that an object held with the arm at 90 degrees would feel heavier than when the arm is relaxed by the side at 0 degrees.

In order to find whether arm posture affects weight judgements, we carried out a psychophysical study in which we asked participants to judge the heaviness of two weights held with precision grip (using index finger and opposed thumb) at two different arm positions. Each experimental trial consisted of three phases (Figure 1.3). In the first phase, the experimenter placed one of eight variable weights (ranging from 168 to 242 grams) or a standard (200 grams) weight in the participant's hand with the arm positioned at 0 degrees or 90 degrees. In the second phase, the experimenter removed the first weight and then placed the standard weight (if the first weight was one of the variable set) or one of the variable weights (if the first weight was the standard) in the participant's hand with the arm now positioned in the other posture (e.g. at 90° if it was initially at 0°). In the third phase, the second weight was removed and the participant was asked to indicate which weight felt heavier: first or second?

Preliminary results collected from six participants show that people perceive objects held with the arm at 90 degrees as heavier than objects held with the arm in the relaxed 0-degree position (see Figure 1.3a). This happened even when the object held with the arm at 90 degrees was 28 grams lighter than the object held with the arm at 0 degrees. These early results suggest that weight judgements are affected by the effort to support our arm against gravity. It appears that the brain has difficulty in separating the information about weight from the effort used in supporting the object and arm against torques due to gravity.

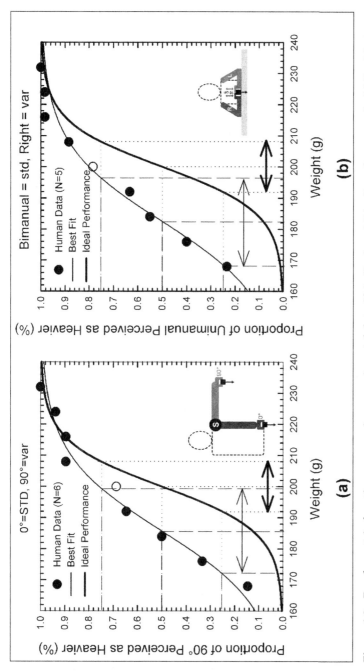

Figure 1.3 Psychometric functions comparing experimental data (thin line) and 'ideal' performance (bold line) in two separate experiments. The x-axes show the range of variable weights compared with the 200 g standard held (a) with arm vertical, (b) bi-manually. The y-axes show proportion of 'heavier' responses when the variable weight is (a) held with shoulder angle of 90 degrees, (b) lifted uni-manually.

Study II: Weight Perception Using One or Two Hands

When carrying out a manual task, such as moving an object, our decision to employ both hands is based on a number of object properties including size and weight. For instance, experience suggests that a large object requires using both hands in order to ensure adequate manipulation, while a heavy object requires bi-manual handling to increase lifting effectiveness by sharing the load between the two hands. This may sound obvious but it raises interesting questions about the way the brain interprets cues to weight when we use two hands. When lifting an object bi-manually, its weight is shared between the hands and the grip force used by either hand is less. This should, in effect, generate weight signals from each hand of half the magnitude experienced in lifting with one hand. So the object might be expected to feel lighter, unless the brain correctly integrates the information across the two hands. Alternatively, it might be argued that using two hands requires more effort because the weight of both arms must be supported as well as the weight of the object. So holding an object with two hands might be expected to increase its apparent weight. In order to compare these two contrasting predictions we are currently conducting a study to test for differences between uni-manual and bi-manual weight judgements.

So far, we have tested five participants on their judgement of the difference in weight of two successively lifted objects (the same weights as used in the previous study), lifted either with just the right hand or with both hands together. The participants sat in front of a table and were asked to lift two weights one after the other (a variable and a standard), either with one hand or both hands, using precision grip between thumb and index finger. For example, first they lifted a variable weight with one hand and then the standard weight with both hands. They were then asked to indicate which weight they felt to be heavier. Results obtained to date show that weights lifted with one hand are experienced as heavier than weights lifted with both hands (see Figure 1.3b). In one-hand lifting, the grip force used is greater than in two-hand lifting, but the effort to hold up just one arm rather than two is less. This suggests that the brain is biased towards local cues from one hand rather than more general cues from the arm in judging weight.

In summary, the initial results from these two studies on weight perception are beginning to show us how information from both the arm and the hands can affect heaviness judgements. When we hold an object against gravity, and at the same time the arm is held at a distance from the body, the brain must produce both hand grip forces, to keep the object in the hand, and arm forces, to maintain arm posture and take the weight of the object. The effect of arm posture on weight judgements in the first experiment indicates that the brain integrates cues to weight from hand and arm. When we use two hands to hold an object, more effort is required to hold both arms against gravity than to hold one arm against gravity when taking the object in one hand. However, in the second case the weight taken by each hand is halved. Since the results of the second experiment show objects held in one hand feel heavier, it seems the brain is more strongly influenced by hand grip cues to weight, and arm effort is discounted. Perhaps the key to the contrasting results from the two experiments is that the brain operates differently depending on qualitative (one vs. two arms) or quantitative (arm angle) changes in lifting conditions. Clearly our research is only a beginning and there are many further studies to be carried out in this interesting area of sensory function.

Summary

In this chapter, we have outlined some of the peripheral sensory and central neural mechanisms for touch that allow us to perceive our world and act upon it effectively. Even simple tasks like preparing a cup of tea, or picking up and examining an object, require the collection and integration of considerable amount of information about physical properties and events (temperature, size, weight) sensed through the tactile and proprioceptive mechanoreceptors in the skin and muscles converting physical energy to neural impulses. These sensory signals may be used to support effective interactions with the objects, such as holding them securely despite destabilising forces such as gravity or inertia that tend to cause them to slip from grasp. At the same time, the information from muscle and skin contributes to our sense of touch, which allows us to judge object attributes such as size and weight. Following our review of the brain mechanisms underlying touch perception, we turned to experimental studies of weight judgement. In showing that these are affected by postural factors, we have pointed to the importance of the way that the brain may select from multiple touch cues when handling objects.

References

Flanagan, J.R. 1996. Action-perception coupling in judgements of hand-held loads. In A.M. Wing, P. Haggard, J.R. Flanagan (eds.), *Hand and Brain: Neurophysiology and Psychology of Hand*. San Diego: Academic Press, 415–30.

Flanagan, J.R., Wing, A.M., Allison, S., Spenceley, A. 1995. Effects of surface texture on weight perception when lifting objects with a precision grip. *Perception & Psychophysics* 57:282–90.

Gordon, A.M., Westling, G., Cole, K.J., Johansson, R.S. 1993. Memory representations underlying motor commands used during manipulation of common and novel objects. *Journal of Neurophysiology* 69:1789–96.

Johansson, R.S., Vallbo, A.B. 1983. Tactile sensory coding in the glabrous skin of the human hand. *Trends in Neurosciences* 6:27–32.

Kandel, E.R., Schwartz, J.H., Jessell, T.M. 2000. *Principles of Neural Science.* New York and London: McGraw-Hill Medical.

Kawato, M. 1999. Internal models for motor control and trajectory planning. *Current Opinion in Neurobiology* 9:718–27.

Macefield, V.G., Hager Ross, C., Johansson, R.S. 1996. Control of grip force during restraint of an object held between finger and thumb: Responses of cutaneous afferents from the digits. *Experimental Brain Research* 108:155–71.

Penfield, W., Rasmussen, T. 1950. *The Cerebral Cortex of Man.* New York: McMillan.

Servos, P., Stephen, C.A., Engel, A., Gati, J., Menon, R. 1999. fMRI evidence for an inverted face representation in human somatosensory cortex. *NeuroReport* 10:1393–95.

2

MAKING SENSE OF TOUCH: A MULTISENSORY APPROACH TO THE PERCEPTION OF OBJECTS

Charles Spence

Introduction

The majority of textbooks on human perception consider each of the senses (vision, hearing, touch, olfaction, and taste) in isolation, as if each represented a separate and independent perceptual system. In most situations, however, our senses receive correlated information about the same external objects and events, and this information is typically combined to yield the multisensorially determined sensations that fill our everyday lives (see Spence 2002; Calvert et al. 2004; Schifferstein & Spence in press). This chapter provides a brief overview of the literature on multisensory perception designed to demonstrate just how dramatically the various senses can influence people's tactile perception.

Touch constitutes a genuinely multi-dimensional experience (e.g. Katz 1925/1989; Bergmann et al. 2006), and our perception of objects consists of an awareness of both their substance and structural properties (Klatzky et al. 1989; Picard, et al. 2003). The substance properties of an object involve such things as its hardness, weight, temperature, and texture, while an object's structural properties consist of its size, three-dimensional shape, and volume. Our perception of the properties of objects appears to rely on different parts of the brain (Roland et al. 1998). An extensive body of empirical research now shows that visual, auditory, and olfactory cues can all modulate people's tactile perception of the substance properties (such as the texture) of haptically explored objects and surfaces (i.e. explored through active touch).

Visual cues have also been shown to dominate touch when people evaluate an object's structural properties (Gibson 1943; Rock & Victor 1964), and all of our senses appear to contribute to an object's perceived pleasantness and functionality (see Spence & Zampini 2006; Schifferstein & Spence in press). Taken together, this empirical research from the fields of experimental psychology and multisensory product design shows that whenever people think about the factors that affect people's touching and handling of objects, as in cultural heritage contexts (e.g. Oppenheimer 1972; Field 1975; Koran et al. 1984; and the other chapters in this volume) they need to consider the variety of sensory inputs that may be contributing to people's evaluation and appreciation of those objects. As Hornik (1992, 457) puts it: 'There is more to touch than "meets the hands"'.

Visual Contributions to Tactile Perception

According to the traditional view, touch was thought to educate vision (see Hooke 1705/1971, 338; Berkeley 1709/1957; Arnold 2003; Classen 2005). However, when psychologists first started to address the question of how the senses influence each other experimentally they found that vision appeared to dominate touch completely (e.g. Gibson 1943; Rock & Victor 1964; Rock & Harris 1967). For instance, Gibson (1933, 4–5) reported that when people ran their fingers up and down a straight meter stick they perceived it as being curved if they simultaneously looked through lenses that made the stick look curved. As soon as the participants closed their eyes, however, or turned away, the stick felt straight again. Gibson noted that this visual dominance over touch (or, more correctly, haptics, i.e. active touch) was so strong that it could not easily be overridden by instruction. Rock and his colleagues (Rock & Victor 1964; Rock & Harris 1967) reported a series of experiments in which their participants had to rate their impression of the size of a small object which they could either see, feel, or both see and feel at the same time. Taken together with other findings being published around the same time, such as those emerging from prism experiments (e.g. Hay et al. 1965), Rock and Harris (1967, 96) concluded that, contrary to the traditional view (as expressed by, say, Berkeley 1709/1957; Arnold 2003), 'vision completely dominates touch and even shapes it'.

Many other experiments have since been reported showing that vision modulates, and often dominates, tactile and haptic perception when the senses are put into some kind of conflict (see Warren & Rossano 1991 for a review). Various theories have been put forward to try and account for the ubiquity of visual dominance, including the modality appropriateness hypothesis (i.e. the idea that we rely on the sense that is most adept for a particular task; Freides 1974; Welch & Warren 1980) and the directed attention hypothesis (Posner et al. 1976). According to Posner et al.'s directed attention hypothesis, people tend to direct their attention more towards the visual sense (in order to compensate for the poor alerting, or arousing, qualities of visual stimuli). This attentional bias tends to result in attended visual inputs (those sensory impressions on which people are concentrating) being weighted more heavily than those from the other relatively less attended sensory modalities (e.g. touch). By contrast, according to the modality appropriateness hypothesis, our brains tend to favour information from the sense that is most appropriate to the task at hand. According to this view, the reason why visual information dominates so frequently is simply that vision is the sense that normally provides the most accurate information concerning the judgement being made (at least for the kinds of perceptual judgements that psychologists are fond of asking their participants to make).

A few exceptions to the generalization that vision will always dominate over touch have been reported over the years. For example, by placing a mirror perpendicular to a letter display, Heller (1992) was able to create a situation in which his participants touched a series of embossed letters while looking at them in a mirror. Using this set-up, Heller created a conflict situation whereby, for example, the participants touched the letter 'p' while seeing themselves in the mirror apparently touching a letter 'b'. The majority of the participants showed tactile dominance (i.e. they identified the letter in front of them as a 'p' in the above example). The responses made by several of the other participants suggested a compromise between the senses, and only one participant showed visual dominance. Heller accounted for these results in terms of an attentional explanation of sensory dominance.

Researchers investigating the multisensory perception of surface texture have shown that both vision and touch appear to contribute to people's perception of the felt texture (or roughness) of a surface (see Lederman & Klatsky 2004 for a review). For example, Lederman and Abbott (1981) reported that participants made compromise judgements when vision and touch were put into conflict, their results suggesting that participants weighted the two modalities about equally (see also Guest & Spence 2003b). Meanwhile, Lederman, et al. (1986) have shown that the extent to which one sensory input is preferred over another depends on the nature of the task that participants have to perform.

Guest and Spence (2007) recently reported a study in which touch was shown to exert a greater influence over participants' judgements of the surface texture of fabric samples than did visual texture cues. Participants had to discriminate between pairs of pilled fabric samples using touch, vision, or both senses together. (Pilling results from the abrading of a fabric's surface through wear.) The participants were able to discriminate between the pilled fabric samples more accurately using touch alone than using only vision. When fabric samples having slightly different pill values were presented to the participants' eyes and fingertips in the bimodal condition, the tactile cues were found to completely dominate participants' perception of how pilled the samples were. These results demonstrate that tactile cues can sometimes dominate over vision in the perception of fine surface textures. Heller (1989) also reported touch to be superior to vision for judgements of very smooth textures in an experiment using Japanese abrasive sharpening stones.

While these results might appear to contrast with the numerous previous studies that have reported visual dominance, Guest and Spence (2007) argued that their results could also be explained in terms of the modality appropriateness hypothesis (Freides 1974; Welch & Warren 1980). For, while vision may dominate when people have to make judgements regarding the macrogeometric properties of an object or surface, touch may dominate when they have to make judgements concerning the microgeometric properties of a surface (see also Heller 1992; Guest & Spence 2003b). This is consistent with the modality appropriateness hypothesis if one considers that vision provides more accurate information regarding macrogeometric object properties (structural properties of the object, or relatively coarse surface texture information) while touch can sometimes provide more accurate information regarding the microgeometric features (in particular, when trying to discriminate very fine surface texture).

Ernst and Banks (2002) recently brought some mathematical rigour to the field of sensory dominance research by showing that the maximum likelihood estimation provided an excellent quantitative account of the integration of visual and tactile/haptic cues in a height judgement task (where the participants had to judge the height of a bar that they could see and also feel between the thumb and index finger of one hand). Research conducted in the last few years has shown maximum likelihood to provide a surprisingly good account of the relative contribution of each of the senses to multisensory perception in a variety of different settings (e.g. Alais & Burr, 2004;

see Ernst & Bülthoff 2004 for a review). However, it is worth pointing out that some residual role for directed attention still appears to be necessary (see Heller 1992; Battaglia et al. 2003; Guest & Spence 2003a), suggesting that there may ultimately be some truth to both the directed attention and modality appropriateness hypothesis accounts of sensory dominance in humans.

Auditory Contributions to Tactile Perception

A number of studies has demonstrated that manipulating the sounds people hear when they touch a surface can have a dramatic effect on the perceived roughness of the surface (Jousmäki & Hari 1998; Guest et al. 2002). More recently, applied researchers have shown that our perception of the pleasantness, powerfulness, and forcefulness of everything from electric toothbrushes to aerosol sprays can also be influenced by the sounds made when they are used (Zampini et al. 2003; Spence & Zampini 2007; see Spence & Zampini 2006 for a review).

Jousmäki and Hari (1998) reported a particularly dramatic demonstration of the auditory modulation of tactile perception, which they labelled the 'parchment-skin' illusion. They showed that people's perception of the skin on the palms of their own hands could be changed simply by changing the sounds they heard when they rubbed their hands together. Participants rated the perceived roughness/dryness of their own hands while rubbing them together (using a 'rough-moist/ smooth-dry' scale). The participants heard the sounds made by their hands (picked up by a microphone placed nearby) over headphones. This auditory feedback either consisted of the actual sound of their hands being rubbed together, or the sound was manipulated to reduce the overall sound level or to amplify or attenuate just the high-frequency components of the hand-rubbing sounds. Many of the participants reported their skin to feel 'smoother/dryer' (like parchment paper) when either the overall sound level was increased, or when just the high-frequency sounds were amplified. They also judged their hands to feel 'rougher/moister' when sounds in this frequency range were attenuated, or when the overall sound level was reduced.

Guest et al. (2002) both replicated and extended these findings using more rigorous psychophysical testing procedures. Once again, the hand-rubbing sounds that participants heard over the headphones were manipulated, but now they had to make separate ratings of how rough or moist their hands felt. Analysis of participants' responses indicated that their hands felt dryer when the concurrent hand-rubbing sounds were either played back more loudly or when just the high-frequency sounds were boosted. However, while the amplification of the auditory feedback led to an increase in 'smooth/dry' responses in Jousmäki and Hari's (1998) study, the same auditory manipulation only led to a significant increase in 'dry' responses in Guest et al.'s study (i.e. this auditory manipulation had no effect on participants' roughness judgements). Given Jousmäki and Hari's use of a *composite* response scale ('rough/moist to smooth/dry'), it is unclear which response dimension was actually driving the participants' responses in their study. In light of Guest et al.'s results, it would seem most likely that the participants based their responses on the 'wet-dry' dimension rather than on the 'rough-smooth' dimension. Despite this discrepancy, both sets of results clearly highlight the significant role played by auditory cues when people evaluate the feel of a surface, even for something as familiar as the feeling of the skin on their own hands.

Guest et al. (2002) have also shown that people's perception of the texture of sandpaper can be modified simply by varying the auditory feedback that they hear (Figure 2.1). The participants in this experiment made speeded discrimination responses regarding the roughness of

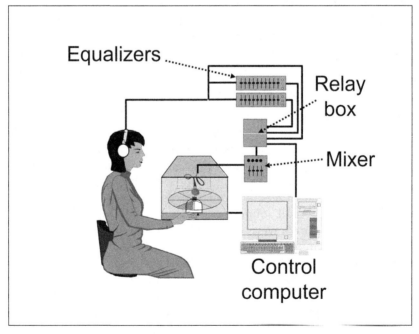

Figure 2.1   Equipment used in Guest et al.'s (2002) study investigating the influence of auditory cues on tactile perception of surface roughness of sandpapers.

various abrasive sandpapers (i.e. rough or smooth). Analysis of the responses indicated that the participants' perception of the roughness of the sandpaper samples was modulated by the frequency content of the auditory feedback of the sandpaper-rubbing sounds. The amplification of the high-frequency sounds appeared to result in an increase in the perception of sandpaper roughness, while the attenuation of these sounds appeared to make the surfaces feel smoother.

Other apparently uni-sensory 'tactile' phenomena may also reflect the consequences of changes in auditory perception. For example, Gordon and Cooper (1975) showed that people's ability to discriminate the orientation of an undulation embedded in an otherwise smooth surface improved if they held a piece of paper under their fingertips, rather than touching the surface directly. This 'paper effect' (Green 1981) has been known and used by skilled craftsmen (furniture makers, automotive panel beaters) for many years, and has been attributed by psychologists to the paper's possibly 'masking' the activity of certain classes of receptors in the skin (Gordon & Cooper 1975), or to changes in the shear forces on the skin (induced by the paper) somehow facilitating tactile perception (Lederman 1978a, 1978b). However, one of the most noticeable changes induced by the use of the paper is how much more one can hear with the paper in place (Why not try this for yourself?). Given the results of Guest et al.'s (2002) study, it would seem likely that the improved tactile sensitivity may have been attributable to the fact that the paper acts as a sort of amplifier, and that the touch-related sounds elicited when people touch a textured surface influence their judgements of how it feels (at either a conscious or subconscious level).

Olfactory Contributions to Tactile Perception

Far less research has been directed at investigating the nature of any cross-modal interactions between olfaction and touch. One of the first studies in this area was conducted by Laird (1932), who conducted a house-to-house survey in which each of 250 housewives was presented with four pairs of silk stockings, each pair in a separate box. The housewives were given the following instructions:

> Here are four pairs of hose that are very much alike. They are the same colour, and all are made in exactly the same pattern and style. Which pair do you judge to be the best quality? Feel them in your fingers, look through them, stretch them, look at the seams. Do anything you would ordinarily do to pick out the best for your own use. (Laird 1932, 244)

In fact, the stockings were identical except for the fact that each had a different smell (a 'natural' slightly rancid fragrance, a complex fruity fragrance, a faint synthetic scent with narcissus predominating, and a 'sachet' scent). Fifty percent of the housewives reported that they preferred the narcissus-scented hosiery over the others (24% preferred the fruity scent, 18% preferred the sachet scent, and 8% preferred the 'natural' scent). Interestingly, the majority of the women attributed their preferences not to the smell of the scented hosiery (which only six of the women noticed), but to tactile and/or visual attributes such as the texture, durability, sheen, weight, or weave of the stockings.

More recently, Demattè et al. (2006; experiment 1) investigated whether the presence of an odour (either pleasant or unpleasant) would also modulate people's perception of the *softness* of fabric samples under rather more controlled laboratory conditions. Participants were seated in front of a carousel on which ten different cotton terry–towelling fabric swatches were mounted (Figure 2.2, upper left panel; note that the swatches were hidden from the participant's view during the experiment itself). The swatches had been chemically treated to

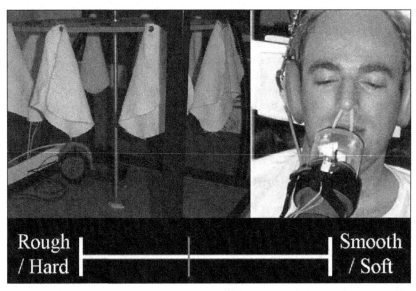

Figure 2.2   Experimental set-up used in Demattè et al.'s (2006) investigation of effects of smell on tactile perception of fabric softness.
The upper left panel shows the fabric swatches hanging from a computer-controlled carousel. On each trial, participants had to feel a fabric swatch, then rate its perceived softness using a visual analog scale (the lower panel). An olfactory stimulus was delivered by a computer-controlled olfactometer direct to the participant's nose (the upper right panel).

alter their softness. On each trial, the participants had to feel one of the swatches and rate its perceived softness using a visual scale presented on a computer monitor (Figure 2.2, lower panel).

The participants were able to discriminate between the different fabric swatches fairly accurately in the absence of any odour. While participants were evaluating the feel of a swatch, the computer could also deliver a specific odour (either a lemon odour or an animal-like odour) directly to the participant's nostrils; then, the participants were asked to report on the perceived softness of the fabric they were feeling using a twenty-point rating scale.

Participants who felt the fabric swatch while experiencing the 'pleasant' lemon odour rated the fabric as significantly softer than when the swatch was paired with the 'unpleasant' animal odour.

An important question for future research will be to determine whether the olfactory modulation of tactile perception is restricted to the perception of fabrics (i.e. to surfaces/materials that are commonly scented), or whether such crossmodal influences also extend to people's perception of other surfaces (e.g. sandpaper) that may not typically be associated with any particular fragrance. It is interesting to note that many studies have demonstrated the significant effect that olfactory cues have on people's perception of (and responses to) many different kinds of products (e.g. see Byrne-Quinn 1988; Bone & Jantrania 1992; Gulas & Bloch 1995). Researchers have also shown that ambient odours can influence people even when presented at such low levels that they are not perceived consciously (see Spence 2002). The studies reviewed in this section highlight the important, if often unrecognized, role that olfactory cues can play in determining our reactions to many different products, materials, and surface qualities.

Individual Differences in Multisensory Integration

One area of research that has received relatively little attention, but which is of particular importance to the themes of this volume, relates to the question of whether there are substantive individual differences in multisensory perception. In other words, are there certain individuals for whom the non-visual senses have a bigger impact on their tactile perception than they do for others. Are there, for example, individual differences in the extent to which vision dominates tactile perception? Over the years, several researchers have made such claims, albeit anecdotally (e.g. see Binns 1937; McDonnell & Duffett 1972; Samuel 1981; Heller 1992), but there has been little systematic attempt to account for what may underlie such individual differences, should they prove to be reliable.

A number of factors may play a role here, including both age- and sex-related differences in sensory perception (e.g. Corso 1971; Baker, 1987; Velle 1987), genetic differences in sensory perception (Hollingham 2004), individual differences in sensory style (Wober 1966, 1991), differences in the level of expertise (Binns 1937), and differences in terms of how long people have been in possession of a particular item (Fenko et al. 2007). Cultural factors may also play an important, if as yet understudied, role (see Howes 1991, 2005; MacDonald 2002). It is, for example, well known that sensory acuity declines as people get older (Corso 1971; Nusbaum 1999). However, the rate at which our perceptual abilities decline differs quite dramatically across the various senses. Note also that sensory prostheses (hearing aids, glasses) can correct for certain kinds of sensory loss when they occur. While tactile, auditory, and visual perceptual abilities already show clear signs of decline by the time we reach middle age, taste and smell sensitivity do not show any marked deterioration until we reach 60 to 70 years of age, whereupon aging takes a greater toll on smell than on taste (see Corso 1971; Doty et al. 1984; Nusbaum 1999).

Shimokata and Kuzuya (1995) conducted a very large study in which they examined the tactile acuity of 2000 people using a two-point discrimination task. The results showed that tactile acuity, measured in terms of the minimum spatial separation between two points needed for people to reliably judge there to be two stimuli rather than one, started to decline even in adolescence and continued its decline at least to middle age. Recalling the maximum likelihood estimation model of sensory dominance described earlier, we might expect that the inevitable decline in visual acuity over the lifespan (if left uncorrected) would result in an increased dominance of the visual modality over the increasingly insensitive (and inaccurate) sense of touch (see Heller 1983, 1992, 659).

There have been suggestions that individuals may vary in their sensory style, that is, in the sensory modality that they prefer to use when learning or when interacting with an object (e.g. see Wober 1966, 1991). In terms of the models of sensory dominance outlined earlier, we might attempt to explain such differences in sensory style (or 'sensotype') in terms of individual differences in the sense a particular individual attends to preferentially (e.g. Posner et al. 1976; Battaglia et al. 2003; see also Heller 1992). This, of course, might interact with expertise, since people may have learned to use one sense more efficiently than another through experience.

The early work by Henry Binns (1937) at the Bradford woollen mills regarding people's judgements of wool textiles is pertinent in this regard. Binns showed that those individuals charged with assessing the quality of the wool-tops (wool-tops consist of a mass of fibres, the whole about an inch thick and the individual fibres lying parallel one to another in a rope-like, untwisted 'sliver') initially tended to base their judgements on the tactile attributes of the wool-tops (in particular, on their softness). However, the more-expert assessors were found to weight vision (in particular, the visually perceived 'fineness' of the wool-tops) more heavily (Binns 1937, 407).

By contrast, Power and Graham (1976) showed that a tactually experienced group of subjects (potters) showed just as much visual dominance over touch in a form-perception task (similar to the intersensory conflict experiments conducted by Rock that were described earlier) as a tactually inexperienced group of participants (university students). When vision was denied to both groups, the potters (who had to make fine haptic discrimination judgements as part of their training and practice) were able to perform the task more accurately than the university students. These findings appear to conflict with those of Binns (1937) in suggesting that tactual training does not necessarily lead to reduced visual dominance when the senses are put into conflict. It is worth noting that the two studies differ in that Binns tested his participants using the stimuli which they had become expert at judging (wool-tops), whereas Power and Graham tested their potters with stimuli unrelated to their expertise (namely, squares whose size was distorted by a lens). Further work on the interaction between expertise and sensory dominance will be needed to resolve this important issue.

Recent questionnaire-based research by Fenko et al. (2007) has shown that the dominant sensory modality in our interactions with everyday products may actually change as a function of usage (and stage of ownership of a product). According to the reports of the 51 participants tested in the study, vision appears to be the most important sensory modality at the moment of purchase for most new products. However, within a week of purchase, the tactile/haptic attributes of the products were found to have become just as important as the visual attributes. When a month had elapsed there was no longer any significant difference between the rated importance of the various sensory product attributes. We need only think of purchasing a new pair of shoes to see the plausibility of these findings: While visual cues often dictate our behaviour at the point of purchase (how fashionable or beautiful the shoes look), the tactile attributes of the shoes (whether they are comfortable or rub our feet) soon come to the fore in determining if and when we will decide to wear them. How the hierarchy of sensory dominance relating to our perception and/or appreciation of particular objects changes during ownership, as a function of changes in expertise, and over the course of a lifetime, would all seem to be particularly germane areas for future research.

Cortical Plasticity and Sensory Reorganization Following Sensory Loss

Much research has also been directed at the question of how the residual senses function, both individually and together, following the complete loss of (or in congenital absence of) a particular sense (usually vision; see Hötting & Röder 2004). The latest findings suggest that the loss of a sense may actually result in somewhat improved sensory acuity in the residual senses. For example, Röder et al. have shown that blind individuals have more acute hearing in the periphery than the sighted (Röder et al. 1999). Tactile perception also appears to be enhanced in the blind compared to the sighted in certain tasks (Röder et al. 2004), as does olfactory sensitivity (see Spence 2002 for a review). These individual differences in sensitivity following the loss of input from a particular sense appear to result from changes in the brain attributable to cortical plasticity. Cognitive neuroscience research has now shown that in blind individuals the part of the brain (known as the occipital cortex) that is normally used for processing what sighted people see appears to be partially taken over by touch to augment the tactile information processing taking place in the somatosensory cortex (e.g. see Sadato et al. 1996; Cohen et al. 1997).

The latest research from Mehrabiat and his colleagues (Mehrabiat et al. 2005) has shown that normal sighted individuals who have been blindfolded for no more than five days will actually start to show the very first signs of such cortical reorganization. That is, their brain scans show evidence of the visual cortex being recruited to perform purely tactile tasks after blindfolding. Perhaps even more remarkably, it has now been shown that spending as little as 90 minutes in complete darkness can result in a significant short-lasting improvement in both tactile spatial acuity and sound localization in sighted people (Facchini & Aglioti 2003; Lewald 2007).

Conclusions

Taken together, the evidence reviewed in this chapter highlights the fact that there is more to the sense of touch than simply what is going on at the skin surface. In fact, a large body of cognitive neuroscience research now supports the view that our tactile/haptic perception of both the structural and surface properties of objects, as well as their perceived functionality (Schifferstein & Spence, in press), can be profoundly influenced by what we see, as well as what we hear—and even, on occasion, what we smell—when touching, interacting with, or evaluating an object, product, or artefact. The tactile/haptic perception of objects/artefacts really ought to be considered a genuinely multi-sensory experience (see Warren & Rossano 1991; Calvert et al. 2004), whether we realize it or not.

It is worth noting that these multisensory contributions to tactile perception tend to be more pronounced when the various sensory stimuli are presented from the same position (Miller 1972; Stein & Meredith 1993; Gephstein et al. 2005; Congedo et al. 2006), and at more or less the same time (Stein & Meredith 1993; Guest et al. 2002). An observer's beliefs concerning whether or not certain sensory impressions belong together, a phenomenon known as the 'unity assumption' (Welch & Warren 1980; Vatakis & Spence in press) has also been shown to influence how the senses are combined (Miller 1972; Spence 2007), and this represents an increasingly important area of research.

Finally, optimizing the multisensory nature of our tactile experiences with objects/artefacts in the future would appear to be a particularly worthwhile pursuit, given that multisensory experiences are generally richer, more pleasurable, and more memorable than unisensory experiences (e.g. see Knasko 1993; Stein & Meredith 1993; Hoffman et al. 1998; Pine & Gilmore 1998; Dinh et al. 1999; Spence 2002; Howes 2005; Vlahos 2006; Schifferstein & Spence in press).

References

Alais, D., Burr, D. 2004. The ventriloquist effect results from near-optimal bimodal integration. *Current Biology* 14:257–62.

Arnold, K. 2003. Skulls, mummies and unicorns' horns: Medicinal chemistry in early English museums. In R.G.W. Anderson, M.L. Caygill, A.G. MacGregor, and L. Syson (eds.), *Enlightening the British: Knowledge, Discovery and the Museum in the Eighteenth Century*. London: British Museum Press, 74–80.

Baker, M.A. 1987. Sensory functioning. In M.A. Baker (ed.), *Sex Differences in Human Performance*. Chichester: Wiley, 5–36.

Battaglia, P.W., Jacobs, R.A., Aslin, R.N. 2003. Bayesian integration of visual and auditory signals for spatial localization. *Journal of the Optical Society of America* 20:1391–97.

Bergmann Tiest, W.M., Kappers, A.M.L. 2006. Analysis of haptic perception of materials by multidimensional scaling and physical measurements of roughness and compressibility. *Acta Psychologica* 121:21–41.

Berkeley, G. 1709/1957. *A New Theory of Vision*. London: J. M. Dent.

Binns, H. 1937. Visual and tactual 'judgement' as illustrated in a practical experiment. *British Journal of Psychology* 27:404–10.

Bone, P.F., Jantrania, S. 1992. Olfaction as a cue for product quality. *Marketing Letters* 3:289–96.

Byrne-Quinn, J. 1988. Perfume, people, perceptions, and products. In S. Van Toller and G. Todd (eds.), *Perfumery: The Psychology and Biology of Fragrance*. New York: Chapman and Hall, 205–16.

Calvert, G.A., Spence, C., Stein, B.E. (eds.). 2004. *The Handbook of Multisensory Processes*. Cambridge, MA: MIT Press.

Classen, C. 2005. Touch in the museum. In C. Classen (ed.), *The Book of Touch*. Oxford: Berg, 275–86.

Cohen, L.G., Celnik, P., Pascual-Leone, A., Corwell, B., Faiz, L., Dambrosia, J., Honda, M., Sadato, N., Gerloff, C., Catala, M.D., Hallett, M. 1997. Functional relevance of cross-modal plasticity in blind humans. *Nature* 389:180–83.

Congedo, M., Lécuyer, A., Gentaz, E. 2006. The influence of spatial delocation on perceptual integration of vision and touch. *Presence: Teleoperators and Virtual Environments* 15:353–57.

Corso, J.F. 1971. Sensory processes and age effects in normal adults. *Journal of Gerontology* 26:90–105.

Demattè, M.L., Sanabria, D., Sugarman, R., Spence, C. 2006. Cross-modal interactions between olfaction and touch. *Chemical Senses* 31:291–300.

Dinh, H.Q., Walker, N., Hodges, L.F., Song, C., Kobayashi, A. 1999. Evaluating the importance of multi-sensory input on memory and the sense of presence in virtual environments. *Proceedings of IEEE Virtual Reality Conference 1999*, Houston, TX., 13–17 March, 222–28.

Doty, R.L., Shaman, P., Applebaum, S.L., Giberson, R., Siksorski, L., Rosenberg, L. 1984. Smell identification ability: Changes with age. *Science* 226:1441–43.

Ernst, M.O., Banks, M.S. 2002. Humans integrate visual and haptic information in a statistically optimal fashion. *Nature* 415:429–33.

Ernst, M.O., Bülthoff, H.H. 2004. Merging the senses into a robust percept. *Trends in Cognitive Sciences* 8: 162–69.

Facchini, S., Aglioti, S.M. 2003. Short-term light deprivation increases tactile spatial acuity in humans. *Neurology* 60:1998–99.

Fenko, A., Schifferstein, H.N.J., Hekkert, P. 2007. Which senses dominate in various stages of user-product interaction? *Submitted*.

Field, B. 1975. *Hands-on Museums: Partners in Learning*. New York: Educational Facilities Laboratories.

Freides, D. 1974. Human information processing and sensory modality: Cross-modal functions, information complexity, memory, and deficit. *Psychological Bulletin* 81:284–310.

Gephstein, S., Burge, J., Ernst, M.O., Banks, M.S. 2005. The combination of vision and touch depends on spatial proximity. *Journal of Vision* 5:1013–23.

Gibson, J.J. 1933. Adaptation, after-effect, and contrast in the perception of curved lines. *Journal of Experimental Psychology* 16:1–31.

Gordon, I.E., Cooper, C. 1975. Improving one's touch. *Nature* 256:203–204.

Green, B.G. 1981. Tactile roughness and the 'paper effect'. *Bulletin of the Psychonomic Society* 18:155–58.

Guest, S., Catmur, C., Lloyd, D., Spence, C. 2002. Audiotactile interactions in roughness perception. *Experimental Brain Research* 146:161–71.

Guest. S., Spence, C. 2003a. What role does multisensory integration play in the visuotactile perception of texture? *International Journal of Psychophysiology* 50: 63–80.

——— 2003b. Tactile dominance in speeded discrimination of pilled fabric samples. *Experimental Brain Research* 150:201–207.

——— 2007. Tactile dominance in fabric texture perception. *Submitted*.

Gulas, C.S., Bloch, P.H. 1995. Right under our noses: Ambient scent and consumer responses. *Journal of Business and Psychology* 10:87–98.

Hay, J.C., Pick, H.L. Jr., Ikeda, K. 1965. Visual capture produced by prism spectacles. *Psychonomic Science* 2: 215–16.

Heller, M.A. 1983. Haptic dominance in form perception with blurred vision. *Perception* 12:607–13.

——— 1989. Texture perception in sighted and blind observers. *Perception & Psychophysics* 45:49–54.

——— 1992. Haptic dominance in form perception: Vision versus proprioception. *Perception* 21:655–60.

Hoffman, H.G., Hollander, A., Schroder, K., Rousseau, S., Furness, T.I. 1998. Physically touching and tasting virtual objects enhances the realism of virtual experiences. *Journal of Virtual Reality* 3: 226–34.

Hollingham, R. 2004. In the realm of your senses. *New Scientist*, 31 January, 40–43.

Hooke, R. 1705/1971. *The posthumous works of Robert Hooke*, R. Waller (ed.), 2nd facsimile ed. London.

Hornik, J. 1992. Tactile stimulation and consumer response. *Journal of Consumer Research* 19:449–58.

Hötting, K., Röder, B. 2004. Hearing cheats touch, but less in congenitally blind than in sighted individuals. *Psychological Science* 15: 60–64.

Howes, D. (ed.). 1991. *The varieties of sensory experience: A sourcebook in the anthropology of the senses*. Toronto: University of Toronto Press.

——— 2005. Hyperesthesia, or, the sensual logic of late capitalism. In D. Howes (ed.), *Empire of the Senses: The Sensual Culture Reader*. Oxford: Berg, 281–303.

Jousmäki, V., Hari, R. 1998. Parchment-skin illusion: Sound-biased touch. *Current Biology* 8:869–72.

Katz, D. 1925/1989. *The World of Touch*. Hillsdale, NJ: Erlbaum.

Klatzky, R.L., Lederman, S., Reed, C. 1989. Haptic integration of object properties: Texture, hardness, and planar contour. *Journal of Experimental Psychology: Human Perception and Performance* 15:45–57.

Knasko, S.C. 1993. Lingering time in a museum in the presence of congruent and incongruent odors. *Chemical Senses* 18:581.

Koran, J.J., Jr., Morrison, L., Lehman, J.R., Koran, M.L., Gandara, L. 1984. Attention and curiosity in museums. *Journal of Research in Science Teaching* 21:357–63.

Laird, D.A. 1932. How the consumer estimates quality by subconscious sensory impressions: With special reference to the role of smell. *Journal of Applied Psychology* 16: 241–46.

Lederman, S.J. 1978a. Heightening tactile impressions of surface texture. In G. Gordon (ed.), *Active touch: The mechanism of recognition of objects by manipulation. An interdisciplinary approach.* Oxford: Pergamon, 205–214.

——— 1978b. 'Improving one's touch' ...and more. *Perception & Psychophysics* 24 :154–60.

Lederman, S.J., Abbott, S.G. 1981. Texture perception: Studies of intersensory organisation using a discrepancy paradigm and visual versus tactual psychophysics. *Journal of Experimental Psychology: Human Perception & Performance* 7: 902–15.

Lederman, S.J., Klatzky, R.L. 2004. Multisensory texture perception. In G.A. Calvert, C. Spence, and B.E. Stein (eds.), *The Handbook of Multisensory Processes.* Cambridge, MA: MIT Press, 107–22.

Lederman. S.J., Thorne, G., Jones, B. 1986. Perception of texture by vision and touch: Multidimensionality and intersensory integration. *Journal of Experimental Psychology: Human Perception & Performance* 12:169–80.

Lewald, J. 2007. More accurate sound localisation induced by short-term light deprivation. *Neuropsychologia* 45:1215–22.

MacDonald, A.S. 2002. The scenario of sensory encounter: Cultural factors in sensory-aesthetic experience. In W.S. Green and P.W. Jordan (eds.), *Pleasure with Products.* London: Taylor & Francis, 113–23.

McDonnell, P.M., Duffett, J. 1972. Vision and touch: A reconsideration of conflict between the two senses. *Canadian Journal of Psychology* 26:171–80.

Merabet, L.B., Maguire, D., Warde, A., Alterescu, K., Stickgold, R., Pascual-Leone, A. 2004. Visual hallucinations during prolonged blindfolding in sighted subjects. *Journal of Neuro-ophthalmology* 24:109–13.

Miller, E.A. 1972. Interaction of vision and touch in conflict and nonconflict form perception tasks. *Journal of Experimental Psychology* 96:114–23.

Nusbaum, N.J. 1999. Aging and sensory senescence. *Southern Medical Journal* 92:267–75.

Oppenheimer, F. 1972. The exploratorium: A playful museum combines perception and art and science education. *American Journal of Physics* 40: 978–84.

Picard, D., Dacremont, C., Valentin, D., Giboreau, A. 2003. Perceptual dimensions of tactile textures. *Acta Psychologica* 114:165–84.

Pine, B. J. II, Gilmore, J.H. 1998. Welcome to the experience economy. *Harvard Business Review* 764:97–105.

Posner, M.I., Nissen, M.J., Klein, R.M. 1976. Visual dominance: An information-processing account of its origins and significance. *Psychological Review* 83:157–71.

Power, R.P., Graham, A. 1976. Dominance of touch by vision: Generalization of the hypothesis to a tactually experienced population. *Perception* 5:161–66.

Rock, I., Harris, C.S. 1967. Vision and touch. *Scientific American* 216:96–104.

Rock, I., Victor, J. 1964. Vision and touch: An experimentally created conflict between the two senses. *Science* 143:594–96.

Röder, B., Rösler, F., Spence, C. 2004. Early vision impairs tactile perception in the blind. *Current Biology* 14:121–24.

Röder, B., Teder-Salajärvi, W., Sterr, A., Rösler, F., Hillyard, S.A., Neville, H.J. 1999. Improved auditory spatial tuning in blind humans. *Nature* 400:162–66.

Roland, P.E., O'Sullivan, B., Kawashima, R. 1998. Shape and roughness activate different somatosensory areas in the human brain. *Proceedings of the National Academy of Sciences U.S.A.* 95:3295–3300.

Sadato, N., Pascual-Leone, A., Grafman, J., Ibañez, V., Deiber, M.-P., Dold, G., Hallett, M. 1996. Activation of the primary visual cortex by Braille reading in blind subjects. *Nature* 380:526–28.

Samuel, J.M.F. 1981. Individual differences in the interaction of vision and proprioception. In R.D. Walk and H.L. Pick, Jr. (eds.), *Intersensory perception and sensory integration*. New York: Plenum, 375–98.

Schifferstein, H.N.J., Spence, C. In press. Multisensory product experience. To appear in P. Hekkert & H.N.J. Schifferstein (eds.), *Product Design*. London: Taylor & Francis.

Shimokata, H., Kuzuya, F. 1995. Two-point discrimination test of the skin as an index of sensory aging. *Gerontology* 41:267–72.

Spence, C. 2002. *The ICI report on the Secret of the Senses*. London: The Communication Group.

—— 2007. Audiovisual multisensory integration. *Acoustical Science & Technology* 28: 61–70.

Spence, C., Zampini, M. 2006. Auditory contributions to multisensory product perception. *Acta Acustica united with Acustica* 92:1009–25.

—— 2007. Affective design: Modulating the pleasantness and forcefulness of aerosol sprays by manipulating aerosol spraying sounds. *CoDesign* 3 [Suppl 1]: 109–23.

Stein, B.E., Meredith, M.A. 1993. *The Merging of the Senses*. Cambridge, MA: MIT Press.

Vatakis, A., Spence, C. In press. Crossmodal binding: Evaluating the 'unity assumption' using audiovisual speech stimuli. *Perception & Psychophysics*.

Velle, W. 1987. Sex differences in sensory functions. *Perspectives in Biology and Medicine* 30:490–522.

Vlahos, J. 2006. The smell of war. *Popular Science* 8:72–95.

Warren, D.H., Rossano, M.J. 1991. Intermodality relations: Vision and touch. In M.A. Heller and W. Schiff (eds.), *The psychology of touch*. Hillsdale, NJ: Lawrence Erlbaum, 119–37.

Welch, R.B., Warren, D.H. 1980. Immediate perceptual response to intersensory discrepancy. *Psychological Bulletin* 3:638–67.

Wober, M. 1966. Sensotypes. *Journal of Social Psychology*, 70:181–89.

—— 1991. The sensotype hypothesis. In D. Howes (ed.), *The Varieties of Sensory Experience: A Sourcebook in the Anthropology of the Senses*. Toronto: University of Toronto Press, 31–42.

Zampini, M., Guest, S., Spence, C. 2003. The role of auditory cues in modulating the perception of electric toothbrushes. *Journal of Dental Research* 82:929–32.

3

ARCHAEOLOGY OF TOUCH: BABYLONIAN MAGIC AND HEALING

Mark Geller

There is a limit to what we can discover today about the significance of ancient objects simply by handling them. Although icons, relics, and amulets obviously have religious and healing properties, the significance and use of such objects can only be determined by living informants or texts. Ancient Mesopotamia, one of the very richest areas of archaeological inquiry, has produced an abundance of magical plaques, gems, amulets, figurines, and other objects for use in magic and therapy, all of which were presumably to be seen or touched in order to be effective. Were these objects touched, and if so, how, and for what purpose? The precise uses of cultic objects can only be known to us from non-archaeological sources.

The main question before us is how we assess the power/effect of touch beyond the realm of artifacts and items. We need to know what touching means in reference to magic and healing, and why touching a ritual object should effect reality or a perception of reality. The idea of touching can be both positive and negative, depending on whether we are looking for protection ('touch wood') or have been 'touched' by events, either emotionally or physically. If touching can be both positive and negative, how would we know if an object is to be touched or is forbidden to be touched, unless texts tell us so? A well-known illustration of this comes from the Bible, when David was bringing the

Ark of the Covenant from Philistia to Jerusalem and it was touched by a non-priest, who died instantly (2 Samuel 6:7).

Ancient Mesopotamia is an ideal region to study magical objects and magical practices, partly because the past century of archaeology has uncovered myriads of relevant artifacts, and partly because magic itself forms such a major part of Mesopotamian literature. Incantations begin to appear already in the third millennium BCE in both Sumerian and Akkadian, and by the second millennium we find elaborate magical texts and rituals describing many different types of healing practices and spells. The magical corpus consists of incantations, from simple spells designed to counter fears and neurotic anxieties against snakebite, dog-bite, and scorpions stings, to long and complex compositions aimed at treating other kinds of physical and psychological distress, such as paranoia, excessive guilt, insomnia, impotence, depression, and low self-esteem. The incantation priest possessed an impressive repertoire of magical texts, some hundreds of lines long, and these existed in tandem with an equally large corpus of medical texts, dealing with diagnosis and prescriptions, drugs and treatments, in a non-magical system of therapy. In both these genres, the idea of 'touching' appears in many different contexts and with different connotations. Many of the texts were widely circulated over a long period in antiquity.

Magical Touching

The word *touch* is a key term within ancient Babylonian magic and medicine, both for describing the effects of demons and disease, and as a therapeutic strategy for treating illness. The terminology is not simply a linguistic curiosity but tells us something about the psychology of illness in Mesopotamia.

Philologists specialising in the languages of Mesopotamia have so far paid insufficient attention to the idiomatic uses of terms for *touch* and *touching* (Sumerian *tag*, Akkadian *lapâtu, liptu*). The word for touch is used in incantations and medical texts in Akkadian in the negative sense of 'afflicting' (literally, touching) the victim and in the positive sense of 'treating' (literally, touching) the patient. Negative meanings associated with touch appear early on in Sumerian, since the abstract noun *nam-tag-ga* (literally, touching) takes on the meanings of 'guilt', 'offence', and 'punishment', and is often used to define the relationship of the perceived sinner to the gods. For this reason, treatment of *nam-tag-ga* 'guilt' (or feelings of guilt) became one of the primary objectives of magical spells.

To an outside observer, the use of such ambiguous terminology can be confusing. A good example of this, in ancient terms, is the proper name of the Sumerian king, who bore a Semitic name, Lipit-Ishtar, and is famed for producing one of the first law codes in Mesopotamia, pre-dating Hammurabi and his more famous code by more than a century. The meaning of Lipit-Ishtar's name is clear—touch of Ishtar—but is it positive or negative? As a newborn baby, was his mother influenced ('touched') by Ishtar and became pregnant, or was the baby himself 'touched' by Ishtar because he had some physical deformity or defect? We are not told by the ancients, and we are left to find the answers for ourselves among the many uses of our term for 'touch'.

Negative Touching

The Akkadian word *lapâtu*, 'to touch', and its associated noun *liptu*, frequently appears in both incantations and medical texts referring to the touch of demons, meaning that the victim has come in contact with a demon. (*Chicago Assyrian Dictionary* L 88ff; Heeßel 2000, 413). As Nils Heeßel points out,

> The 'hand of the gods' is only one, albeit the most frequent, phrase used to name the supposed divine involvement. The gods can also 'seize' … , 'touch' … , 'strike' … , or 'reach' … the human being and these verbs can even be combined with the phrase 'hand of the god'. It should be remarked that a 'touch by the divine' is common to all these expressions and we should not ignore this fact. Here, so it seems, is a trace of how the Babylonians saw the process of falling sick. It apparently required physical contact between the god and the human being. (Heeßel 2007, 125)

Heeßel's remarks are based upon the very common term for disease as the 'hand' of a god or demon or ghost in Babylonian diagnosis and therapy, suggesting on one level at least that contact with a god or demon was responsible for the illness. (The expression 'hand of a god' became used as a generic term for disease, without much in the way of religious overtones.)

The 'touch' of the demon was one of the primary expressions for demonic attack in Mesopotamia. Here are some examples from Sumerian-Akkadian bilingual incantations:

> May you, evil Utukku-demon (and) ghost who have *touched* the man,
> (and) you, Fate-demon, who *touched* the man's head,
> (along with) the evil mouth and evil tongue which swear (falsely),
> the evil Utukku-demon who gazed at the man,
> and magic and evil sorcery of a man under oath—
> (all) be smashed like a pot and poured out like water.
> (Utukku Lemnutu Incantations Tablet VI 141'–146', to be published in the author's forthcoming *Canonical Utukku Lemnutu Incantations*, Helsinki University Press)

A familiar description of demons within these incantations, warning that the demons 'approached that man and *touched* his hand, chased after him and went to his house, and made the man neglect his body (literally, limbs)' (Utukku Lemnutu Incantations VII 34–36). In the same vein, the demon is ordered as follows: 'You must not place your head upon his head, your hand upon his hand, your foot upon his foot. You must not *touch* him with your hand' (Utukku Lemnutu Incantations IV 179'–182'). Likewise, the feared demon Lamashtu, who attacks women during childbirth and newborn infants, attacks by touching the bellies of women in labour (see *Chicago Assyrian Dictionary* L 85b). One medical text describes a woman in this same condition: 'If a woman has been "touched" by a "touch", the foetus is [dead(?)] in her belly' (Stol 2000, 54).

The touching of gods or demons is only one aspect of the evidence, since medical texts frequently refer to the patient being 'touched' (or 'affected') by diseases, without reference to demons or personifications of illness. In the same way, Babylonian Aramaic *nega^c* means both 'to touch' and 'to be afflicted with leprosy' (Sokoloff 2002, 729f.). In general terms, the Akkadian verb *lapâtu* can simply mean 'to hurt', referring to any part of the body, such as, 'if a man's ears hurt him' (Herrero 1984, 36). Hence a patient might have been touched by an illness, as in the following examples: 'If a man has pain in his kidney, his groin hurts him and his urine is white like donkey urine, and later on his urine shows blood....', or 'if a man's groin hurts him either when he walks or lies down' (Geller 2005, 49, 87). There is no intended reference to any etiology of disease in these contexts, as if diseases were manifestations of demonic contact, since the term is used here in strictly medical contexts referring to symptoms, without reference to magic. This general negative sense of touch can regularly be found in Babylonian omen literature, in which the term *lapâtu* simply means 'to be unfavourable' when referring to predictions (Starr 1990, 336ff).

The associated noun *liptu* 'touch' further reinforces this point, since it can also refer to a plague (*Chicago Assyrian Dictionary* L 201f.), as can Classical Hebrew *nega^c*. In physiognomic omens, the term *liptu* refers to a reddish spot or blemish on the body, and in fact an entire tablet of such omens is dedicated to the subject of the reddish *liptu*-spot on various parts of the human face and head (Böck 2000, 174f.). In Babylonian medical literature, *liptu* 'touch' became a generic term for disease in general. The Babylonian Diagnostic Handbook, which lists symptoms of illnesses from head to foot, refers in some cases to the 'nature of the "touch" (i.e. disease)' (Labat 1951, 108, 168) or to the 'touch of Fate' (Heeßel 2000, 363) or, specifically, to the touch of the patient's cheek (Heeßel 2000: 220, 224, 260). The general meaning of disease probably derives from the literal meaning of 'touch' within magical contexts, such as the statement in the Akkadian incantation series *Maqlû* against witchcraft, which describes the witch with the epigram, 'whose touch is death' (Maqlû III 81, with the reading corrected in *Archiv für Orientforschung* 21 [1966] 74).

Even within magic itself, examples of 'touching' in Mesopotamian magic can be positive or negative, depending upon whether the touch was that of a benevolent god or harmful demon. Two incantations from the same archive illustrate this point, both referring to Gula, patron goddess of medicine. One begins, 'O Gula, doctor to the people, your incantation is a cure, your *touch* is healing, (and) wherever I place my hands, you grant well-being' (Finkel 2000, 202). A second incantation in the same group of school texts was aimed against the demon Shulak, demon of the toilet, and begins, 'Shulak, who struck the young man and stole his life, angry *gallû*-demon, who spilled the blood of the young man .... You *touched* him, and he no longer enjoys good health' (Finkel 2000, 195). The same demon occurs again in an incantation (not yet edited) known as *bit meseri*, which refers to 'Shulak, whose touch is death' (see *Chicago Assyrian Dictionary* L 201).

The act of touching also conveys the notion of contagion in both magical and medical contexts, through coming into contact with someone or something bewitched or unclean. Even with ancient medical texts this contact is likely to be more magical than medical, in the sense that the patient is advised against touching something that can cause disease; he is specifically told that 'he should not touch an unclean person' (nu kù nu *i-lap-pat*, Thompson 1930, 129).

Positive Touching

In liver divination, during which the entrails of sheep are examined for omens, the 'touch of the hand' (*lipit qâti*) refers to performing a ritual accompanying the omens, and hence is positive (see *Chicago Assyrian Dictionary* L 202). Similarly, another positive use of Akkadian *lapâtu* is to 'smear', specifically in ritual contexts. This usually includes such actions as smearing gypsum onto the door frame of the victim's house to prevent demons from entering: 'I have smeared (literally, touched) the threshold of the house with bitumen and gypsum' (Utukku Lemnutu incantations Tablet IX 75). Alternatively, the same word can refer to rubbing (literally, touching) some part of the patient's body with a salve or ointment, or 'touching' sexual organs to arouse desire, in potency incantations (Biggs 1967, 40; Goltz 1974, 69). In one magical ritual to ward off ghosts, the *materia medica* is to be *smeared* (literally, touched) on the patient's temples so that the 'hand of the ghost' (disease) will never return and 'touch' the patient again; the word *lapâtu* in this context refers both to the positive application of the ritual (smearing) and the feared attack (touch) of the demon (Scurlock 2006, 328).

The same term for touch also occurs in incantation rituals, as in the scapegoat ritual in the same Utukku Lemnutu incantations cited above, in which the incantation priest ties a goat to the patient's bed, after which the incantation priest 'touches' the goat's throat and sacrifices it, placing the dead goat's body upon that of the patient (to transfer the disease from one body to another). The touch of the incantation priest is the effective component of the ritual process.

The recitation of an incantation referring to touching is only one part of the process, but what about touching the object itself? Does touching an incantation tablet have any kind of healing power? One cylinder seal in the British Museum shows the healing goddess Gula with her dog and holding a tablet, as if the tablet itself is one of the instruments of healing, as an object (Collon 2001, no. 238). There is nothing comparable, however, within Mesopotamia to touching a relic, the bone of a holy person or priest, mostly because bones were considered impure and touching them could spread impurity, and the bones of the dead were expected to be buried as a complete corpse. Nevertheless, there are exceptional cases within Babylonian medical recipes in which *materia medica* include human bone as an ingredient, usually in the case of leather amulets to be worn by the patient, but without any hint of venerating the bones of holy persons.

Nevertheless, no archaeological object speaks for itself, and we have no way of knowing whether it was forbidden to touch such an amulet or ritual accoutrement. For instance, we find a long list of taboos within incantations known as *Shurpu*, among which are taboos associated with various musical instruments, such as the drum and kettle-drum, timbrel and cymbal, lyre and harp, lute and pipe, or a taboo associated with the skipping rope and astragal (see Reiner 1970, 21f.). These taboos, although vaguely referred to in the text, probably indicate the misuse or touching of objects that belonged to the temple and cult and should not be used for profane purposes; hence, touching them in non-sacred contexts would have been a sin.

Similarly, if a priest or diviner had touched a holy object, such as a sacrificial animal, while wearing soiled garments or street clothes, he would have put himself in mortal danger by committing a serious cultic offence (see *Chicago Assyrian Dictionary* I/J 56a, and Starr 1990, 198, no. 198).

Symbolic Touching

We occasionally encounter symbolic acts of touching the patient during the course of magical treatments. One such medical text, against depression (*kis libbi*) contains the following remedy:

> You place (the patient's) head below and you raise his feet high, in this *limp posture* you strike (his) cheek and in his *limp posture* you rub him down, and you should say to yourself that 'it is good'. With your left thumb you should touch his rectum 14 times, you should touch his head 14 times, and you should touch the earth. (Cadelli 2000, 109)

This type of ritual procedure is unusual, even within the context of some bizarre Mesopotamian healing rituals, and it seems clear that it is intended to be symbolic rather than therapeutic. This ritual, however, is not entirely unlike another ritual associated with an incantation addressed to Dumuzi, the dying god and lover of Ishtar. The ritual calls for the patient to be made to crawl under the bed, lying flat on his face. The therapist or exorcist turns the patient's face towards his feet and then 'touches' the patient seven times with a seven-knotted reed, and each time the patient must rotate himself around while the exorcist recites the phrase, 'May Ishtar your beloved go to your side' (Farber 1977, 155). The sympathetic power of this ritual resides in the reversal of the patient's position and being touched by the magic wand, in order to reverse any harmful magic and encourage the protection of the goddess.

In other instances, touching can have both symbolic meaning and refer to contamination. A good example are the omens referring to the man who encounters an unclean woman or a prostitute in the street. One text states that if a man touches an unclean woman in the street, he will remain impure for six days. Another omen, however, gives a more symbolic use for touching, explaining that 'if there is an unclean (i.e. menstruating) prostitute in front of him (in the street), if he touches her breast he will be released (from any evil omen resulting from this encounter)' (Köcher & Oppenheim 1957, 58, 71).

Negative Results from a Positive Touch?

'Touching of the hand' on a patient is, as expected, a normal part of the magical and medical treatment, even within Babylonian therapy in which surgery is hardly attested. The exorcist expresses the hope that 'when I approach the patient, and lay my hand on the patient's head, may the good spirit and good genius be present at my side' (Utukku Lemnutu Incantations Tablet III, 111f.). In other cases, however, 'touching the hand' on the patient or 'carrying the hand' to the patient refer specifically to medicine rather than exorcism, and not always in the most favourable light. Hemerologies, for instance, which specify lucky and unlucky days of the month, often declare that on certain unlucky days the physician 'is not to bring his hand to the patient' (Labat 1939, 62 et passim). An oracular text that addresses queries to the sun-god Shamash states, 'if you make an extispicy for the practice of medicine, the physician shall not touch the patient: the diviner shall not make a prognosis' (Starr 1990, 295, no. 317). In other words, if you take the trouble to go directly to the god and seek an oracular answer to a medical question, it is then better to avoid any other approach to healing (which may be less effective), such as going to the doctor or a diviner for a second opinion.

An unpublished stele from eighth-century BCE Syria records an autobiographical account of the life of the local ruler, who complains about the chronic illnesses he has suffered throughout his life [this information is courtesy of Prof. M.G. Massetti-Rouault, Ecole Pratique des Hautes Etudes, Paris]. The ruler mentions that no healing arts helped him, that he benefited neither from the 'touch of the hand of medicine' nor from the exorcist casting spells. The 'touching of hand' refers to the medical practices of the day, which the ruler found insufficient for his needs, and the usage in this text may well have pejorative connotations. I suggest that the ruler is being ironic here, with medicine of his day being hinted at as a useless enterprise (in his case at least) by being called the 'touch of the hand', since in other contexts the connotations of this phrase are clearly negative.

'Touch of the hand' (*lipit qâti*), indicating injurious activities, appears *inter alia* in Maqlû anti-witchcraft incantations. In one passage cataloguing various detrimental encounters in everyday life, the incantation lists sorcery and witchcraft, 'bad things done by people, "touching of the hands", "strangling of sheep" (disease), sacrifices and performing of divination' (Maqlû VII, 125f.; see also *Journal of the American Oriental Society* 59, 1939, 13). Although 'touch of the hands' may not be intrinsically negative, in some contexts it can have unpleasant results, in the same way that sacrifices can be ineffectual or divination may provide unwanted predictions. This idea is also expressed in another text, a series of litanies in which the patient lists all sins he may have committed unwittingly, and for which he is now being punished. The patient prays to the sun-god Shamash for any evil to be erased, and these evils include bad signs and omens, 'touching of the hands', and even performing divination, all of which have created obstacles for the patient (Reiner 1956, 143). Although touching may refer in other contexts to normal and necessary activities, within the context of these litanies, 'touching of the hands' is construed (together with divination) as something that 'blocks' the patient's progress. The idea appears to be that even worthwhile acts can have negative results.

Conclusion

To return to a question we posed earlier, whether Lipit-Ishtar's name could be positive or negative, we cannot be sure, but it seems likely that such a name was attached to a baby who was deemed to be ill or abnormal at birth, or perhaps whose mother had died in childbirth.

The effect of touching in Babylonian magic and medicine is often psychological rather than physical, in the same way that English slang sometimes refers to someone who is 'tetched', referring to be mentally ill or unstable. The significant point is that the touch of demons in Babylonia implies contact but not 'possession', in the Western sense of this word. The type of demonic possession known from the New Testament, in which the demon inhabits a person's body and speaks through the patient's mouth, is so far unattested in Babylonian magic (Stol 1993, 52). Even Aramaic magic bowls from the same region dating from late antiquity show no evidence for demonic possession like that in the New Testament, maintaining this distinction between Western and Mesopotamian magic. 'Touching' is as close as we come to the physical contact between humans and demons in Babylonian magic, and the 'hand of the god' expresses a similar idea within Babylonian medicine, but in neither case does the demon or god inhabit the body of the patient.

References

Biggs, R. 1967. *Ancient Mesopotamian Potency Incantations*. Locust Valley, NY: J.J. Augustin.

Böck, B. 2000. *Die babylonisch-assyrische Morphoskopie*. Vienna: Institut für Orientalistik, Universität Wien.

Cadelli, D. 2000. *Recherche sur la Médecine mésopotamienne* (unpub. Ph.D, Sorbonne, Paris).

Collon, D. 2001. *Catalogue of the Western Asiatic Seals in the British Museum, Cylinder Seals*, vol. 5. Neo-Assyrian and Neo-Babylonian Period. London: British Museum Press.

Farber, W. 1977. *Beschwörungsrituale an Ishtar und Dumuzi*. Wiesbaden: Franz Steiner Verlag.

Finkel, I.L. 2000. On Late Babylonian medical training. In A.R. George and I.L. Finkel, (eds.), *Wisdom, Gods and Literature*. Winona Lake, IN: Eisenbrauns, 137–223.

Geller, M. 2005. *Renal and Rectal Disease Texts*. (Babylonisch-assyrische Medizin, VII). Berlin: Walter de Gruyter.

Goltz, D. 1974. *Studien zur altorientalischen und griechischen Heilkunde*. Wiesbaden: Franz Steiner Verlag.

Heeßel, N. 2000. *Babylonisch-assyrische Diagnostik*. Münster: Ugarit Verlag.

——— 2007. The hand of the gods: Disease names and divine anger. In I.L. Finkel and M.J. Geller (eds.), *Disease in Babylonia*. Leiden, Boston: Brill, 120–30.

Herrero, P. 1984. *Thérapeutique mésopotamienne*. Paris: A.D.P.F.

Köcher. F., Oppenheim, A.L. 1957/58. The Old-Babylonian omen text VAT 7525. *Archiv für Orientforschung* 18:62–77.

Labat, R. 1939. *Hémerologies et Ménologies d'Assur*. Paris: Adrien Maisonneuve.

——— 1951. *Traité akkadien de diagnostics et pronostics médicaux*. Paris, Leiden: Academie Internationale d'Histoire des Sciences.

Reiner, E. 1956. *Lipshur* litanies. *Journal of Near Eastern Studies* 15:129–49.

——— 1970. *Shurpu, a Collection of Sumerian and Akkadian Incantations*. Osnabruck: Biblio-Verlag.

Scurlock, J. 2006. *Magico-Medical Means of Treating Ghost-induced Illnesses in Ancient Mesopotamia*. Leiden, Boston: Brill.

Sokoloff, M. 2002. *Dictionary of Jewish Babylonian Aramaic*. Baltimore: Bar Ilan University Press.

Starr, I. 1990. *Queries to the Sungod: Divination and Politics in Sargonid Assyria*. Helsinki: Helsinki University Press.

Stol, M. 1993. *Epilepsy in Babylonia*. Groningen: Styx.

——— 2000. *Birth in Babylonia and the Bible*. Groningen: Styx.

Thompson, R. 1930. Assyrian medical prescriptions against *Shimmatu* 'poison'. *Revue d'Assyriologie* 27: 127–36.

4

FOR YOUR EYES ONLY?
THE MAGIC TOUCH OF RELICS

Jan Geisbusch

Introduction

'It hit the spectator like a bullet, it happened to him, thus acquiring a tactile quality.' Walter Benjamin is alluding to the way Dadaist art had exploded the solemnity and intellectual detachment that formerly characterised the reception of artworks (1937/1999, 231). Whatever the merits of this particular appraisal, we are interested here in the connection Benjamin establishes between impact and tactility. It is this kind of sensuous 'drive-by shooting' that I explore here, though its ammunition is sacred objects rather than art (notwithstanding some overlap between the two categories, as discussed in this chapter). Our central concern is what might be termed 'modalities of perception' and their experiential and social implications with regard to the sacred.

Seeing and touching—as well as hearing, tasting, and smelling, though these are not our focus—represent complementing, but more often competing, modes of sensory experience. This chapter argues that they are implicated in broader issues over the development of a Western subject, its agency within the world, and, more specific to the topic, how it has conceptualised the sacred.

Relics

First of all, we need to clarify what is meant by 'relics'. The *Oxford Dictionary of the Christian Church* provides a workable definition: 'In Christian usage the word is applied to the material remains of a saint after his death and to sacred objects which have been in contact with his body' (Livingstone 1996, 433). Historically, such relics, especially the major ones, present themselves to us boxed into reliquaries, permanently installed in tombs and shrines. Typically, scholarly literature addressing the subject understands relics primarily as fixed, localised objects. Even analyses such as Geary's *Furta Sacra* (1978) and *Sacred Commodities* (1990), which show medieval relics in motion through gift giving, theft, or trade, assume that this state is only temporary, a movement between two points of immovability.

The natural condition of relics, it is implied, is that of motionlessness as the centre of sacred space. Their occasional movement is something of a liminal state, erasing, or at any rate threatening, the relic's ascribed cosmological position and authority; this authority has to be reconfirmed once the relic is installed in a new location—through miracles or heavenly signs, and through the incorporation into the new physical and institutional setting (the shrine and the religious community).

Yet there are also relics, and a vast multitude of them, the purpose of which is not to stay put but to circulate. These are the sort of relics that are available from religious congregations, religious goods shops, and even eBay, the Internet auction house. The Carmelite Sisters of Lisieux, for example, distributed an estimated 17 million (!) relics of their co-sister, St Theresa of the Child Jesus (1873–1897), between 1897 and 1925 (Figure 4.1) (Erret 2003, 12). Even today, religious congregations often use the distribution of relics to promote the cause of a candidate for sainthood or foster the devotion to a saint already canonized. Orders may give away actual particles of the body, typically bone fragments placed in a *theca*, a small metal locket secured by a wax seal; or they issue prayer cards or medals of inexpensive material carrying particles of cloth that was either used by saints during their lifetime or touched to a body relic. Relics such as these can be manufactured cheaply on a large scale and, in the case of contact relics, ad infinitum. They are the kind of relic that is destined to serve private devotions, or at any rate often enough ends up in private hands.

The Magic Touch

What role does touch play in these devotional practices? The mittens of Padre Pio serve as an illustration (Figure 4.2). Born Francesco Forgione

Figure 4.1   Examples of relics: Prayer card of St Theresa with contact
relic (centre); contact relic in plastic pocket (top left); two relic
medals (front and back, centre left); paper slip containing matter
from the birthplace of St John the Baptist (bottom left); *theca*
with bone relic (top right); plaque with contact relic (bottom
right). (author's collection)

in 1887, Padre Pio was a priest and Capuchin friar living in Southern
Italy. In 1918 he received the stigmata, the wounds of Christ, and soon
his reputation as a mystic and miracle worker began to spread. This
brought him into conflict with the Church hierarchy, which accused
him of various sorts of misdeeds, from financial fraud to sexual abuse
of female parishioners. With his name eventually cleared, he became
the centre of a popular cult[1] during his lifetime. While working for the
spiritual salvation of his flock, Padre Pio also managed to turn around
the economic fortunes of San Giovanni Rotondo, the rural backwater
where he lived, by founding a large hospital. After his death in 1968, this
'hospital industry' was further complemented by a 'pilgrimage industry', which today draws pilgrims in numbers comparable to Lourdes
or Fatima. In 2002 Padre Pio was canonized, in one of the most high-
profile cases of recent times (see McKevitt 1991).

Relics of Padre Pio, especially cards and medals (sometimes of
dubious origin) are widely and easily available from his order, religious
goods shops, or eBay. Not so easy to obtain—in fact highly limited

Figure 4.2   Prayer card with contact relic of Padre Pio, showing him wearing his mittens. (author's collection)

in their availability—are more substantial relics, such as his mittens (which he used to cover the stigmata in his hands), although quite a few of them are extant. At least one such pair of mittens is in the UK, in the possession of MD, a devotee who uses the mittens in her pastoral work. Being partly of Italian stock, MD had known of Padre Pio since her childhood, though he became a significant presence in her life only after the sudden death of her husband, which left her in deep and lasting distress. It was during a special Padre Pio Mass, held at a church in her vicinity, that something like a healing process dramatically set in. It was at this point that the 'magic touch' made itself felt. In her words:

> At the close of the Mass, the priest placed a mitten of Padre Pio on the head of each individual. This was the first time for me. As soon as the mitten was placed on my head, I can only describe the feeling as a bolt of lightning going through me. I felt as though I was stuck to the floor and could not move away. I also felt I was standing there for a long time, although this could not have been possible. I made my way to the back of the church, turned to my friend [who had brought her there], and instantly burst into tears. I asked her if she felt anything. She replied 'Wow, did I feel that.' It was a very emotional night. (pers. comm. 2004)

MD then became a regular worshipper at this Mass and eventually was given a mitten of Padre Pio as a gift:

> She placed the mitten in my hand and then her hand on top. I felt the plastic covering the mitten very cold, yet the mitten was burning hot. I cannot explain that. She prayed to Padre Pio to make his presence known to me and show me I was not alone. (pers. comm. 2004)

MD then became increasingly involved with the friars of San Giovanni Rotondo, working as a translator for them and distributing information material on Padre Pio. The mittens continue to play an important part in her local pastoral activities:

> Mainly, people ask us to visit friends/relatives who are sick. . . . Many feel the comfort of holding the mitten. As far as I know, other mittens used (which have been 'entrusted' and are eventually returned to the Friary) are encased in plastic. My mitten was gifted to me, and so I have chosen not to cover it. I have never believed that Padre Pio would put his hand inside a plastic bag before he would allow people to touch him. . . .Also, my mitten had some crusts/scabs from Padre Pio's hand inside it, and I know it comforts people to see these. (pers. comm. 2004)

There were also occurrences when the mittens made themselves felt in a different way, emitting a scent of violets—a phenomenon known as 'odour of sanctity' and a well-worn hagiographic topos also reported by other sources on Padre Pio. It is not necessary here to determine the veracity of this phenomenon or explain its occurrence; what is interesting is the appeal to senses other than visual perception, which is perhaps the sense most commonly associated with relics in particular, and with Roman Catholicism more generally.

What, then, are we to make of these practices? For an answer, or at least for some suggestions, we turn to the notion of magic. While the work of Frazer has lost much of its significance in anthropology, his writings on magic (notwithstanding the theoretical problems relating to the term) are still useful. The notion of 'contagious magic' can especially help to focus attention on the very materiality of the object, making it clear that the connection between the relic, the saint, and the saint's power is not metaphorical. The relic is remarkable (and potent) because it has been in actual physical contact with, or is indeed derived from, the very substance of the saint.

Though the theology behind them is subtler and more complex, often downplaying the material aspect, relics are typically perceived not just as reminders but remainders, not *like* but *of* the saint. While doctrinally not quite correct, the relic thus frequently evokes an image of being inhabited, animated, by the saint, imbued with something like a 'real presence' (Dinzelbacher 1990). As MD put it to me: 'I understand what you say about praying only [when asked about the relation to praying of internal faith as opposed to external objects], but I think it helps the sick to feel "closer" to the Saint from whom they ask intercession' (pers. comm. 2004).

Visual Piety: When Seeing Is Believing

We need to remember that relics are not only experienced through touch but also, and perhaps more so, through sight. *Schaufrömmigkeit* (visual piety) is a core element of Catholic devotion with a most venerable tradition, reaching back at least to the mid-to-late twelfth century, when reliquaries first became transparent through the use of crystal windows that allowed a view of the relic inside. As Diedrichs points out, this was a development with far-reaching art historical and devotional consequences: 'The medium of veneration turns into its object; the believer becomes spectator. . . . Face to face with the new kind of reliquary the observer confronts, as subject, the object of his contemplation' (2001, 9; translation my own). Diedrichs regards this development as the starting point of a growing externalisation of devotion and an increase in superstitious practices, a case of popular piety subverting the spiritual and intellectual principles of the Church's teachings.

We might ask whether the rise of visual piety as characterised by Diedrichs did not rather prefigure the first dawn of our uneasy, incomplete modernity. What we witness is the slow rise of an 'era of art' after an 'era before art' (Belting 1994) that would no longer recognise objects serving as conduits of the sacred, but only objects of (supposedly) disinterested contemplation. Heidegger speaks of the 'world as picture', distinguishing the modern age, where 'man' is no longer 'the one who is looked upon by that which is', but instead 'that which is ... come[s] into being ... through the fact that man first looks upon it' (quoted in Pinney 2002a, 360).

Apart from Heidegger, a substantial body of scholarship (e.g. Merleau-Ponty 2002 [1962]; Foucault 1975; Jay 1988) critically connects the emergence of the modern Western subject with the rise of sight as the privileged mode of perception, thus engendering a relation of detachment from the world. Disembodied and disinterested, the world is positioned as the passive subject of man's dissecting eye. Of course, as Pinney notes, there are still aspects of Western visual culture that are predicated on an engaged beholder (citing pornography and the iconography of sport, to which I add advertising. They constitute not so much an aesthetics—a system of scholarly, disengaged reflection—but what Pinney terms *corpothetics*, the 'sensory embrace of images, the bodily engagement that most people (except Kantians and modernists) have with artworks' (2001, 158).

Arguably, Catholicism too has always been responsive to corpothetic practices. At the same time as we see the rise of visual piety, there is ample evidence that the sacred retained its material quality: we may think of the (alleged) comb of St Hildegard (1098–1179), now kept at the Bayerisches Nationalmuseum, which was used by the Benedictine nuns of Eibingen (Hesse, Germany) to cure their headaches (van Os 2001, 157ff); or of the German altar piece, *The Blood Miracle of the Franciscan Martyrs of Morocco* (ca. 1460; Germanisches Nationalmuseum Nürnberg) that shows the faithful crouching around the saints' shrine, rubbing off its power with pieces of cloth (a type of contact relic known as *brandea* since antiquity). Similar evidence can be found on a Dutch altar piece (ca. 1500; Museum Catharijnenconvent, Utrecht) depicting the shrine of St Kunera, from the railings of which hang strips of cloth to be wrapped around injured limbs by devotees seeking a cure. Even today, liturgy, the images of saints, the architectonic splendour of churches, incense, music, and, of course, relics can be seen as constituting a network in which the believer, instead of being an aloof observer, willingly gets caught up with all senses.

Exactly how comfortable are institutions like the Church hierarchy (or the museum, as we shall discuss later) with the 'performative dimension of the artefact' (Pinney 2001, 157)? Do they not rather assert 'those European subject/object distinctions which have insisted on the triumph of discourse over figure as part of its strategy to degrade the agency of objects' (2002b, 139f)? Already in the 1960s Mary Douglas argued that, due to an overly intellectual training, large parts of the Catholic hierarchy are debilitated in that they 'cannot conceive of the deity as located in any one thing or place' (2003 [1970], 52).

I would argue that there is a strong inclination within the Catholic Church to disentangle the religious self from the 'sticky touch' of objects, to marginalise certain devotional forms (tellingly subsumed under the heading 'popular piety') and, animated by the same dynamics, to displace certain objects from the shrine to the museum. During fieldwork I often noticed how aesthetics rather than corpothetics resonate with the sensibilities of many of today's clergy. They prefer to 'read' the relic, to understand it in a symbolic fashion as a sign of exemplary virtue, of hope, of salvation, of historic continuity, or of institutional memory. It is rarely (and only if carefully hedged by theological subtleties) a repository of a tangible and powerful presence.

Making the Sacred Tangible

In contrast to the ideology of the eye, touch recognises that subjects are not really detachable from the world. It is the only sensual perception that works as a mutual, two-way process—while touching I am being touched, while being touched I touch the other—allowing the experience of the world as contingent and interconnected, questioning the sharp divide between object and subject. It is eminently human and potent, as is shown in the case of Padre Pio's mittens: the close and prolonged contact with the unprotected relic, its plastic cover removed, creates a deeper intimacy between saint and devotee than could sight alone.

I would argue that touch remains central to certain religious practices like, for example, the cult of relics. For what are relics if not touch made permanent? The whole concept of the relic is based on the idea of transfer through physical proximity. Once the sacred has entered the world, has taken residence in the bone and flesh of a holy person, it spreads through contact, through contagion. Certainly, devotees may and do converse with the sacred through vision, yet often enough it is the tactile, corporeal encounter that prompts visual piety as, for example: with the shroud of Turin, or the *sudarium* (Veronica's veil upon which Christ left an impression of his face), or the blood-stained bandages from Padre Pio's hands, which were shown to me at the Capuchin headquarters in Rome. These are remarkable (or holy, if you are a believer) not because they depict or signify something but because they have been in actual contact with something (or rather, someone).

'*Dreikönigenzettel*' (literally, Three-Kings slips) are just printed pieces of paper or fabric and their linguistic/pictorial representations may stimulate piety and devotion. Yet their capacity to protect from 'dangers while travelling, falling sickness, headaches, sudden death, poison and witchcraft' derives from the fact that they have been touched to the 'heads and relics of the Magi at Cologne'" (Beer & Rehm 2004, 1; translation my own). *Thecas* usually have little loops so they can be worn as a pendant or attached to a rosary, which of course encourages their handling.

Visual contemplation thus easily blurs with other forms of perception: a *theca* may be fondled during prayer; holy pictures given away at pilgrimage sites are proof that the devotee has undertaken not just a spiritual but a geographical journey, experiencing all the attendant physical sensations and discomforts of such an undertaking; little devotional prints (*Schluckbilder*, literally, swallow pictures) could be ingested for purposes of healing and protection, a practice that draws an intriguing connection to medical drugs, whose distribution and dispensation, like that of relics, can also be fraught by disputes between experts and lay users.

Touch reminds us how much the sacred is predicated on the material and the corporeal, how much it is a corpothetics rather than an aesthetics (or a theology)—a matter of engagement, interest, desire, captivation, manipulation rather than dispassionate contemplation, study, or belief. Sight *can* do this too, as demonstrated in detail by Pinney (2001, 2002a, 2004) and Morgan (1998, 2005). But in the West at least sight is also deeply implicated in the radical subject/object divide of our supposed modernity that privileges the dissociating vision of contemplation over the associating vision that permeates popular cultures. As Miller (2005, 1) reminds us, '[t]here is an underlying principle to be found in most of the religions that dominate recorded history. Wisdom has been accredited to those who claim that materiality represents the merely apparent, behind which lies that which is real. . . . Nevertheless, paradoxically, material culture has been of considerable consequences as the means of expressing this conviction.' No wonder, then, that hands-on experiences are often frowned upon or seen with concern as prone to slippage into heterodoxy and superstition. It is the unease felt at the return of the repressed.

The recalcitrant sensuous cannot but assume a haunting and troublesome aspect to a disembodied gaze that has imagined itself to be rid of the world and its things and is therefore now unable to recognise what confronts it. The fetish—often disparagingly invoked by clerical informants as the pitfall of the naïve believer—is thus indeed a figure of misapprehension, but less a misapprehension of the fetishist (so-called) than of its enlightened critic. Magic, superstition, fetishism—those traps into which relic practices are apparently so liable to fall—thus come to be seen as disparities of perception and at the same time as disparities of social interests: elite interests that are (can afford to be) conceptual, intellectual, cosmological, one step removed from everyday necessities—ocularcentric; and 'popular' interests that are (cannot escape being) down-to-earth, pragmatic, and banal, but pressing nonetheless—tangible in more than one sense. As Bourdieu put it: 'Each dominated practice or testimony of belief is condemned to appear as a profanation to the extent that it represents, through its mere existence and even without profane intent, an objective contestation of the monopoly to administer the sacred, that is to say of the legitimacy of the owners of this monopoly' (Bourdieu 2000, 66; translation my own). Differences in sensory experience thus have their specific material and institutional locations; in fact, they could be said to be expressive as well as constitutive of these locations.

Magic behind Glass

Like the Church hierarchy, the museum is another site where touch is relegated to the margins. In the UK, and possibly in most countries outside the Catholic Mediterranean, relics are today usually encountered in museums rather than in their natural habitat—they have become museological artefacts. More precisely, what one encounters (and what is privileged) is inevitably the *reliquary*, the container, with little or no mention of whether it still contains any relics and what their nature may be. Given the precious and intricate design of many medieval and early modern pieces this is understandable, and yet it is somewhat perverse. It is like preferring the gift box to the gift. Furthermore, what tends to be collected and preserved are the outstanding pieces of craftsmanship, those of high material and aesthetic value, as, for example, the Eltenberg Reliquary at the Victoria and Albert Museum or the Holy Thorn Reliquary of Duke Jean de Berri at the British Museum.[2]

Often overlooked are the myriad devotional objects of humble appearance and little value—the ones we consider here—the medals and prayer cards, the *thecas* and paper sachets containing a bit of holy dust that belong to the ill-defined domains of private devotion and popular religion. While there can be no doubt that museums have saved many sacred objects, they have done so *in their fashion*, preserving their physical existence, yet bleaching them of energy and meaning. It is the museological gaze that Foucault saw as emblematic of Western modernity, imprisoning the object within discourse, 'abstracted in a space beyond touch' (Pinney 2002b, 140).

The question is: Can our museums be more than just dutiful but impassive guardians content to salvage the raw material for monographs on twelfth-century enamel techniques or seventeenth-century goldsmithing? Indeed, curators themselves are aware that something may be amiss. The catalogue of a French exhibition opens with the statement that 'more and more have reliquaries become an object of the museological type. . . . One admires the art work, the technique; one studies the messages revealed through iconography; but the sacred has today nearly vanished' (Musée d'Art Sacré du Gard 2000, 5; translation my own). But has it? Or is the museum simply ill-equipped for its presentation? In a poem on the ethnographic collection of the Pitt Rivers Museum in Oxford, James Fenton brings out the fascination that objects can hold, even within this classical space of Enlightenment rationality. Tellingly, though, it is a childhood experience he recalls, not yet organised by the quest for meaning and its control, but open to an 'affective intensity' (Pinney 2002b, 132), that is to say, to fascination, enchantment, and desire. The poem mixes the exotic—witches' hair, earth from a grave, tigers—with the danger of encountering the unknown and getting lost in it; yet, with the danger also comes the allure of imagination, of creating one's own magical world (Fenton 1983, 83).

Looking at the questions of whether and how relics could be featured within the museum or heritage sector, three main issues confront us: presentation, conservation, and propriety.

If the sacred has vanished, part of the reason is that the typical museum setting is not especially conducive to its aura. As the bourgeois temple of elite culture, the museum's cult is a secular one (Duncan 1995). To let devotional objects shine will therefore, at least in part, be a matter of presentation. While educational requirements must be taken into account, so should sensuous qualities. The presentation of devotional objects should allow the visitor not only to learn but also to experience. Curators, exhibition designers, and architects may want to address this question. While there is a long tradition of visual piety, there is a crucial difference between the vision of worshippers, who are immersed in a numinous presence, and the vision of the curator, who strongly influences how the visitor is going to look at an object.

Hands-on Experience: Enabling a Culture of Touch

Visual presentations, of course, have the advantage of causing the least wear and tear and are therefore the preferred solution from a conservator's point of view. Yet, to look at a relic is only half the story. That it is possible to create a more physical experience is illustrated by the example of Louis Peters. A lawyer from Cologne, Germany, he owned until recently one of *the* major relic collections not in ecclesiastical hands,[3] one containing around five hundred pieces, ranging from tiny *thecas* to sizeable shrines, dating mostly from the eighteenth and nineteenth centuries. The collection was shown in a number of exhibitions around Germany and Austria during the 1980s and 1990s.

The 1989 show at the renowned Schnütgen Museum for medieval art in Cologne marked something of a watershed because it generated renewed interest in relics and popular piety among curators and scholars alike. Peters himself has always attached great importance to the haptic dimension of his pieces and he has been scathing of 'overprotective' curators. He deplores the decline of our 'culture of touch', due to the 'fixation of our art historians and conservators who would much prefer to let their objects rot in deserted rooms, protected from light and breath. And yet our relic and shrine culture is utterly a cult of touch, badly in need of rejuvenation' (Peters 1994, 104; translation my own).

During the exhibition of 1989 many objects were therefore freely accessible, and in guided tours Peters would pass around *thecas* to be handled by visitors. Obviously, we would not want to find the Eltenberg Reliquary passed around a class of sixth formers; but the sacred objects that concern us here—the *thecas*, holy cards, relic medals—are usually neither rare nor valuable. Within certain limits, it is therefore possible to allow greater proximity between visitors and objects. Of course, objects will be worn out in this process. But perhaps we can contemplate the possibility that using up an object in this way is not the museum's loss so much as the visitors' profit.

If this is an unusual concept for curators and art historians, it is not necessarily so for anthropologists. Susanne Küchler (1988) points out, in an article on *malanggan*, how time can be confounded and memory produced through destruction rather than preservation. Wooden sculptures created for funereal ceremonies by the natives of New Ireland, Papua New Guinea, *malanggan* are intentionally left to rot as part of the ritual process, transforming the sculpture into a memorised image. I would argue that relics can activate a similar process. As they carry a strong message of *vanitas*, the remains of the saints, ingeniously, speak not only of life everlasting but also of the fact that all things must come to perish. They present death as the mirror in which to reflect on ourselves.

Conservation does not need to be an intractable problem. We could look instead at propriety: how appropriate is the presentation of sacred objects in a museum context and what difference does it make if we allow or even encourage their touching by visitors? Recalling incidents like the condemnation by Christian groups of the BBC's broadcasting of *Jerry Springer: The Opera*, or the cancellation of a production of *Idomeneo* in Berlin over fears of possible violent actions by Muslim extremists, it is clear that religion and its representation within the culture industries has become a touchy issue.

In a related, though less threatening way, many museums have been under pressure from indigenous groups to sort out their holdings of

sacred objects and human remains, through removal from display, repatriation, or by allowing native worshippers access to them on museum
premises. The British Museum's *A'a*, for example, the wooden sculpture
of a deity from Rurutu, Polynesia, is still being visited by Rurutuans to
pay homage through song, performance, and offerings. Another good
example even closer to this subject matter is the 1999 exhibition 'La
mort n'en saura rien—Head Relics from Europe and Oceania' at the
Musée National des Arts d'Afrique et d'Océanie (MNAAO) in Paris.
A colloquium of curators, scholars, and government officials discussed
the questions of whether these artefacts could be exhibited at all (and,
if so, how). Since these head relics, the skulls of ancestors, are regarded
as highly potent, curators first obtained the agreement of elders, who
released them for display after having ritually removed the skulls' in-
dwelling 'souls' (to be reinstalled upon their return). In the particular
case of Christian relics, the relevant interest groups to consult might
include the local ordinary, the Vatican Congregation for the Causes
of the Saints (which has technical authority over relics), the religious
community to which the saint belonged, or the place of worship from
which the relic originally came, if it can be identified.

Conclusion

I have presented an analysis of religious practice centered around two
modalities of perception: vision and touch. Visual piety has a long and
vital tradition, and vision possibly constitutes the dominant mode of perception in our society, being nearly coterminous with the project of
modernity and the emergence of a particular modern subjectivity. But
touch remains a central part of religious practice, a transmitter of equally
powerful and possibly more intimate experiences of the sacred.

Relics play an important part in this experience, notwithstanding
a theology that tends to aestheticise their function, that is to say, to
read them in an abstract symbolic fashion, thus distancing them from
all-too-physical experiences. Yet the intimacy of the religious touch is
often beset with unease: Does its sensual, affective quality imply an
inherent power? Can it be contained within the religious field or is it
destined to be marginalised as magic, fetishism, and superstition from
an institutional point of view? Unlikely candidates, perhaps, for such
an assessment, yet in their very characterisation of certain practices
as magic, fetishism, or superstition, both theology and the Church
hierarchy appear strongly committed to the project of modernity. In
this contest over orthopraxis (could one say, ortho-perception?) the
respective significance of vision and touch is revealed as a function of
social position.

The corporeal nature of the relic poses certain problems to the Catholic Church. The relic offers a direct route to the sacred, bypassing institutional mediation, and thus necessitating institutional control and ideological safeguarding. One such measure of control was the medieval directive that the remains of the saints must be kept in reliquaries (Fourth Lateran Council, 1215). On the whole, it would seem to me that visual piety is a safer alternative to channel religious desires than tangible experience.

Next to the Catholic hierarchy, I have described the museum as the other locus of modernist ocularcentrism. No longer the *Wunderkammer* of the sixteenth and seventeenth centuries, the museum has nonetheless often become the repository of the miraculous—or, more exactly, the once-miraculous. For practical as well as ideological reasons (if a neat separation can be made), touch is usually discouraged by the museum. Thus the magic of touch may be just as much the (supposed) antithesis of science as it is of religion. Yet, I argue, there are objects—relics among them—that need to be met and experienced in a different way, a way that allows fascination and fetishism to flourish alongside science, learning, and education. The sacred, after all, is not for your eyes only.

Notes

1. 'Cult' is the technical term used by the Catholic Church; it implies systematic and continuous veneration based on a reputation of holiness. It does not have the derogatory connotations of the colloquial English usage.
2. The Eltenberg Reliquary must be one of the museum's most precious treasures: a large reliquary of bronze and copper gilt in the shape of a domed basilica, decorated with enamel, ivory, and figures of prophets and apostles (Rhenish, ca. 1180). The Holy Thorn Reliquary is a rather theatrical construction of gold and enamel, depicting the Last Judgement, and lavishly adorned with rubies and pearls (French, ca. 1410).
3. The collection has since been acquired by the French government, which apparently plans to present it in a specifically dedicated museum.

References

Beer, M., Rehm, U. 2004. Die Macht der kleinen Bilder. Zur Sammlung Kleiner Andachtsbilder im Museum Schnütgen. In Manuela Beer and Ulrich Rehm (eds.), *Das Kleine Andachtsbild: Graphik vom 16. bis zum 20. Jahrhundert*. Hildesheim: Georg Olms Verlag, 1–5.

Belting, H. 1994. *Likeness and Presence: A History of the Image before the Era of Art*. Chicago: Chicago University Press.

Benjamin, W. 1999 [1937]. The work of art in the age of mechanical reproduction. In Hannah Arendt (ed.), *Illuminations*. London: Pimlico, 211–35.

Bourdieu, P. 2000. *Das religiöse Feld: Texte zur Ökonomie des Heilsgeschehens.* Konstanz: Universitätsverlag Konstanz.

Codex Iuris Canonici (CIC). 1983. London: The Canon Law Society of Great Britain and Ireland.

Diedrichs, C. 2001. *Vom Glauben zum Sehen: Die Sichtbarkeit der Reliquie. Ein Beitrag zur Geschichte des Sehens.* Berlin: Weissensee-Verlag.

Dinzelbacher, P. 1990. Die 'Realpräsenz' der Heiligen in ihren Reliquiaren und Gräbern nach mittlealterlichen Quellen. In Peter Dinzelbacher and Dieter R. Bauer (eds.), *Heiligenverehrung in Geschichte und Gegenwart.* Ostfildern: Schwabenverlag, 115–74.

Douglas, M. 2003 [1970]. *Natural Symbols.* London: Routledge.

Duncan, C. 1995. *Civilizing Rituals: Inside Public Art Museums.* London and New York: Routledge.

Erret, G. 2003. *Die heutige Bedeutung und Anziehungskraft des Reliquienkultes.* Retrieved 26 April 2004 from [http://www.pfarrer.at/reliquien_buchenhuell.pdf]

Fenton, J. 1983. *The Memory of War and Children in Exile: Poems 1968–1983.* Harmondsworth: Penguin.

Foucault, M. 1975/1995. *Discipline and Punish: The Birth of the Prison.* New York: Vintage.

Geary, P. 1990. Sacred commodities: the circulation of medieval relics. In Arjun Appadurai (ed.), *The Social Life of Things.* Cambridge: Cambridge University Press, 169–91.

—— 1978. *Furta Sacra: Thefts of Relics in the Central Middle Ages.* Princeton: Princeton University Press.

Jay, M. 1988. The scopic regimes of modernity. In S. Lash and J. Friedman (eds.), *Modernity and Identity.* Seattle: Dia Press, 178–95.

Küchler, S. 1988. Malangan: Objects, sacrifice, and the production of memory. *American Ethnologist* 15(4): 625–37.

Livingstone, E. (ed.). 1996. *The Concise Oxford Dictionary of the Christian Church.* Oxford: Oxford University Press.

McKevitt, C. 1991. San Giovanni Rotondo and the shrine of Padre Pio. In J. Eade and M.J. Sallnow (eds.), *Contesting the Sacred: The Anthropology of Christian Pilgrimage.* London, New York: Routledge, 77–97.

Merleau-Ponty, M. 2002 [1962]. *Phenomenology of Perception.* London: Routledge.

Miller, D. 2005. Materiality: an introduction. In D. Miller (ed.), *Materiality.* Durham and London: Duke University Press, 1–50.

Morgan, D. 2005. *The Sacred Gaze: Religious Visual Culture in Theory and Practice.* Berkeley: University of California Press.

—— 1998. *Visual Piety: A History and Theory of Popular Religious Images.* Berkeley: University of California Press.

Musée d'Art Sacré du Gard. 2000. *Reliquaires* (exhibition catalogue). Nîmes: author.

Os, H van. 2001. *Der Weg zum Himmel: Reliquienverehrung im Mittelalter.* Regensburg: Schnell & Steiner.

Peters, L. 1994. Reliquien und ihr Publikum. In Diözesanmuseum Paderborn (ed.), *Heilige und Heiltum: Eine rheinische Privatsammlung und die Reliquienverehrung der Barockzeit in Westfalen* (exhibition catalogue). Paderborn: Diözesanmuseum Paderborn, 103–105.

Pinney, C. 2004. *'Photos of the Gods': The Printed Image and Political Struggle in India*. London: Reaktion.

———— 2002a. The Indian work of art in the age of mechanical reproduction or, what happens when peasants 'get hold' of images. In F.D. Ginsburg, L. Abu-Lughod and B. Larkin (eds.), *Media Worlds: Anthropology on New Terrain*. Berkeley: University of California Press, 355–69.

———— 2002b. Creole Europe: The reflection of a reflection. *Journal of New Zealand Literature* 20: 125–61.

———— 2001. Piercing the skin of the idol. In C. Pinney and N. Thomas (eds.), *Beyond Aesthetics: Art and the Technology of Enchantment*. Oxford and New York: Berg, 157–79.

5

DON'T TOUCH! HANDS OFF!
ART, BLINDNESS AND THE
CONSERVATION OF EXPERTISE

Fiona Candlin

Watch the crowds in any museum and, despite the prohibitive ropes and signs, somebody will be touching something. Once the guards' backs are turned, museum visitors touch precisely because it is forbidden; but they also use touch to investigate an object's surface, to verify what they have seen, or in an attempt to make a connection with the past. Increasingly, museums are recognising this desire to touch and acknowledging the value of sensory experience.

The impetus behind this sensory shift is highly over-determined. Embodiment theorists have convincingly argued that knowledge is not detached from the body, suggesting instead that the body is the ground of culture and thought (Csordas 1994; Lingis 1994; Merleau-Ponty 2000) and similarly concepts of physical intelligence and bodily learning have become accepted within educational theory (Gardner 1993). Handling sessions and other forms of sensory engagement are therefore in line with current thinking on learning and make good pedagogical sense for museums. Crucially, however, the introduction of haptic experience, and of interactivity more broadly, is also motivated by current government policy.

For most national museums, funding is now closely tied to audience statistics, particularly to the numbers of visitors categorised as C2 and

DE (skilled working class and unskilled working class as well as those with limited incomes) and to educational provision. Rather than functioning as storehouses or centres of scholarly knowledge, museums are now being characterised as resources for informal learning and for social inclusion (Anderson 1999; Department of Culture, Media, and Sport 2000) so they simply cannot *afford* to alienate their visitors. On the contrary, museum staff need to make sure that the displays are appealing to a wide range of age and class groups, including non-traditional museum goers. By introducing sensory and interactive components into exhibitions and events programmes, museums hope to encourage both learning generally and those visitors who would be repelled by scholarly approaches. More specifically, opportunities to touch also help satisfy government requirements on physical access for blind people, which, under the Disability Discrimination Act 1995 (DDA), are now legal requirements.[1]

At the same time, interactive and sensory elements within museums can contribute significantly to negotiating and containing damage. Providing handling material at an exhibition is explicitly intended to protect the larger collection by discouraging visitors from touching other more delicate or valuable items, and organised handling sessions or touch tours can be viewed in a similar light. Allowing people to touch selected objects from the collection in supervised circumstances is a way of granting access through touch without giving people choice or control over what they touch. Like interactive elements in displays or programmes that only permit the visitor a closely prescribed set of responses, this level of access is arguably palliative. Instead of developing haptic experience as a source of knowledge and pleasure in its own right, handling material is used to demonstrate that the museum is accessible to blind people without impinging upon the museum's remit to preserve the collections.

Handling is one area where the right of the individual to learn from and enjoy public collections is in tension with the duty of the museum to care for its objects in perpetuity. Thus, as Hetherington points out, 'access often has to respond to the demands of conservation rather than the other way around' (2002, 195). Unlike sight, touch is a threat to conservation, and for Hetherington it thereby has the potential to undermine the very idea of the museum. In consequence, he positions blind people and their demand for haptic learning outside of ocularcentric museum practices (2000, 462; 2002, 195). Hetherington's comments are certainly echoed by museum curators, for whom reference to conservation usually curtails any further discussion on access through touch other than to posit the collapse of the museum as we know it (CV, 17/5/02; D 31/06/01).[2]

This chapter, however, focuses on the issue of *who touches* rather than touch per se and seeks to move the discussion past its current stalemate, in which conservation is always the contrary of access. This has implications for access by the blind and for the way museum practice is conceptualised; it is thus of consequence for all museum visitors, for how they understand the collections, and how they literally articulate that knowledge.

Conservation and Art through Touch

Although museums rarely use touch as a means of learning about art and objects (handling sessions are often considered an opportunity to *look* more closely) all of us, blind or otherwise, experience and understand the world through touch. Touch is not just a single sense, rather it requires a combination of inputs from our skin, from the movement of fingers, hands, and arms, as well as information about how our limbs move and are positioned in relation to our body as a whole and to that which is touched. Touch involves the interrelation of rhythm, movement, contact, proprioception (postural or bodily awareness), articulation, and pressure, and with it we can perceive shape, space, size, texture, temperature, vibration, and response (Heller 2000). Touch cannot be a substitute for sight; though they will certainly produce overlapping information, there will also be perceptions particular to each sense. Fine touch, for example, enables us to feel what is not always accessible to sight; the quality of fabric or a smooth wood surface is usually better judged with the fingertips and hands than with the eyes.

Touch is used pre-consciously and is also a skill that, like a perfumer's trained nose, can be learned and developed. As with the other senses, touch is used with varying degrees of acuity and is not an ability that blind people somehow acquire automatically or in which they necessarily excel. People who have been taught Braille often develop a very acute sense of touch; indeed, there is some evidence that prolonged haptic experience results in a certain degree of cortical reorganisation and specialisation, but this happens through extensive practice and not by some magical process of sensory compensation (Millar 2000).

In the interviews that were conducted as part of this research, the majority of museum visitors who were blind or partially sighted stressed the importance of touch. Whatever their level of skill, touch formed a primary means of learning about art objects and artefacts. Touch supplemented poor sight and confirmed or contradicted ambiguous visual inputs. Visitors who had various types of partial sight used touch exactly as 'fully' sighted people do, to fill in the inevitable gaps and uncertainties of vision (Merleau-Ponty 2000). Notably, touch was often used to help the visitor build up a *visual* picture:

Imagine yourself with very low vision ... that person's face is so broken up, you can't see it properly. So when you touch that person's face ... and every contour of the ears, eyes, mouth, you get a photographic memory ... of what that person looks like, so put that to a statue's face, and it makes a big difference, because you can visualise what that (statue) actually looks like, from whether the eyes have got - say Asian eyes, Chinese eyes, or whether they have got round eyes, or droopy eyes. And the nose, and the ears ... you have got a picture to construct, a face shape. (QE, 11/12/01)

For other visitors touch was not a supplementary activity:

Well for me (touch) is the only method of appreciating what's there. . . . Unless you can touch, the visit is more or less meaningless because even if you get a description you are getting someone else's interpretation or account of the object ... which one could quite easily get through a book or a programme indoors. (CL, 3/5/02)

Both this respondent and one of his colleagues described a visit to a Rachel Whiteread exhibition at the Serpentine Gallery in terms of spatial relations. Rather than characterising the artwork by the way it looked, they discussed how Whiteread's casts of empty spaces were themselves situated in space. This set of observations could equally have been made by someone who *saw* the show and, in this instance, touch and sight perceptions could be thought of as potentially overlapping or existing in parallel. In other cases, however, touching artwork elicits responses not amenable to those who only see.

You don't just look at shape and form, you look at the texture of things, temperature. You are sensing all of it ... cold for bronze work, maybe, if it is inlaid, the different grains. (recorded group discussion 2002)

For many of the interview respondents, touch worked at numerous interlocking levels. In addition to a pre-conscious use of touch, which was part of the way in which individuals lived in the world, it was a means of consciously examining an unknown object in detail. Touch enabled those people who had seen or who retained some sight to build up a visual image of an art object, while visitors who were congenitally blind, or who had increasingly begun to understand the world in non-visual ways, could develop a spatial or tactile figure through handling. Those few people who managed to negotiate museum restrictions on touch to a degree that allowed them to develop a thorough knowledge of form and texture then used touch as a means of identifying objects or making comparisons and judgements.

Despite touch's being an important and at times irreplaceable way of understanding art objects and artefacts, museums rarely encourage touch outside of designated handling sessions or occasional touch tours. Many artefacts are far too fragile to be handled regularly, and even relatively sturdy art objects can be adversely affected both by the erosion of repeated handling and by the residue of sweat and oil from people's hands. Thus, the opportunity for blind people to learn through touch is ostensibly in tension with the preservation of art objects. Yet, on closer examination the case is not as clear-cut as it might first appear.

At a seminar held by Arts Through Touch, a group that campaigns for blind people's access to museum and gallery collections, Ken Uprichard, a senior conservator from The British Museum, commented that:

> One of the primary functions of the museum is to preserve the collections ... that is a clear principle in the museum. But there is also a need for access. If we just had to preserve the collections, we'd put them in a room, we'd lock them in a controlled environment and throw away the key, but we don't do that, we put them on display. (recorded seminar 31/6/01)

While the exhibition of objects is itself a negotiation between conservation and access, the question of touch highlights this tension even further. At the same meeting, David Rice, the chairman of Arts Through Touch, argued that:

> Being totally blind, the only way I can appreciate the national heritage is by touch. You keep saying it's being saved for future generations; well, I'm sorry, but this is my generation and I need to appreciate my national heritage. (31/6/01)

Both these comments implicitly raise the question of a museum's purpose and institutions vary in their response. Michael Harrison, the Director of Kettle's Yard in Cambridge, a small museum based on the collection established by Jim Ede and housed in his former home, noted that the approach to conservation and access at Kettle's Yard was markedly different from that in the national museums:

> For a conventional curator, Kettle's Yard might seem something of a nightmare. Objects are on open display and daylight—though UV filtered—is one of its essential qualities. Visitors are encouraged to sit on chairs and are able to walk on wonderful rugs, so there is inevitably some wear and tear. We discourage the touching of objects except under supervised conditions but some visitors can find the temptation too great. (31/6/01)

At Kettle's Yard the emphasis is on preserving the accessibility and original ambience of this domestic collection.

Even in more conventional museums, however, the needs of the current generation are not necessarily in stark opposition to conservation. At present there are two main ways for blind people to access museum collections through touch; organised handling events that take a different theme in every session, and permanent touch tours (on educational provision for blind museum visitors, see Candlin 2003). In both cases the number of blind visitors making use of these facilities is minute. For instance, in 2002 the British Museum (BM) held six educational events for adults that averaged six visitors each and, while the permanent touch tours are being reorganised in light of gallery and exhibition changes, they were previously taken by about fifteen people a year. At the Victoria and Albert Museum (V&A) there were twelve classes, each attended by an average of thirteen people. Given that handling sessions usually use different objects on each occasion, the amount of contact between blind people and art objects is negligible, particularly when the number of visitors is compared to the size of these museum collections—the British Museum holds approximately eight million objects and the V&A, four million. Even discounting two-dimensional works and objects that are extremely fragile, the amount of contact with individual art and artefacts remains minimal.

Some materials are virtually unaffected by touch. Granite and basalt can bear any amount of handling. Bronze will discolour but will not erode easily, so the use of surgical gloves or hand wipes is sufficient to prevent damage, as is the case with many other metals. Moreover, although art objects are often unique and therefore irreplaceable, museums often have many versions of the same object held in reserve collections, some of which could be, and occasionally are, designated handling material. The damage that might be done to objects by blind people thus seems disproportionate to the resistance it elicits. Why then, this anxiety about blind people learning through touch?

Touch and Status

There is often a conflation between blind people's touching objects and the general public's mishandling the collections. At the Arts Through Touch seminar, conservators recognised the difference between the general visitors' casual touching and the touching that a visually impaired person needs to do to understand the object; however, this acknowledgement segued almost seamlessly into concerns about the damage perpetrated by millions of visitors a year to objects that are displayed within reaching distance:

> For both the BM and the Tate, the fear is that if you allow one person to touch everybody's going to touch, hence (there are only) twenty-two things available to touch. (Michael Harris 31/6/01)

Those attending the seminar raised issues such as graffiti and security that clearly have little to do with blind people and much more to do with the general public's contact with objects. It is clear that part of the reason for restricting access by the blind is not because they might damage objects but because the vast numbers of non-blind visitors apparently do. *Apparently* do, because, throughout the history of museums, the general public has been characterised as unruly, unwashed, as a threat to both the preservation of objects and to other visitors' proper enjoyment of the collections. The following comment made by the art historian Gustav Waagen in 1853 is by no means uncommon:

> I have … been in the National Gallery when it had all the appearance of a large nursery, several wet nurses having regularly encamped there with their babies for hours together, not to mention persons whose filthy dress tainted the atmosphere with a most disagreeable smell. . . . It is highly important, *for the mere preservation of the pictures*, that such persons should in future be excluded from the National Gallery. The exhalations produced by the congregation of large numbers of persons, falling like vapour upon the pictures, tend to injure them, and this mischief is greatly increased in the case of the two classes of persons alluded to. (Trodd 1994, 42–43; my emphasis)

It is not simply that the working class visitors behaved in ways unapproved of by the upper middle classes, but that they visited a territory that Waagen assumed to belong to his class without removing the traces, literally the smells, of their foreignness. Clearly, judgements about preservation, damage, and dirt are not always logical or practical but in this instance derive from social boundaries being crossed by working class visitors. Is there then a similar politics of pollution at play when blind visitors enter contemporary museums?

Damage done to art objects in the contemporary context is often inflected by a sense of whose touch is appropriate. In reference to the damage done to objects on open display, Uprichard from The British Museum noted:

> One of the things that is very obvious on objects that are touched on a regular basis, particularly touched, is the soiling … where you can get the handling grease on the objects, the handling grease itself then attracts dirt … I think that we all have experienced the dirt on the door, where, you know, your hands aren't dirty but after five years you can see where people touched the door … Indeed when we cleaned the Rosetta Stone recently, everybody thought it was a black and white object. The white was easily explained because in 1980 one of our curators sat and inked in the whole inscription in white ink. The black we had analysed and … most of that black … was simply as a result of handling. It was handling grease. (recorded seminar 31/06/01)

What is considered good practice is of course historically specific and conservators obviously cannot be held responsible for their predecessors' actions, but it is noticeable that it is the handling grease that Uprichard emphasises and not the curator's white lettering, although both have resulted in discoloration. Inappropriate touching thus is considered more damaging than the legitimate intervention made by a curator.

The curator's touch is perceived to be qualitatively different from that of the casual visitor. Museum curators often research or work with the same collections for many years and their ensuing expertise entitles them to handle objects. This expertise is not, however, the only issue at stake. In *Touching: The Human Significance of Skin*, Montagu Ashley (1986) notes that who can touch whom is deeply inflected by status; employers can make physical contact with their employees but junior staff rarely pat the hand of their boss. Touch is hierarchical and proprietorial. We touch what we have relative power over and, conversely, in touching we establish our rights to that person or thing. Likewise, the curator's rights over an object are connected in part to expertise but also to status (the one not necessarily guaranteeing the other). Museum curators do not necessarily touch objects in accordance with how much they know, but because being a curator entitles them to do so. The fact that they do touch reinforces their status and right to touch.

How much direct contact curators have with objects depends both on the fragility of the object and the institution for which they work, and for many curators handling objects is a necessary part of their research and role. Still, it is notable that their touch is rarely considered damaging in the way that the public's is. The curators' status and perceived rights over what are often public collections enables them to touch because, as the object's appropriate guardians, their traces cannot be harmful. The curators' clean hands recall Mary Douglas's (1966) descriptions of high priests who, alone amongst their tribe, can come into contact with sacred objects. This characterisation was echoed by Suzanna Taverne's comment on resigning her directorship at The British Museum. Referring to the 'priesthood of curators', Taverne said that:

> There is this notion that only they can be the intermediaries between the relics and the public. . . . They carry the sacred flame of the institution—the museum. These same people question when anybody doubts the apostolic succession. (Gibbons 2001)

In contrast, the public—those people who are not entitled to touch— have grubby hands that potentially render objects filthy.

The degree to which damage through touch is not simply a matter of fact is perhaps best illustrated by instances of positive damage when people of importance are perceived to change an object for the better. While describing the difficulty of getting access to objects through touch, one interview respondent said:

> Have you ever been to the House of Commons? They have got Churchill in there … it is a bronze statue, it has a green finish colour, but his left foot is really polished, a kind of brassy colour, because when all of the MPs go in to make their first speech, they always rub their elbow on his foot, saying 'Can you give me some of your powers of oratory?' (JE 27/11/01)

Unlike other quasi-magical objects such as the Blarney Stone, where power moves from the object to the subject, this touch involves an exchange of power. Touching Churchill's statue potentially conveys something of his power to the new Member of Parliament while the MPs' touch incrementally transforms and adds to the history and power of the statue. Notably this exchange of touch is not open to everyone; only the elect are allowed to receive the possible power of the statue and, equally, only those of importance can change that object positively. The marked statue becomes the archive of an elite tradition.

Touching leaves a trace of the body on the object, so the constitution, status, or quality of that body matters. Depending upon whose body it is, the object will be damaged, unaffected, or even transformed. Within classical literature, blind people are closely associated with spiritual insight although, as Barasch (2001) points out, these prophetic abilities are often highly ambiguous, for they are usually acquired as a result of having transgressed and watched something forbidden to human eyes. It is significant that the Judeo-Christian tradition loses the image of the blind seer but retains the connotations of sinfulness. In Leviticus it is made clear that blind people cannot be priests:

> Say to Aaron, None of your descendants throughout their generation who has a blemish may approach to offer the bread of his God. For no one who has a blemish shall draw near, a man blind or lame. (Leviticus 21:17–18)

Both sacrificial animals and the people who approach the temple had to be physically perfect. All bodily discharges were potentially defiling and had to be either ritually cleansed or were banned from sacred spaces. The whole and perfect body literally acted as a container for the body, so if this body were perceived to be incomplete it could conceivably *leak*. Blind people were thus potentially more polluting than those people with supposedly intact bodies (Douglas 1966, 52–54).

The faultiness of blind people's bodies is reinforced in New Testament teaching, where blindness is linked to sinfulness and ignorance of God. Saul was blinded for his lack of faith and had his sight restored upon gaining it, while stories of Jesus' healing the blind by touching their eyes (another example of the power of touch) are key within a Christian tradition as symbols of the transition from ignorance to belief. Consequently, within this tradition, blindness is elided with wilful ignorance, sinfulness, and error.

From the classical era onwards, blind people have been associated with sin, ignorance, faithlessness, lasciviousness, and error (Barasch 2001). Blind people's hands do not therefore confer power, nor have they been considered clean. These negative connotations of blindness do not remain conveniently in a historical past but inform our sense of blindness today.[3] I am not suggesting that curators or conservators *consciously* think that blind people's hands are more damaging than their own or those of the general public, but that touch in the museum is inseparable from both a cultural history of public pollution and of blindness which inflects an inherited sense of whose touch is appropriate. As a congenitally blind member of Arts Through Touch said:

> This whole infrastructure of myths and, shall we say, the way it is duplicated and believed is not unrelated to social services provision. You know, going back to the physical disability and the idea of someone's disability being somehow dangerous is at the root of the whole idea of incarceration: Put these people away! (CL, 3/5/02)

Or, in the case of museums, don't let them touch.

Aesthetic Repressions

Touching objects within museums is not wholly prohibited but it is only permitted to those individuals who have the correct institutional status. Yet even as curators pick objects up and, in touching, understand that piece differently, the knowledge and pleasure they derive from handling artefacts *must* be repressed within the institutional framework of the museum.

Within a Western philosophical tradition both the acquisition of knowledge and aesthetic pleasure are potentially disrupted by anything not associated with the higher faculties of judgement. In the first instance, academic distance, empirical thought, and objective observation have all been predicated on the concept of the disembodied eye and the supposed capacity to transcend base bodily desires or lapses. Blind people are not, however, perceived as possessing the ability to do this because they are seen as being irrevocably attached to their bodies.

Both Jacques Derrida and David Applebaum have used Milton's lines from *Samson Agonistes*—'Which shall I first bewail/thy bondage or thy lost sight/prison within prison/inseparably dark'—to draw a parallel between blindness and being literally locked into your body. Applebaum writes that:

> Being blind he is confined. Being confined he is returned to the confines of his own body. To move forward, toward the world, he must stumble or be led ... Blindness returns Samson to the earth, where ... he dwells in the cave of his being. (1995, 3)

While Derrida points out that bodily confinement might be rich, full of smells and sounds, this sensory experience remains an insular one, leaving blind people unable to shed their embodied existence in the search of pure knowledge (Derrida 1993). As Applebaum puts it, 'Contrasted with the clarity of an unimpeded line of sight, blind groping is of questionable value. Philosophical method is achieved by stepping back, thereby extending the world beyond our focus' (1995, 5).[4] Within that framework of Western philosophy, blindness makes intellectual clarity impossible.

Likewise, inescapable embodiment outlaws access to aesthetic experience. The British art historian Clive Bell made the opposition between aesthetic understanding and the body only too clear in the following passage:

> When an ordinary man speaks of a beautiful woman he certainly does not mean that she moves him aesthetically. . . . With the man in the street, 'beautiful' is more often than not synonymous with 'desirable'. . . . Perhaps they have never had an aesthetic emotion to confuse with other emotions. (Bell 1982, 70)

Here, physical desire actually suggests an incapacity for aesthetic experience. Within the history of art, touch is often equated with sexual rather than sublime pleasure. Whereas looking at art theoretically allows the disinterested viewer to appreciate it at a seemly distance with no ulterior motives, touch brings the body into direct contact with the art object.

The association between blindness, touch, body, and desire and, in turn, their opposition to aesthetics and transcendence, is made quite excruciatingly clear in 'Sight versus Touch', where James Hall discusses the uncouth, 'gross and gloomy' associations connected to touching sculpture (1999, 84). It is noticeable, however, that Hall's comments on images of people touching rapidly veer away from historical accounts and make his own discomfort only too apparent. Describing Caravaggio's 'Doubting Thomas' (1602–1603), Hall writes:

> Thomas parts the thick *labial* skin and plunges his finger inside. Here touch is not just nauseating; it is an admission of ignorance and faithlessness. (1999, 85; my emphasis).

Hall's equation between touch and sexual penetration similarly informs his discussion of Luca Giordano's painting, 'Carneades with the Bust of Paniscus' (1650–1654), about which he writes:

> ...so disturbing is the bust's uncanny fleshiness and greasiness. It seems horribly alive. Carneades' *unashamed* fingers prod its lower lip and the corner of its eye. Pan was the god of lust but even he seems alarmed by the blind man's ministrations. Touch gets us too close for comfort. (1999, 87; my emphasis)

Anybody's touch would potentially threaten aesthetic pleasure or intellectual contemplation, but blind people's contact with art objects poses particular problems not least because it is construed as being un-ashamed. In this text the assumption is that the inability to see equates to immodesty.[5] Derrida has made a similar point, writing that:

> More naked than others, a blind man virtually becomes his own sex, he becomes indistinguishable from it because he does not see it, and is not seeing himself exposed to the *other's gaze*, it is as if he has lost even his sense of modesty. (1993, 106; my emphasis)

That the issue is not so much blindness as the other's gaze becomes increasingly clear when Hall claims that the image of blindness actually *enables* erotic touching. The blank pupils of Canova's sculptures are, for Hall, 'an alibi for exotic sensory experiences', while the narcissistic intertwining of 'The Three Graces' is only made possible by 'their blindness and their corresponding lack of self-consciousness'. The lack of self-consciousness is in fact the sighted viewers'; faced with a blind subject, spectators can become the ultimate voyeurs because their own lascivious stares cannot be acknowledged within the logic of the artwork.

In these paintings and sculptures, blindness is used as a way of exonerating looking but it also opens up the overlap between physical de-sire and art. For Hall, 'Carneades with the Bust of Paniscus' is uncanny and disturbing because the image of a blind man touching sculpture is too close to that of a blind man touching flesh. A similar elision between sculpture and flesh was evident in one of our recent interviews. Asked if he ever touched artworks, this respondent replied:

> Um, oh! Now that is a very interesting, that's a very interesting proposition. But my dear, in our country that would be disgusting. I am an expert in life drawing and they are all nudes, dear. I mean (laughing) touching a nude, no I wouldn't. I remember before the war, before the Second World War, darling, I was at school and I was in a life class. And the model fainted and she was cold and clammy and wet. And I think this was about 1936 when I was fairly new to all this 'being an artist' stuff and I didn't know what the hell to do and there was no older student just at that moment and I had to go and pick her up. And that I think did tend to put me off picking, uh, touching models. (JRE, 25/3/02)

Sculpture becomes flesh, the connotations of one slide into those of the other, so much so that Hall can read Carneades fingers as intruding into the openings of the (stone) face, conjuring images of sexual investigation that go too far even for the god of lust. The blind man's exam-ination threatens literally to penetrate the smooth surfaces of classical sculpture. Through touch the marble ceases to exist as only a surface for the pleasures of vision. It is as if the blind man's body, historically considered imperfect, could disrupt the perfection of these ideal bodies and make them fleshily material, thereby casting doubt on their status as aesthetic objects.

In order for the aesthetic experience to function as such (and there is considerable doubt as to whether it functions at all; see Connor 1999), bodily desire and contact must be repressed. In Hall's text and the examples he documents, touch and desire re-emerge through the figure of the blind man who makes the bodily responses, so fiercely outlawed by the aesthetic, only too visible. Within these aspects of the history of art, the illicit desire to touch is displaced onto the blind man, who allows for the return of the repressed in a manner that the sighted can both judge and enjoy.

If touch is the repressed other of the aesthetic, then it is unsurprising that, despite the capacity of touch to produce different and by no means lesser perceptions to those acquired through sight alone, museums still regard blindness as a major impediment to understanding art objects and artefacts. In contrast, restrictions on touch are not considered to be a loss for museum visitors. Sight is privileged to the extent that, despite the various sensory attributes of art objects, they become synonymous with the visual and curators work within a paradigm where touch is not only an antithesis, but is quite literally repellent, to the conjuncture of vision, aesthetics, and knowledge. Even as they do touch, it is thus extremely difficult for curators to conceive of learning about or appreciating art through touch, and it is clear from the interviews that many curators were surprised by blind people's ability to do this in any competent way.

The Limits of Expertise

Preservation and conservation is part of the founding logic of many museums. The British Museum's Plan for 2001/2 to 2002/3, for instance, notes that 'the stewardship of the collections and their contribution to the enrichment of cultural heritage is fundamental to every aspect of the Museum's purpose' (2001, 13). Yet in interview several education officers commented that while conservators were generally helpful in establishing which objects could or could not be touched safely, it was the curators who resisted touch being used more widely within the museum. Nobody disputes that some objects would be damaged by handling but what is at stake here is not only the vulnerability of the collections but also the professionalism and standing of the curatorial staff.

In order for a professional to master a specific aspect of knowledge, it is important that what counts as knowledge be clearly defined.

To become an expert, you must have a specialised field—a point that Samuel Weber makes:

> A professional was—and is—a specialist ... who has undergone a lengthy period of training in a recognised institution (professional schools), which certified him as being competent in a specialised area; such competence derives from his mastery of a particular discipline. . . . Professionalism lends its practitioners their peculiar authority and status: they are regarded as possessing a monopoly of competence in their particular field. (2001, 25)

To construct or defend those boundaries is to assert a right to the territory; it is to claim that art historians, for example, know what art history is and what methods are appropriate within it. Expertise and professional standing are thus dependent on the differentiation of specific intellectual and methodological grounds. The demarcation of the art world in relation to vision explicitly includes only certain ways of apprehending art and establishes visual competence as being of primary importance. Smell, taste, hearing, and touch are not within the register of necessary skills; indeed, they are understood as detracting from the study of art.

Viewed in this context, touch is deeply oppositional to the structure of museum professionalism as we currently understand it, and it would be easy to characterise blind activists as attempting to undermine the founding logic of both conservation and aesthetics. To read the situation as a choice between the museum as a disembodied and optic space *or* as embodied and haptic is, however, to miss its already hybrid nature and the possibilities of heterogeneous practice. The notion of aesthetic pleasure and knowledge in museums *is* predicated upon sight functioning in isolation from touch, but touch is still actively desired, achieved, repressed, and displaced within the institution. Just because the museum *claims* that touch is other doesn't mean we have to believe them.

Blind people do not, then, introduce a new form of knowledge into the museum; rather, they insist on its recognition, validity, and democratisation. Such an acknowledgement does not discredit sight as a mode of learning and pleasure because haptic and optic experiences can and are already used in mutually productive ways, not least when visual images are informed by a recollection of texture (Klatzky & Lederman 2001). Nor does haptic experience automatically threaten conservation, for, as suggested here, some objects can be touched with relative impunity while other more fragile artefacts could still be analysed and discussed within a haptic framework without being as freely available to direct touch.

Relinquishing the notion of the museum as a purely optical space does come at some cost, particularly in relation to institutional expertise. This could be understood in relation to the challenge of accepting lay opinions and the necessity of mastering new skills. It would require a paradigm shift, in that curators would need to accept that sight is not the sole route to aesthetic experience and knowledge and that embodiment is not disassociated from thought. Yet, given that the validity of pure aesthetic experience has already come under considerable criticism, it would not necessarily be a momentous jump to adopt a more relative position on visual knowledge. In all probability, once curators and academics began to develop linguistic, analytic, and bodily skills in relation to touch, the borders of what constitutes expert knowledge within the museum and art establishment would be slowly extended and, after some mild controversy, the question of expertise would recede into the background.

In this instance the borderlines of professionalism swell and are reoriented to include touch, but the resistance to touch may be symptomatic of a far greater shift in the parameters of expertise. Bruno Latour (1993) has argued that academic practice until recently accepted a series of divides between nature and society and, by extension, between different disciplines; physics is apparently unrelated to politics, for example, or, in this case, culture supposedly exists in a different sphere from touch, the body, and biology. In practice, however, these disciplinary separations do not work but precipitate hybrid conjunctions. Instead of dismissing these hybrid forms of knowledge as aberrant, Latour suggests that academic disciplines have never actually maintained their apparent separation; thus, instead of conceiving knowledge to be a series of discrete areas it should be conceived to be a network.

Latour's work provides us with a way of understanding the status of touch within museums. Ocularcentric learning and its correlative forms of professionalism have been predicated upon the separation of sight from a broader sensory-conceptual matrix but this does not mean that touch (or the other senses) have ceased to operate in this context. Rather, curators use touch while simultaneously denying it. These official and unofficial forms of learning do not remain in separate zones but interweave. In museums, as elsewhere, touch cuts across the apparently optic circuits of knowledge, responding to and counterbalancing visual cues, implicitly disputing the separation and integrity of optic knowledge.

Admitting that optic knowledge is not reified has consequences for the attribution of knowledge within the museum. If, as Weber maintains, expertise is based on a conception of a field that can be mastered, then the separation of the different disciplines is key to the foundation of academic authority; whereas, when knowledge is thought about in relation to networks rather than fields, the usual basis for establishing expertise is lost. No approach or object is automatically excluded from a given network; indeed, any one thing can potentially be related to another, so by definition there are no clear boundaries or fields over which mastery can be demonstrated. Acknowledging touch within the museum may therefore induce resistance, not because it pressures staff to learn new skills and to re-establish the parameters of their subject, but because it indicates that there are no fixed parameters to learning and that their authority is never an accomplished fact.

Blind people's demand for access through touch is not just a challenge of one paradigm to another: haptic versus optics, access versus conservation, embodied versus intellectual thought; instead, it questions the accreditation of authority per se. As such it forms part of a wider institutional shift with regards to expertise. That blind people are lobbying for greater access to collections and that they now have some legislative muscle is itself indicative of changing power relations that involve museums. Current government policy pushes curators towards educational programmes and consultation with user groups while discouraging unilateral research projects and decision making. Despite the lack of prior training or educational background, curator's jobs are moving away from familiar academic grounds towards a much wider and more accountable remit. This not only makes problematic their authority in relation to skill but, by insisting that lay experience must be central to museums' plans, current policy implies that expert knowledge of an area is insufficient. Thus, it is not only that the demand for touch destabilises accepted paradigms of knowledge and the corresponding ascription of expertise, but that the demand can be seriously made is symptomatic of how authority within the museum is already under question. In effect, the emphasis on consultation and social inclusion means that an equation between disciplinary expertise and institutional authority is no longer automatic.

The move away from traditional patterns of expertise signals the possibility of new networks of learning and improved levels of access for blind and non-blind visitors alike. At the same time, these changes provoke high levels of resistance from those people who fear the loss of their territory. Yet a complete institutional overhaul and dispossession of experts would be to simply reverse an injurious structure and therefore perpetuate it. Academic knowledge is necessarily exclusionary and often oppressive but it undoubtedly has great value; the problem comes when it is assumed to be the *only* way of approaching a subject, when it is considered to exist in isolation, and where authority is given unquestioned precedence. Conversely, lay knowledge should not be over-valourised, for it is equally capable of bias and exclusion (Wynne 1996, 77).

Moreover, the notion of replacing one paradigm with another remains within the logic of separate spheres of practice. Conceiving of knowledge as a network may foreclose on the seductive possibility of academic mastery but it equally implies that one paradigm of knowledge cannot replace another one. Lay experience cannot oust scholarly expertise nor haptic knowledge supersede optic learning. It may come as some comfort to academics and curators that territory, authority, and expertise are therefore not entirely lost. Nevertheless, they do have to be negotiated and shared.

Notes

1. For DDA legislation see http://www.opsi.gov.uk/acts/acts1995/1995050. htm.
2. These and subsequent initials and dates refer to interviews undertaken in the course of this research.
3. For example, Joseph Grigley (2000) has pointed out that remarks such as Elaine Showalter's comment that 'We have so long lamented the blindness, the deafness, and indifference of the male critical establishment towards our work' demonstrates the elision between not being able to see or hear and not *wanting* to see or hear.
4. However, this image of 'blind groping' is not a particularly accurate one. Throughout the history of visual images, blind people have been depicted as clumsy and stumbling. Georgina Kleege (2000) argues in relation to film that this representation is pervasive, not because it is necessarily truthful but because it is the only way to make blindness visible to the non-blind.
5. In fact, Stephen Thayer (1982, 276) reports that blind people use social touching less than sighted people for fear that they will make mistakes and appear foolish.

References

Anderson, D. 1999. *A Commonwealth: Museums in the Learning Age, A Report to the Department of Culture, Media and Sport*. London: The Stationary Office.

Applebaum, D. 1995. *The Stop*. Albany: State University of New York Press.

Barasch, M. 2001. *Blindness: A History of Mental Image in Western Thought*. London, New York: Routledge.

Bell, C. 1982/1914. The aesthetic hypothesis. In F. Frascina and C. Harrison (eds.), *Modern Art and Modernism: A Critical Anthology*. New York, Cambridge: Harper & Row, 67–74.

The British Museum. 2001. *Plan 2001/2 to 2002/3*. London: British Museum.

Candlin, F. 2003. Blindness, art and exclusion in museums and galleries. *International Journal of Art and Design* 22(1): 100–10.

Connor, S. 1999. *What if there was no such thing as the aesthetic?* Steven Connor home page. [http://www.bbk.ac.uk/eh/eng/skc/aes] (10.10.02)

Csordas, T.J. 1994. *Embodiment and Experience: The Existential Ground of Culture and Self.* Cambridge: Cambridge University Press.

Department of Culture, Media and Sport. 2000. *The Learning Power of Museums: A Vision for Museum Education.* London: DCMS.

Derrida, J. 1993. *Memoirs of the Blind: The Self-Portrait and Other Ruins.* Chicago, London: University of Chicago Press.

Douglas, M. 1966. *Purity and Danger: An Analysis of the Concepts of Pollution and Taboo.* London, New York: Routledge.

Gardner, H. 1993. *Multiple Intelligences: The Theory in Practice.* New York: Basic Books.

Gibbons, F. 2001. British Museum turns to national treasure [online]. [www.theguardian.co.uk] (09.15.01)

Grigely, J. 2000. Postcards to Sophie Calle. In S. Crutchfield and M. Epstein (eds.), *Points of Contact: Disability, Art and Culture.* Ann Arbor: University of Michigan Press, 31–58.

Hall, J. 1999. *The Changing Status of Sculpture from the Renaissance to the Present Day.* London: Chatto and Windus.

Hetherington, K. 2002. The unsightly: Touching the Parthenon frieze. *Theory, Culture, Society* 19: 187–205.

—— 2000. Museums and the visually impaired: The spatial politics of access. *The Sociological Review* 48(3): 444–63.

Heller, M. (ed.). 2000. *Touch, Representation and Blindness.* Oxford: Oxford University Press.

Klatzky, R.L., Lederman, S. 2001. Modality specificity in cognition: The case of touch. In H.L. Roediger et al. (eds.), *The Nature of Remembering.* Washington, D.C.: American Psychological Association, 233–46.

Kleege, G. 1999. *Sight Unseen.* New Haven, London: Yale University Press.

Latour, B. 1993. *We Have Never Been Modern.* Harlow, Essex: Longman.

Lingis, A. 1994. *Foreign Bodies.* London, New York: Routledge.

Merleau-Ponty, M. 2000. *The Phenomenology of Perception.* London, New York: Routledge.

Millar, S. 2000. Modality and mind. In M. Heller (ed.), *Touch, Representation and Blindness.* Oxford: Oxford University Press, 99–142.

Montagu, A. 1986. *Touching: The Human Significance of Skin.* New York: Harper & Row.

Thayer, S. 1982. Social touching. In W. Schiff and E. Foulke (eds.), *Tactual Perception: A Sourcebook.* Cambridge: Cambridge University Press, 263–304.

Trodd, C. 1994. Culture, class, city: the National Gallery and the spaces of education 1822–1857. In Pointon, M. (ed.), *Art Apart: Art Institutions and Ideology across England and North America.* Manchester: Manchester University Press.

Weber, S. 2001. *Institution and Interpretation.* Stanford: Stanford University Press.

Wynne, B. 1996. May the sheep safely graze? A reflexive view of the expert–lay knowledge divide. In Lash et al. (eds.), *Risk, Environment, Modernity: Towards a New Ecology.* London: Sage, 27–43.

6

EXPLORING THE ROLE OF TOUCH IN CONNOISSEURSHIP AND THE IDENTIFICATION OF OBJECTS

Sally MacDonald

Contexts for the Study of Specialist Touch

Within the field of material culture studies, and particularly in museum studies, we might expect to find a well-developed understanding of the role of handling in learning from objects. As Classen has demonstrated, privileged visitors to early European museums saw touch as a vital adjunct to visual appreciation (Classen 2005b). Touch functioned as a means of verifying visual impressions, gave visitors the pleasure of an intimate encounter, and 'allowed them to access the mysterious powers popularly associated with the rare and the curious' (Classen 2005b, 278). Classen argues that, as museums gradually opened up to wider audiences, and particularly to middle and working class audiences, so the restrictions on touching increased. Stallybrass and White (2005) describe the nineteenth-century bourgeois perception of the 'contaminating touch' of the poor. As museums became more publicly accessible, concerns for the preservation and security of collections increased, and opportunities for visitors to touch artefacts almost ceased. In the UK in recent years the Labour government has exerted strong pressure on museums to 'open up' access to their collections. Nevertheless, the opportunity for the visitor to touch the collections is normally confined to special 'hands-on' areas of the museum, which focus on children's learning and house pre-selected 'sacrificial' objects. The right to touch freely remains restricted—very much as it did in the seventeenth and eighteenth centuries—to privileged users, such as curators, researchers, or sponsors.

In line with these developments, the literature on object-based learning has tended to focus on the visual appreciation of objects behind glass and almost exclusively on children's learning (Hein 1998; Paris 2002). Evaluations of learning through handling museum artefacts have again focused largely on children's experiences (Hooper-Greenhill 1993; Mitchell 1996; Curtis 1997). The question of how a sense of touch underpins the knowledge that 'object experts' such as curators, collectors, and antique dealers apparently acquire is articulated surprisingly infrequently.

At the same time, it is generally accepted that, within museums, object-based skills and research have been waning for some years; the decline of the specialist curator coinciding with the growing ascendancy of the generalist manager. A recent report by the UK Museums Association (Wilkinson 2005, 26) refers to the dearth of curatorial expertise, commenting that 'museums need to reassert the development of knowledge and research as a key role'. Museums and those who work in them need to be able to understand and articulate what constitutes curatorial expertise if they are to nurture it.

Since the publication of the first major study of tactile perception (Katz 1925), several significant studies on how people learn through touch have been undertaken in the field of clinical psychology (Gordon 1978; Kreuger 1982; Lederman & Klatzky 1996). These have mainly addressed the physiological aspects of handling; for example, the relationship of tactile to visual perception or the distinction between the perception of vibration and that of pressure. With few exceptions (such as Katz's study of bakers' perceptions of the quality of dough) they have tended to focus on questions of basic shape recognition and identification, or on understanding how haptic perception enables the location of objects in space (e.g. Millar 1994) rather than on more sophisticated uses of handling for fine distinction between similar objects, or on the effects of handling on the emotions. Our understanding of tactile memory and its relationship to visual and auditory memory remains very limited.

Discussion of the role of emotional response in connoisseurship features strongly in the literature on aestheticism (Jaffe et al. 1979; Maginnis 1990; Phillips 1997). As Zerner (1987) has noted, 'the work and knowledge of the connoisseur is often badly expressed, if verbalized at all, so that it appears as a kind of divination or arbitrary authority'. Maginnis goes further to suggest that the skills of the connoisseur have been tainted by association with the marketplace and have therefore come to be despised within academia. Whatever the reason, connoisseurship skills have not been adequately dissected. Within the literature on aestheticism, the tendency has been to focus on connoisseurship as applied to 'high art' (that is, painting) and to privilege visual impact and expertise, focusing on the relationship between seeing and memory.

It is only very recently that attempts have been made to draw together different disciplinary perspectives on touch and handling (Classen 2005a). Clearly, considerably more work will be needed before we can assess what types of object are useful or pleasurable to learn from, or what it is that you can you understand about something from touching it that you cannot understand in any other way. Touch—maybe *feeling* is a better word—is something we in museums routinely deny our audiences; in the interests of conservation and security, touch is heavily managed. Yet we have not really articulated what it is that gets lost in this process.

The Interviewees

I wanted to explore some of these ideas by talking to object experts about the role they think touch and handling plays in their lives and in the honing of their expertise. For this initial investigation I interviewed nine people. Four were dealers, most of whom were also, in a small way, collectors. Five were museum curators, and two of these were also collectors. Most of my interviewees were male, all were white, and all were London-based. Because I located them through museum colleagues, the dealers I spoke to had considerable contact with museums and museum staff. The areas of expertise covered by my interviewees corresponded to several classic Western decorative arts typologies: prints and drawings, coins and medals, decorative arts and sculpture, seventeenth- and eighteenth-century costume, European porcelain, archaeological textiles, German sculpture, furniture, and base metalwork.

The interviews were semi-structured and recorded. Most of the interviewees spontaneously produced objects or tools to show me. What follows is an attempt to summarise what was said, using verbatim quotes where possible. It was agreed that all interviewees should remain anonymous.

Something in the Blood?

Several interviewees referred to object expertise being something of a family tradition, 'in the blood'. One of my interviewees had an antique-dealer father, another had an uncle who was a picture collector, and one had a great uncle who had amassed a huge collection of oriental ceramics. The two interviewees who specialised in textiles had come to the subject through being taught sewing by their mothers, and one of them described still having 'a yearning to be getting on and making things all the time'.

Most of these people collected objects as children: one collected stamps, another dinky toys, another medals and shells in a small home museum. This last-mentioned interviewee commented on the desire to collect and classify things: 'I'd be suspicious of someone in this business who hasn't done it'.

One curator described a colleague who had thrown his first museum out of the window at age six. Another of the curators spoke of having had it drummed into him that 'curators never collect', but most of the people I spoke to still collected something, even if they could not afford to collect what they would really like. One, who admitted to collecting unusual shells and orchids, remarked:

> I'll pick 'em up, the ones that look pretty, and I'll go back home and I'll identify them. And if I find a dead creature which I rather like the look of I'll bring that home and I'll put it in the deep freeze and then I'll get it stuffed.

In every case these were people who had, for a variety of reasons, felt drawn to objects and materials at an early stage in their lives and still got pleasure from having them around. It would be interesting in future to explore whether people who are good with objects have other common characteristics. One of my interviewees commented that in his opinion sculpture connoisseurs tend to be tactile, highly sexed people. Two people noted the number of dyslexic connoisseurs they knew: 'almost anybody one knows who's not just adequate but really good suffers from a form of dyslexia'.

Developing Skills

Handling played a major part in the way the interviewees developed their expertise. Most of them described a combination of some kind of hands-on apprenticeship and independent learning. Two dealers cited the experience of portering at the large auction houses, which involved putting the correct labels on pieces, as forming the bedrock of their understanding of objects. Both spent all their spare time at major museums, looking at things on display. The museum equivalent of portering was curatorial housekeeping; for instance, re-arranging stores with a senior colleague constantly telling one what to look for. Almost everyone cited discussing problematic objects with colleagues as being an effective and enjoyable way to learn, and the way in which to continue to develop their skills.

One former dealer regretted having gone to university, wishing he had spent those three years going through the British Museum's print collections; he said 'with drawings it's the only way to learn—reading books doesn't tell you much'. And two curators bemoaned the lack of hands-on training for museum staff. One recalled Friday training sessions in the Victoria and Albert Museum in the 1960s; each week a different expert would get out a group of objects to discuss with colleagues. Another recommends that her students visit sale previews, or volunteer in charity shops, to get what she describes as 'a very tactile sort of access that you don't get in museums'. As another former curator told me 'Nowadays there's too much reliance on books and not enough playing with the gear'. And one particularly self-motivated interviewee, when asked who taught him to do what he does, replied 'The objects did. As a curator, the collection actually forms you'.

Visual Attribution

Within the interviews, we discussed and attempted to dissect the different processes occurring when an expert encounters an object for identification and assessment. Several people mentioned the spontaneity of attribution, the immediate impression—'like recognising a friend's handwriting'—that is almost always correct. One interviewee described it like this:

> It's a flash thing. I make an attribution instantly, I shoot from the hip. You have this database of information locked away somewhere there and that's what comes screaming out at you and you almost feel it's another person rather than you doing it. I'm an attributional machine, and that's a thing that gives me huge pleasure.

The majority of interviewees have created physical or digital databases to which they have immediate recourse: most of the people I interviewed were working in rooms lined with books and catalogues. Many also use physical references. One dealer collected objects he described as 'touchstones' that he could use for reference. He cited a damaged red lacquer table top, the provenance of which was so good that its authenticity was unquestionable. Other dealers mentioned taking really problematic objects to museums to put them alongside objects whose provenance was unquestionable; one dealer described such museum objects as 'yardsticks'.

All the interviewees spoke about a mental database as their main attributional tool. One said: 'A good eye is a misnomer, it's more to do with having a good database of experiences'. Another described the process of committing an object to memory as 'making an image of it in my head. It's not just a glimpse, it can take a while. There are forty-two busts in Cologne cathedral and it takes you three days to discriminate them. You get faster, but it usually takes 20 minutes to get into a figure'. Most interviewees claim that their mental image includes a memory of the feel, the weight, the texture of an object. Each new object for identification is then compared to the memory of a body of other similar-looking objects, as this interviewee describes:

> I think it sort of comes automatically. Different coins can have different things about them that sort of come to you in time, and so if someone shows me something I would have a preconceived idea of what I was reckoning that thing to look like and feel like and use that against what was coming to me.

Manipulation and Tools

All of the people I spoke to felt that the primary sense they used in identification and assessment was sight. It was primary in that it was the one they used first, and on which that instant attribution was generally based. However all claimed that touch, and to some extent other senses too, were vital adjuncts. One said: 'If I get as far as touching it to identify it then there is an element of doubt'. Another said: 'The eyes do most of work, but if you're trying to puzzle out an object you normally have it in your hands'.

All the interviewees felt that handling (in the sense of manipulation, turning an object around) was almost a part of seeing it, and was essential for proper viewing. Those who worked with textiles, for instance, spoke of the need to 'delve into' them, to see inside the folds without unfolding them, and the experience needed to use your hands to investigate fabrics without damaging them. Others talked of up-ending ceramics to see foot-ring marks, of looking inside sculptures to see whether the screws holding them together were hand-made, of poking pins into furniture inlays to establish whether they were made of composition (which is hard) or wood (which is softer). And in some fields it is considered acceptable practice to deconstruct an object in order to understand its manufacture; taking drawings out of mounts and frames for instance. One curator had a pair of pliers beside him when he registered objects. Another commented, 'clock people take everything to bits'.

All the people I spoke to relied on hand tools to help them to assess objects. Magnifying glasses, torches, and tape measures were the most widely employed, with scales used for the fine assessment of coins and medals, toothpicks for cleaning out hallmarks, and magnets for testing for the presence of iron. One of the textile experts regarded her linen tester (a fixed magnifying glass) as being 'like another limb'. One of the interviewees has only recently and reluctantly resorted to the magnifying glass, his only supporting tool, because of failing sight, having regarded it all his life as 'the tool of phonies' because it buys attribution time.

Sensory Attribution

Did the interviewees use the other senses—hearing, smell, and taste—in their work? Most said they did, though in a limited way. The porcelain dealer uses resonance (flicking vessels with his finger) to establish whether they have hair cracks. One interviewee described how he had already catalogued for sale a Renaissance bronze medal with a good provenance, when he idly tapped it with his biro and was alerted by the dull sound to the fact it was an electrotype copy. With that one tap its price fell from a range of £3,000–£4,000 to under £100. Another had identified a cleverly faked seventeenth-century corkscrew, whose handle looked and felt like genuine lacquer, by the sudden smell of cellulose (indicating a date in the nineteenth century or later).

After this we went on to discuss the role of touch. In most cases we were discussing active (haptic) rather than passive touch. Interviewees cited numerous instances where different aspects of touch (pressure, texture, temperature) could be important in identifying materials or techniques.

In more detailed attribution, surface texture can be critical in understanding manufacture or in discerning fakes. The sculpture curator described how different sculptors had different approaches to surfaces. He described how, in the undecorated limewood reliefs by the Late-Gothic sculptor Tilman Riemenschneider, one would expect to find a highly polished surface, especially on areas representing skin, whereas other sculptors would use completely different chisels to roughen the skin surface to achieve a livelier feel. A contemporary sculptor, Viet Stoss, was often forced to use poor-quality wood, which he had to fill. If the wood of a Stoss figure felt smooth, the sculpture curator would doubt the attribution. Such qualities could, he said, only be truly appreciated by feeling the wood.

A former picture dealer described being able to tell an oil painting from an oleograph copy by the comparative roughness of the surface. A coin dealer could tell a cast copy from a struck coin by its comparatively soapy feel. A textile curator could tell animal fibres from plant fibres by their springier feel. A porcelain dealer would take into account the texture and graininess of the glaze in attributing a piece to a particular factory.

In other cases the *weight* of an object was crucial (e.g. distinguishing brass from gold or plated copies from solid metal). Temperature was critical in distinguishing between certain materials that appeared similar; for instance, between cooler linen and warmer cotton, which could often not be distinguished by eye. Temperature was one way of telling hard-paste from soft-paste porcelain, and a quick way to tell marble from plastic imitations.

The textile curators described feeling fabrics much as people do in fabric shops, between thumb and forefinger, to get an idea of the quality of the material and a feel for how it would drape or cling. As one commented, 'You can count the threads in both directions but you cannot tell without touching how thin the threads are'.

In most of these cases people were describing touch through their fingertips, but this was not the only part of the body used for feeling. One dealer described scratching with his fingernail the body of Delft pottery to determine whether it was eighteenth-century, or a nineteenth-century copy (which would be more resistant). He said he could tell whether a ceramic was restored by touching it with his teeth; if it was not restored, he would feel (not hear) a click. Another interviewee said he had a colleague who could tell English-made Samian pottery from that made elsewhere in the Roman Empire because it felt grittier on his teeth.

Perhaps the most forceful illustration of the role of touch in connoisseurship came from one curator who claims many attributions can be made with eyes shut. He said:

> You could tell with your eyes shut whether things were soft- or hard-paste porcelain, and you could tell which factory they were by the profile of the foot-ring and things like that, and by feel a lot could be done. I remember I used to do it as a child, trying to work out what all the different things were. I had a series of little coffee cups and tea cups and saucers and things like that, and one fiddled around with those things in bed at night, trying to work out what they were.

Work or Pleasure?

Some of my interviewees felt that tactile pleasure was not a significant factor in their work or in the development of their expertise. A former picture dealer, and one of the sculpture experts, felt that the pleasure gained from working with objects was primarily visual. The curator dealing with ancient textiles found handling them stressful, as she was so conscious of their fragility. But most of them talked with enthusiasm about the pleasure of handling objects:

> Part of the interest in having a coin is having it in your hand—I mean it's a two-sided object so just looking from a distance you're only seeing half of it. If you've got it in your hand you can flick it over. The one side tends to relate to the other in some way and, you know, that's the way you get enjoyment from handling a coin.

> Sculpture is an incredibly tactile medium and all you have to do is to see sacred images to see how often parts of their anatomy are touched. The most obvious thing is the rubbing of St Peter's foot or toe to such an extent that he has to have a little boot put on. As far as male or female naked figures are concerned, you'll find that there's a natural, magnetic situation where people want to rub their nipples or rub their phalluses or whatever, and you can see that the more powerful the image happens to be—if its not guarded, it'll be shining. It's a touchy-feely thing. And that happens to such an extent that I actually believe it's an important part of sculpture. When you've got a little bronze in your hand one wants to be able to not only feel the weight of the thing, which is terribly important, but also stroke its buttocks, it's a sexual thing.

The second interviewee quoted here also believed that the tactile qualities of an object affect its value. He gave the example of sculptures by the neoclassical sculptor Jean-Antoine Houdon that are made in plaster and marble. The plaster sculptures were autograph, made by Houdon himself, while the marble were made by his studio, but the marble would sell for more, the interviewee felt, because marble is pleasantly tactile and plaster is repellent to touch.

For other interviewees, the ability to touch an object brought about a powerful sense of connection with the original owner of the object. One interviewee said he only experienced this sensation when he saw the actual fingerprints of a particular sculptor: 'That's him! That's his fingerprint!'

The textile curators reported feeling a particularly intimate connection with the original wearers and makers of the clothing they handle. One, who was excavating an archaeological site that had been a Jewish stronghold besieged by the Romans, found herself examining a piece of textile. She said:

> I realised this was a head veil we'd taken out and then you could see it had human hair on it, and then probably a layer of human skin, and it had probably been under the head of the woman as she was dying. You know that was extraordinarily moving and took you zooming right back 2000 years.

Control

I talked with the interviewees about the implications of their experience for the museum and cultural heritage sector, and particularly for the general public as visitors to museums and galleries. They were, of course, well aware of the security and conservation issues continually under debate.

One area that provoked strong responses was the question of whether to wear gloves. Everyone I spoke to was aware of the reasons for doing so, but most deplored their use. None of the dealers wore gloves except when handling certain types of metal or ancient glass, where handling may do immediate and obvious damage, and several of the curators were resisting their conservator colleagues and refusing to wear gloves; this was a fraught area for them. One spoke about conservators 'really getting in the way' by treating objects as though they were sanctified. Often interviewees cited the increased danger of dropping objects, or of inlay snagging on cotton gloves, as evidence that gloves could be harmful. The following quotes give an impression of the collective attitude:

> They're frightfully scared of small amounts of acid on your hand, sweat or whatever, but I mean its such an infinitesimally small amount that we disregard that and I think most collectors would say the same. You don't have that same direct feeling for the piece of metal that you're touching.

> I'm a bit careful with the over-use of gloves because certain objects, particularly bronzes, have been made for handling, and suddenly we in our super-scientific world say, Oh, the surface will be destroyed!

> Your fingertips are incredibly sensitive and they are actually working in association with your mind and your eye all the time; now, if you're going to cover that with a glove, it's much worse than a Durex [condom], isn't it?

The opposition to the use of gloves underlines the importance attached by interviewees to direct physical contact with the objects. However, most were assuming that such contact would naturally be restricted to experts.

Touch in the Museum

Interviewees were universally aware of the fact that as curators and dealers they had privileged and immediate access to objects, the kind of access that others are routinely denied by a glass barrier. As a curator put it:

I have collected Renaissance medals and, honestly, looking at them from 6 inches away through glass, you wouldn't be able to tell whether the thing's an electrotype or an original. In fact, you wouldn't be able to tell from three inches away. Sometimes you can't tell until you pick the bloody thing up. You've got to get that feeling for the weight of the thing.

This interviewee also remarked that museums took advantage of this distancing to dupe their audiences. According to him, until recently some Italian galleries routinely hung reproductions instead of Old Master drawings. It was impossible to tell that they were not genuine through the glass, and the galleries did not admit this, so that the public were unwittingly fobbed off with copies.

Of course, most museums would not be so duplicitous, but other sorts of conflicts arise in decisions about what to display. Another curator noted that displaying an object—particularly an elaborately mounted object such as a costume—effectively makes it inaccessible for detailed study; thus, one form of access prevents another.

While such conflicts may be hard to overcome, other comments hint at ways forward. An experienced curator recalled the thrill of handling, in discussion with a conservator, the entire contents of the Basel treasury—the kinds of objects that would normally be displayed behind thick glass. A dealer commented that the privilege of his experience enabled him to 'feel' through the glass: 'With the benefit of one's experience and knowledge you can go to a museum and, even when you can't handle it, you know what it *does* feel like'.

This supports the experience of many who work in museums that offering the public opportunities to handle things is likely to prove exciting and memorable, and that the memory of touch may in some circumstances inform an appreciation of similar objects in other displays. To make this experience purposive, it may be appropriate to focus on the kinds of questions that experts use handling to answer; to make it pleasurable, it may be appropriate to select particularly tactile objects—for instance, objects made to be handled.

Loss of Expertise

The interviewees also had much to say about what they perceived as a worrying skill shortage in museums. One of my interviewees was a retired dealer who is now helping to review attributions at the British Museum, and another was a retired curator who returns to the Victoria and Albert Museum once a month for an 'opinions afternoon' when members of the public bring in objects for identification. There was a general feeling that object-based expertise is no longer based in museums, but outside, where these skills have an obvious value. As one curator put it, if he had a problematic object he would be more likely to take it to an antique shop on the corner than to a major museum because, he said:

> The average bloke round the corner would give a more intelligent answer to start off with because that guy has to live by it, so he's got to get it right. And the average pompous kid one meets in a museum hasn't an effing clue. They're not inquisitive enough. They might know an enormous amount about echinoids or bivalves, but you move away from that one iota and they've had it.

Most of the people I spoke to (probably because of the way I selected them) had contacts with other specialists in their fields, whether these were based in museums, auction houses, or dealers' showrooms, and some referred to specialist societies, such as the Silver Society [www.thesilversociety.org], which encourage the sharing of expertise. Another interviewee felt there was a strong case for a formal apprenticeship system, and wondered whether there was a case for developing par-ticular skills not within individual institutions but on a national basis, perhaps through specialist networks.

More than one interviewee spoke sadly of a sharp divide between academics—who work mainly from documentary and picture sources—and curators working with objects. She cited the fact that, while academics are given time and incentives to publish, most curators are not, leading to a dearth of object-based studies.

Summary and Further Work

It appears from these interviews that touch and handling play an important role in object-expertise, although sight appears to be the primary sense used in identifying objects, and touch is almost always used as an adjunct to it. Most of the interviewees had collections of their own. They enjoyed handling objects, and the pleasure in handling was likely to be closely connected with the development of expertise. All respondents were concerned about the future training of object-specialists and the decline of the curatorial apprenticeship. Few of the respondents could identify easily with the museum visitor, denied the privilege of touching, but in their abhorrence of the use of gloves they were passionate about the importance of direct contact with artefacts and rather dismissive of what they saw as an over-emphasis on conservation.

This very preliminary study suggests that we need to know more about the role of touch in specialist learning and the enjoyment of objects. Further research could address some of the following questions:

- Does touch play a more significant role in the identification of particular types of object?
- How do short-term and long-term tactile memories operate in the development of expertise?
- Are there types of object that are widely felt to be more or less pleasurable to touch than others? Is this reflected in the way they are handled, treated, and valued?
- How might we best share haptic experiences online? What effects might this have on the development of object-expertise, the expectations of museum visitors, our perceptions of authenticity?
- How might we offer museum audiences more thoughtful, pleasurable, and inspiring tactile experiences?

As museums seek to differentiate the special experiences they can offer—whether in a genuine effort to democratise knowledge or simply to justify continued funding—such investigations will become increasingly important.

References

Arts and Humanities Research Council (AHRC). Workshop series 2006–2007. *Touch and the Value of Object Learning.* [http://www.ahrc.ac.uk/ahrb/website/images/4_98167.pdf] (Accessed 23.03.07)

Classen, C. (ed.). 2005a. *The Book of Touch.* New York: Berg.

────── 2005b. Touch in the museum. In C. Classen (ed.), *The Book of Touch.* New York: Berg, 275–86.

Curtis, N. 1997. Young children's learning from objects: Research in Mareschal Museum. *Journal of Education in Museums* 18: 31–33.

Danet, B., Katriel, T. 1989. No two alike: Play and aesthetics in collecting. *Play and Culture* 2: 253–77.

Ellen, R. 1988. Fetishism. *Man* 23: 213–35.

Gordon, G. 1978. *Active Touch: The Mechanism of Recognition of Objects by Manipulation: A Multi-Disciplinary Approach.* Oxford: Pergamon.

Hein, G. 1998. *Learning in the Museum.* London: Routledge.

Hooper-Greenhill, E. 1993. A set of criteria to map the development of skills for using objects. *Group for Education in Museum News* 55: 14–15.

Her Majesty's Stationery Office (HMSO) and Museums Association. 2005. *Collections for the Future.* Retrieved from [http://www.museumsassociation.org/asset_arena/text/ns/policy_collections.pdf] (Accessed 23.03.07)

Jaffe, H.L.C., van Leeuven, J.S., van der Tweel, L.H. 1979. *Authentication in the Visual Arts: A Multi-Disciplinary Symposium.* Amsterdam: B.M. Israel BV, 93–102.

Katz, D. 1925. *Der Aufbau der Tastwelt.* Leipzig: Barth.

Kreuger, L.E. 1982. Tactual perception in historical perspective: David Katz's world of touch. In W. Schiff and F. Emerson (eds.), *Tactual Perception: A Sourcebook*. Cambridge: Cambridge University Press.

Lederman, S.J., Klatzky, R.L. 1996. Action for perception: Manual exploratory movements for haptically processing objects and their features. In A. M. Wing, P. Haggard, and J.R. Flanagan (eds.), *Hand and Brain: The Neurophysiology and Psychology of Hand Movements*. San Diego: Academic.

Maginnis, H.B. 1990. The role of perceptual learning in scholarship. *Art History* 13(1): 104–17.

Millar, S. 1994. *Understanding and Representing Space: Theory and Evidence from Studies with Blind and Sighted Children*. Oxford: Clarendon Press; New York: Oxford University Press.

Mitchell, S. (ed.). 1996. *Object Lessons: The Role of Museums in Education*, Edinburgh: HMSO, Scottish Museums Council.

Nemeroff, C., Rozin, P. 2000. The makings of the magical mind. In K. Rosengren, C. Johnson, and P. Harris (eds.), *Imagining the Impossible: Magical, Scientific and Religious Thinking in Children*. Cambridge: Cambridge University Press.

Paris, S. (ed.). 2002. *Perspectives on Object-Centred Learning in Museums*. London, New York: Routledge.

Phillips, D. 1997. *Exhibiting Authenticity*. Manchester: Manchester University Press.

Stallybrass, P., White, A. 2005. Bourgeois perception: The gaze and the contaminating touch. In C. Classen (ed.), *The Book of Touch*. New York: Berg, 289–91.

Wilkinson, H. 2005. *Collections for the Future: Report of a Museums Association Enquiry*. London: Museums Association.

Zerner, H. 1987. quoted in R.G. de Koster, *On Connoisseurship* (1998, website). [http://highlands.com/art/] (Accessed 23.04.07)

7

UNDERSTANDING OBJECTS: THE ROLE OF TOUCH IN CONSERVATION

Elizabeth Pye

Introduction

Conservators handle objects (often fascinating, and sometimes extraordinary, objects) all the time, and it is easy to forget that this contact with objects and discovery of the stories they tell is not available to others. The aim of this chapter is to explore the role of touch and handling in the examination, conservation, and restoration of objects, and to consider the ambiguities inherent in conservators' involvement with touch.

Conservation is the means by which the physical structure and intangible meanings of an object are preserved through repairing existing damage and preventing, or at least limiting, future change. Clearly, understanding of the nature of the object should be a first step in this process; conservators need to know *what* they are conserving. This involves investigating the fabric and condition of the object, and discovering the significance it may hold for different people.

Linked to conservation there is a further process of restoration that is intended to make the meanings of an object understandable, either through restoring something of the original appearance (as in restoring a painting), or original function (as in restoring a clock to working order), or both of these. Conservation and restoration could be described as essentially tactile practices, involving investigation and intervention to modify the 'normal' course of deterioration. Conservation is not a 'one-off' action but a continuing process involving the documentation, monitoring, and management of change (Caple 2000; Pye 2001; Villers 2004).

In this chapter touch is taken to mean direct contact with an object, either through the hand or by means of a tool guided by hand that allows transmission of sensation to the hand. Apart from routine and superficial visual checking, all conservation involves handling objects, but not all involves a more interventive touch. Conservators distinguish between remedial conservation and preventive conservation. Remedial conservation aims to deal with existing damage so as to improve the current condition of an object; it almost always involves physical or chemical treatment of some kind, and so changes the object. Preventive conservation may not involve any direct intervention, but is focused on improving the conditions of housing and use (including, for example, the way an object is handled) in order to prevent or minimise future deterioration.

Understanding through Touch

The starting point in understanding is to examine the object. One of the most important investigative skills a conservator needs is the skill, not just of looking, but of *seeing*—not a casual glance, but a searching examination. This is achieved by careful and systematic exploration of the surface of an object, perhaps using a focused light source, magnifier, or microscope, and registering and reflecting on what is seen. There almost always comes a point when a conservator touches the surface of the object to check what has been seen. Sight and touch are the essential tools for understanding the composition and condition of an object, and the conservation problems it presents.

> Do not underrate the conservator ... by feeling the properties of materials with very accurate instruments (his eyes and his hands) he can cut his way through a multivariable problem more efficiently than the scientist. (Torraca 1996, 443–44)

This form of touching is circumspect and exploratory. With skill and experience, hands are precisely controllable, and their power of touch can be extended with the sensitive use of hand tools. Fingertips are used to focus touch through contact with the surface of an object. In this way it is possible to assess temperature differences, texture, flaking or powdering, moisture or dryness, stickiness, waxiness, resilience, and telling combinations of these characteristics. Knowledge is gained through the touch of the fingertips, the hands, or a hand tool. In many cases this contact with an object is an essential aspect of thinking about the problem. This is not unique to conservators; in interpreting what they excavate, archaeologists also work like this: 'He handed me a trowel and said 'What do you *think?*' (Hodder 1999, 10; original emphasis).

Conservators also gain information from using their hands to manipulate an object—for example, by opening a folded textile or a book to test flexibility and to look at the inside. The resistance or vibration encountered when they use their hands to encircle, lift, and move objects aids conservators in their assessment of weight, density, or flexibility. Weight can be indicative of material, so an apparently gold metal will feel heavy for its size if it is solid gold, but if it is not particularly heavy it is more likely to be a yellowish alloy or a less valued metal with a gilded surface. Handling is, of course, limited by size; it is not possible to estimate by hand the weight of a very large object, and tiny objects such as beads may be impossible to pick up without the aid of tools such as tweezers.

Although sight and touch are probably the most important senses for conservators, the other senses are also informative: some materials have characteristic smells (e.g. rubber, early plastics such as Bakelite, leather). Touching an object to produce a sound can be informative; for example, gently tapping the surface of a ceramic can indicate how dense and high-fired it is. Porcelain 'rings', whereas more-porous ceramics fired at a lower temperature produce a duller sound.

The information gained through touch (and sound and smell) can provide a quick way to discriminate between different materials. So, in the group of matt-black objects shown in Figure 7.1, which might superficially appear to be made of similar materials, it is possible to distinguish differences. Reading from left to right in the back row: the body of the torch is rubber (slightly resilient with a characteristic smell) the clock case is made of dark polished stone (heavy and feels cold); and the barometer stand is painted wood (light in weight and feels warm). In the front row, the photographic timer has a textured, painted metal case (feels cold and has a characteristic 'ring' when tapped); the small box is lacquer on a thin wood base (light in weight and warm to touch); the clock is plastic (also very light and warm to touch); and the teapot is ceramic (feels cool and gives a characteristic 'ping' when tapped). It is clear from these examples that touch alone will not provide a complete identification; it provides one of the many types of information that conservators use to establish the nature of objects (including perceptions from all the senses, together with contextual, stylistic, and technological information).

Figure 7.1 A group of black objects, each of which feels different to the touch.

Exploring Condition

After looking, touch is used to verify (or not) what has been seen. Combined with visual examination, cautious probing or stroking of a surface can be a good indicator of condition (e.g. if a painted surface is cracked and rough rather than smooth and coherent). A damp or 'greasy' surface on glass can indicate a form of deterioration known as 'weeping' glass. Gradual and gentle flexing or slight pressure can be used to test pliable materials such as textiles to discover if they have become stiff (and, probably, brittle), or to test joints in an object made from several components (e.g. a chair). Tentative tapping can indicate discontinuities in a structure, so a cracked porcelain cup will not give a crisp ring but emit a dull sound, and blisters in a wall painting will produce a hollow sound. Some types of deterioration, such as chemical damage to leather ('red rot'), or tarnish on silver, have characteristic acrid smells. The combined senses, finely tuned through experience, serve the conservator as incomparable diagnostic tools.

The Way Things Are Made: The Touch of the Maker

All pre-industrial objects were handled in the making, and examination reveals the hand (the 'touch') of the maker, showing signs of the way the maker manipulated and controlled the raw material and the tools being used. These material traces not only help us to understand the processes of manufacture but also bring us closer to understanding the motives and skills of the people who made the objects. Perhaps some of the most evocative objects to examine are ceramic vessels because, in forming a shape, potters often leave finger and thumb prints in the clay and create spiral furrows (rilling) with their fingers in the walls of pots as they pull the clay up on the wheel (Kingery and Vandiver 1986; Courty 1995).

Each type of tool (e.g. chisel, file, hammer) leaves its own characteristic mark, though some may be microscopic. In one instance, tool marks typical of a sixteenth-century plane on the back of a supposedly fake Renaissance cabinet were one clue that led experts to decide a cabinet was in fact genuine (Getty Museum 2007). Each individual tool leaves its own signature, created by a pattern of imperfections such as the chips or nicks in the edge of the blade. This information has been used to identify marks left by individual axes in prehistoric wood and to make links between different pieces of timber worked with the same tool. Based on the number of different axe signatures found in one phase of activity, it may be possible to speculate on the size of the workforce, though of course with extended use tool signatures will change (Sands 1997).

Metals can show direct evidence of different types of tool, each of which may leave tell-tale signs such as hammer or file marks, or marks of the draw plate left on metal wire (Oddy 1996). Metals may also show evidence of indirect shaping. Objects are frequently formed by pouring molten metal into a mould. A long-established technique involves making the model for the metal object in wax, enclosing it in clay to form the mould, then introducing the molten metal (the lost-wax process). The result is that shaping techniques easy to use on the soft and pliable wax, but that would not be possible on metal (e.g. rolling fine 'sausages' between fingers and palms or on a flat surface), leave tell-tale signs visible in the finished metal indicating how the object was produced. Figure 7.2 shows part of the wax model for the production of a Benin brass, with several fine rolls of wax used to provide surface detail on the model. The way the wax was worked is clearly echoed in the brass after the casting process was completed (seen on the right of Figure 7.2).

Figure 7.2   Close-up of part of a wax model for a modern Benin brass,
showing detail achieved by rolling and applying wax 'sausages'.
The cast brass (seen on the right) shows the sausages translated
into metal. (courtesy of the Horniman Museum and Renata
Peters)

This revelation of the maker's 'hand' is effectively summed up in Doxiadis' description of the stylistic signatures left in ancient Egyptian mummy portraits:

> The subtlety and roughness, the finesse and asperity, seen in the portraits attest to the idiosyncrasy of each individual painter. Although they are unsigned works, the 'handwriting' of each painter is visible in the brush-strokes and tool-marks scored in the thick wax impasto of the ancient faces. (Doxiadis 2000, 31)

Wear and Tear: The Touch of the User

Use often leaves physical evidence and adds to the stories objects can tell. Some objects acquire new surface texture in the form of fine scratches and chips, or deformation such as dents resulting from continued handling; others lose some of their original crisp definition, as may happen with repeated polishing of a medal. These acquired surface changes testify to how the object has been used and impart a look of age (the valued 'natural' aging that some manufacturers attempt to replicate through artificial 'distressing'). Figure 7.3 shows an early twentieth-century silver tobacco box. The surface is covered in a network of fine scratches resulting from daily use, having been kept in a pocket together with coins or keys. Wooden handles of tools in regular use often acquire a glossy surface—a combination of the oils deposited from the hand with the polish of manipulation. Even very ancient objects may show signs of use, as seen in the patterns of damage

Figure 7.3   A silver tobacco box showing signs of use and wear. (courtesy of David Balaam)

and abrasion left on the edge of stone tools; experimental work has suggested that it is possible to identify the different types of material, (e.g. meat, bone) cut with the tools (Vaughan 1985).

Wear may be caused by a ritual touching. The mediaeval Winchester reliquary shows signs of wear to the gilding, some of which may have been caused by touching (Keene 1987; Caple 2006). Signs of use can even include finger marks, such as those discovered by a conservator when she gently removed the lid of a small tin canister from a Roman site in London. It contained the remains of a whitish ointment complete with the finger marks smeared in it by the last user (Peachey 2003).

The Conservator's Touch

The activities of the conservator or restorer can help to reveal the intentions—both the 'hand' and the 'voice'—of the maker through regaining something of the original visual impact, and sometimes also (as in mechanised or motorised objects) the original function.

Discovering the Surface

Beyond its basic form, much of the impact and meaning of an object is conveyed by the character of the surface.

> It is the surface that bears the finishing touches and the finest workmanship of the original artist or craftsman (Van de Wetering 1996, 415).

It is also the surface that carries the look of age and history resulting from burial, use, wear, and repairs. If, however, the surface is so modified or overlaid that the character is obscured by accretions of soil, corrosion, later modifications, or discoloured and dirty coatings, the object may not convey its character effectively.

Skilful removal of these accretions can dramatically alter the perception of an object. In the case of excavated objects, it may reveal the full intricacy of a piece that appeared initially as a shapeless lump. In the case of paintings, removal of later restorations may enable scholars to reassess the attribution, as happened recently with two paintings in the UK Royal Collection that had been considered unimportant copies but on cleaning were pronounced to be by Caravaggio himself (Royal Collection 2007). Figure 7.4 shows a pair of small medieval brooches; the one on the right has been cleaned, revealing both gilding and original tool marks. This cleaning entails direct, intimate contact with the skin of the object involving cautious removal of overlying layers until the desired surface is uncovered.

The process involves achieving a balance between two apparently contradictory aims: to reveal something of the original intent of the artist and to retain a sense of history. There may be no obvious separation

Figure 7.4   A pair of brooches. The one on the right shows the effects of cleaning.

between 'dirt' and 'aged surface', so cleaning involves constant re-evaluation and is a process of interpretation and judgement. It depends on visual clues and on differences of consistency, as well as on contextual and other information. This is perhaps the most intimate and risky of conservation procedures, and the results can be controversial if critics consider the process has removed too much.

Retrieving Shape and Form

The form of a three-dimensional object is also an important aspect of its character. Breakage, crushing, or distortion can rob an object of its identity. Conservators can reinstate three-dimensionality by piecing together fragments or gently manipulating a crushed object back to shape. When pieces of pottery are reassembled, it is possible to appreciate the object as a whole and to interpret its function (such as jug or cooking pot). Fragments of iron and gilded bronze become recognisable as an Anglo-Saxon helmet (Williams 1992), and a crushed and distorted ancient crocodile skin becomes understandable as a piece of Roman armour (Sully 1992). Again this is a matter of judgement, since some distortion such as creases or folds in textiles may be signs of use rather than damage (Brooks 2000); thus, sensitive reconstruction of a pair of medieval leather boots at the Museum of London retained the distortion caused by the uneven tread of the mediaeval wearer (see fig. 45, Pye 2001, 146).

Touching out Damage

Damages and voids in an object can be distracting, so understanding can be enhanced by filling areas of loss or damage and colouring the fills to integrate them visually (this form of restoration is often known as 'retouching'). In a very fragmentary object, this process plays an important role in reinstating the visual impact and, it is presumed, the meaning intended by the artist. A painting conservator describes this transformation:

> In the early stages of ... a complicated treatment of a damaged picture, visitors to the studio usually begin their conversations about the picture with comments about the extent of the damage. . . . But there is usually a point in time when the comments begin to shift, imperceptibly at first. Eventually, though, the conservator realizes that the visitors no longer have any interest in whatever damages there may have been; they have turned their comments and conversations to the impact of the painting itself as a work of art. When this moment is reached ... enough of the problems have been corrected to allow the artist's voice to speak for itself (Leonard 2003, 52–53)

The Conservator's Signature

Conservators' actions are not neutral but add another layer to the history of objects. However much conservators attempt to avoid obtruding themselves, all remedial conservation and restoration involves interpretation and causes some change to an object through removing or adding materials. In this sense, conservators make a personal statement and leave their signatures on the objects they treat (Leitner & Paine 1994; Larson 1997). Sometimes this was literally so: Robert Ready and his son Augustus, employed by The British Museum in the nineteenth century, signed and dated some of the pots they reconstructed (Watkins and Scott 2001). Some conservation methods can be firmly linked to individual people—and were even patented—for example, the work of Amelia Fowler on flags, including the Star-Spangled Banner (Trupin 2001). More often, however, it is a question of style or fashion in conservation treatment:

> Is it not possible to recognise the museum, or at least the country, from which a painting … originated by the manner in which the painting was treated? (Philippot 1996, 217).

Methods and materials used can indicate when an object was conserved. In the early and mid twentieth century it was usual to remove corrosion from excavated metal objects by chemical means, but from roughly the last quarter of the century mechanical methods became the norm, and each of these methods leaves an identifiable appearance. The types of adhesives and gap-filling materials used on ceramics have changed during the last century and can also be roughly identified to period (Thornton 1998).

The Lansdowne Herakles provides an interesting example of the effects of fashion on styles of restoration. This classical marble statue had been restored in the eighteenth century by the restorer Albacini. In the 1970s, Albacini's realistic carved marble limbs were removed and replaced with synthetic additions in a more starkly 'honest' style. These additions did not age well, and eventually the decision was made to remove them and replace the eighteenth-century marble limbs, as being more aesthetically sympathetic to the statue and part of the history of the piece (Podany 1994).

Conservators' interpretations (signatures) may have a profound effect on the status of objects and their consequent influence on wider studies. A large and important collection of Bronze Age ceramics originally reconstructed in the nineteenth and early twentieth centuries was recently re-conserved, resulting in re-evaluation of the shape and decoration on a number of examples (Burden et al. 2004). Similarly, a leather object that had been reconstructed in the form of a jerkin was re-conserved and reinterpreted as a satchel (Lewis 2006). In each case the earlier work had been recognised as inaccurate, and the reinterpretation accepted as nearer to the original form. Even what is seen now as an apparently more meticulous and accurate reinterpretation may be challenged in the future. A well-known example of how influential a conservator's work can be is the Sutton Hoo helmet. This Anglo-Saxon helmet had been restored in the 1950s and, in the absence of other examples, was widely accepted (and published) as typifying helmets of the period. Growing misgivings about the accuracy of the reconstruction led to re-evaluation and re-restoration in the 1970s, in conjunction with extensive research and consultation (Williams 1992). The re-interpretation certainly appears to be more satisfactory as a piece of protective armour, and has become, in its turn, an iconic representation of the Anglo-Saxon helmet.

The conservation of very damaged artefacts can therefore not only alter their status but becomes an essential feature of their character and history (Pye 2006). Speaking of one of the Roman wall paintings from Boscotrecase, Beard and Henderson point out:

> The masterpiece we admire represents an enormous input of care and imagination, to re-create a wonderful painting from bits of plaster. Our evaluation of this painting rests squarely on a judgement on the quality of its *restoration*; and that is a dilemma we face in trying to see how 'good' any ancient painting is. (Beard & Henderson 2001, 53; original emphasis)

Constraints on Touch and Handling

Aware of the effects that conservation can have on objects, conservators try to limit their interventions and are increasingly cautious about touching objects. Over the last 15 to 20 years, conservation has shifted focus from repair and restoration to the preventive measures aimed at controlling the surrounding environment rather than treating the object itself.

Touch and handling may be constrained for other reasons, such as health and safety: lead, asbestos, and radioactive substances are all represented in collections, as are organic objects that have been treated in the past with pesticides such as DDT (Odegaard 2005). A different problem is presented by the growing number of plastic objects in collections, not because they are hazardous but because many are likely to deteriorate, some to the point of disintegration, and are at present difficult or impossible to conserve (Baker & McManus 1992; Heuman 1999). They include late-nineteenth or early-twentieth century plastics used to imitate natural materials such as ivory, as well as much more recent domestic items or art objects. An example is the 1960s sculpture 'Thumb' by Cesar, composed of three different modern polymers, which by the 1990s had visibly deteriorated and posed a complex conservation problem (Sale 1995). This organ of touch and manipulation may eventually become impossible to touch!

Touching some objects is not possible for legal or cultural reasons. Conservators of recent art can be constrained not just by materials but by artists' copyright: the alteration of a work of art even in the name of conservation may infringe copyright. For this reason, conservators of modern collections frequently consult the artists themselves in making conservation decisions (Stone 1990; Fry 1997; Garfinkle et al. 1997). Most conservators are cautious about working on objects of unknown provenance, particularly if there is any suspicion that they may have been looted from ancient sites (Tubb 1995). Cultural constraints may limit handling and conservation of some objects. In their original contexts these objects may have been secret or sacred, and accessible only to certain people. Descendant communities may find it inappropriate or offensive that they are touched by particular groups such as the uninitiated, or women (Drumheller & Kaminitz 1994; Peers & Brown 2003; Ogden 2004).

Some objects are not intended (as opposed to expected) to last, and decay is an essential and welcomed aspect of their meaning, so conservators should hesitate to interfere in this trajectory (Ferguson & Martza 1990). This can be true both of some types of ethnographic objects and some examples of recent conceptual art. Clavir (2002, 153) reports the views of representatives of Canadian First Nations expressed about totem poles:

> They weren't put up for tourists, they were put up there as memorial poles … those memorial poles will stand there until they crumble, and when they crumble, then gone are the memories. The old people say they are not meant to be maintained. (Peggy Svanvik)

> But the pole, when it is lying on the ground, doesn't lose its cultural significance. In time that pole starts returning back to the earth, and that pole may provide what's now known as a nurse log, that little seedlings grow from the pole, that insects and small animals use the pole as a refuge, but in time that pole goes back to the earth. It's a cycle. (Don Bain)

In all these cases, conservators have to negotiate a satisfactory conservation outcome that balances care of the objects with the need to take account of safety, or legal requirements, or cultural concerns.

Prohibition of Touch

Touch is a privilege usually reserved to conservators and curators. It is undeniable that touching and handling objects can be damaging. Many objects in museums are old, fragile, and vulnerable, so the prohibition of touch is seen as another aspect of conservation. Except for selected examples, objects are generally protected from handling by visitors.

> Museum objects are—unfortunately—only there to be *seen*. Thousands of people earn their living preventing untold thousands of others from touching objects. (Van de Wetering 1996, 415; original emphasis)

Most conservation and museum studies programmes include training in handling. Most galleries and museums have rules about who can and who cannot touch, and provide in-house training in handling procedures (e.g. Miles 1992; Rowlison 1994). Despite this caution there are examples of significant objects that are regularly touched. An interesting example is the sixth/seventh century Sultanganj Buddha in Birmingham Museum. Local Buddhists are welcomed to the museum to hold ceremonies, and often touch the statue's left little finger. This is accepted by the museum's conservators despite the fact that this regular touch is visibly affecting the patina on the finger (Birmingham Museum 2007). Another example is the Lord Mayor's coach, which spends most of its existence in the Museum of London, but is taken out and used for its original ceremonial purpose when the Lord Mayor processes through the streets of the City of London (Pye 2001). This form of access is encouraged in other collections, for example, the Smithsonian's National Museum of the American Indian (see Johnson, Chapter 14 in this volume).

In fact, it is generally agreed that a greater danger comes not from touching stationary objects but from the lifting and handling needed to move objects within a museum, or to transport them to another institution (or to another country or continent) when they are lent for exhibition elsewhere. 'The safe moving of objects is worth a book on its own' (Ashley-Smith 1999, 270).

Touching Emotions

We all know how emotive objects can be, even just by seeing them:

> You don't just see an object, you see a whole people and what they must have been about. (Debra Sparrow, quoted in Clavir 2002, 130)

One of the most startling experiences I have had in a museum was to enter a room in the military museum at Les Invalides in Paris and come face to face with Napoleon in the form of his greatcoat and hat displayed on a dummy figure. The impact of the encounter was emphasised by the coat's severe simplicity and drab colour, which contrasted with the ornate and colourful trappings of military splendour surrounding it. An anonymous encounter can be just as emotive; some of the most touching objects I have seen are the small tokens left with babies when their poor mothers abandoned them at the Foundling Hospital in London: half a coin, a dented thimble, a key, or a finger ring. . . . Women hoped they might one day be able to reclaim their child, so the token was a way of identifying the baby (Wedd 2004).

This emotional impact does not necessarily require us to handle the object, but how much more powerful it can be to make physical contact! This contact is unlike the distanced gaze of the viewer. Objects can touch us as much as we can touch them. Handling an ancient object such as a flint tool or copper alloy axe-head brings us closer to its prehistoric maker and also sends a powerful message about the maker's skill in manipulating the raw material.

There is something particularly thrilling about handling an object once owned and used by an exceptional person: a piece of clothing worn by Abraham Lincoln or a manuscript written by Jane Austen. Contact with objects can also be shocking and chilling, as when a Jewish colleague handed me the star he had been forced to wear as a child during the Nazi regime. However, for conservation reasons, this powerful effect of touch is generally denied to everyone except museum professionals.

Managing Touch

Conservators are very conscious of their professional responsibility to protect objects in order that they survive into the future, so are cautious about touching objects themselves and hesitant to encourage touch by others. At the same time they still enjoy—take for granted— the intimacy of handling objects in their daily work.

There are certainly risks in allowing handling, but there are many risks to objects in the museum and heritage context (see Ashley-Smith 1999 for a whole book on the subject). There are risks in allowing visual appreciation because of the damaging effects of light, but because vision has been the dominant mode of experiencing objects the risks of lighting have been accepted and worked with.

It is accepted that objects are lent to other institutions in order to reach new audiences, so the hazards of handling, moving, and transport, as well as the risks of exposing the objects to climate differences, are also accepted. In libraries the touch and handling associated with reading are seen as essential to the appropriate use of books and archives, so it is acknowledged that wear cannot be eliminated. On heritage sites and in historic houses, it is known that visitors have a physical effect on the fabric, eroding paths and imposing increased loading on floors and stairways, but visiting is not banned. It is situations like these that have contributed to the development of the distinct branch of conservation known as preventive conservation.

The risks of exposure to light are dealt with by being selective over what is displayed and by controlling and monitoring light levels and length of exposure. The risks of damage to sites and historic houses are dealt with by limiting visitor numbers and varying access routes. In libraries and archives, access is maximised and handling limited by making as much material as possible available digitally or through microfilm, but old and relatively vulnerable books are also available for consultation, positioned on supporting cradles to minimise stress on the binding.

The desire (or the 'right') to see objects or visit sites is seldom questioned. Access through touch is now becoming more widely accepted. Educational handling collections are well-established (Keene 2005); groups of handleable objects are included in conventional 'visual' exhibitions; more museums are holding touch exhibitions, for example, 'Touch Me' at the Victoria and Albert Museum in 2005 (Victoria and Albert Museum 2007) and 'Raised Awareness' at Tate Modern, also in 2005, which was designed specifically for blind and partially sighted visitors (Tate Modern 2007).

It is interesting to note that, in 2002, Resource (now the Museums Libraries and Archives Council) commissioned a report on the impact of handling on objects (Munday 2002), which concluded that more objects could be made available for touch and handling and to much wider audiences. The consequence of these shifts in opinion must be that eventually the risks of touching and handling objects will be assessed and managed by conservators in much the same way as the risks of exposing objects to light or of reading books. The management of touch will become an increasingly important aspect of preventive conservation.

References

Ashley-Smith, J. 1999. *Risk Assessment for Object Conservation.* Oxford: Butterworth-Heinemann.

Baker, M.T., McManus, E. 1992. History, care, and handling of America's spacesuits: Problems in modern materials. *Journal of the American Institute for Conservation* 31: 77–85.

Beard, M., Henderson, J. 2001. *Classical Art from Greece to Rome.* Oxford: Oxford University Press.

Birmingham Museum. 2007. *Buddha: The Sultanganj Buddha.* [http://www.bmagic.org.uk/objects] (Accessed 7.04.07)

Brooks, M. (ed.). 2000. *Textiles Revealed: Object Lessons in Historic Textile and Costume Research.* London: Archetype.

Burden, L. et al. 2004. The reconservation of 105 Bronze Age ceramics. *The Conservator* 28: 37–46.

Caple, C. 2006. *Objects: Reluctant Witnesses to the Past.* London, New York: Routledge.

——— 2000. *Conservation Skills: Judgement, Method and Decision Making.* London: Routledge.

Clavir, M. 2002. *Preserving What is Valued: Museums: Conservation and First Nations.* Vancouver, Toronto: UBC Press.

Courty, M. 1995. Identification of wheel throwing on the basis of ceramic surface features and microfabrics. *Journal of Archaeological Science* 22: 17–50.

Doxiadis, E. 2000. Technique. In S. Walker (ed.), *Ancient Faces: Mummy Portraits from Roman Egypt.* London: British Museum Press, 30–31.

Drumheller, A., Kaminitz, M. 1994. Traditional care and conservation, the merging of two disciplines at the National Museum of the American Indian. In A. Roy and P. Smith (eds.), *Preventive Conservation: Practice, Theory and Research.* Preprints of the Contributions to the Ottawa Congress, September 1994. London: International Institute for Conservation, 58–60.

Ferguson, T.J., Martza, B. 1990. The repatriation of *Ahayu:da* Zuni war gods. *Museum Anthropology* 14 (2): 7–14.

Fry, R. 1997. Preservation or desecration? The legal position of the restorer. In P. Lindley (ed.), *Sculpture Conservation: Preservation or Interference?* Aldershot, Hants: Scolar Press, 55–62.

Garfinkle, A., Fries, J., Lopez, D., Possessky, L. 1997. Art conservation and the legal obligation to preserve artistic intent. *Journal of the American Institute for Conservation* 36: 165–79.

Getty Museum. 2007. *A Renaissance Cabinet Rediscovered.* [http://www.getty.edu/art/exhibitions/cabinet] (01.03.07)

Heuman, J. (ed.). 1999. *Material Matters: The Conservation of Modern Sculpture.* London: Tate Gallery.

Hodder, I. 1999. *The Archaeological Process.* Oxford: Blackwell.

Keene, S. 2005. *Fragments of the World: Uses of Museum Collections.* Oxford: Butterworth Heinemann.

——— 1987. The Winchester reliquary: Conservation and elucidation. In J.W. Black (ed.), *Recent Advances in the Conservation and Analysis of Artifacts.* Institute of Archaeology, Jubilee Conservation Conference Papers. London: Summer Schools Press, 25–32.

Kingery, D.W., Vandiver, P.B. 1986. *Ceramic Masterpieces.* London, New York: Free Press (Macmillan).

Larson, J. 1997. Sculpture conservation: Treatment or reinterpretation? In P. Lindley (ed.), *Sculpture Conservation: Preservation or Interference?* Aldershot, Hants: Scolar Press, 69–82.

Leitner, H., Paine, S. 1994. Is wall painting restoration a representation of the original or a reflection of contemporary fashion? An Austrian perspective. In A. Oddy (ed.), *Restoration: Is it Acceptable?* British Museum Occasional Paper 99. London: British Museum, 51–66.

Leonard, M. 2003. The artist's voice. In M. Leonard (ed.), *Personal Viewpoints: Thoughts about Paintings Conservation.* Los Angeles: Getty Conservation Institute, 41–58.

Lewis, R. 2006. Interpretation in conservation: A rare leather find from an early historic crannog. *The Conservator* 29: 87–94.

Miles, G. 1992. Object handling. In J. Thompson (ed.), *Manual of Curatorship: A Guide to Museum Practice*, 2nd edn. London: Butterworth Heinemann, 455–58.

Munday, V. 2002. *Guidelines for Establishing, Managing, and Using Handling Collections and Hands-On Exhibits in Museums, Galleries, and Children's Centres.* Report undertaken for Resource. [http://www.mla.gov.uk] (Accessed 23.04.07)

Oddy, A. 1996. Jewelry under the microscope: A Conservators' guide to cataloguing. In A. Calinescu (ed.), *Ancient Jewelry and Archaeology*. Bloomington, IN: Indiana University Press, 185–97.

Odegaard, N. 2005. *Old Poisons, New Problems: A Museum Resource for Managing Contaminated Cultural Materials*. Walnut Creek and Oxford: Alta Mira Press.

Ogden, S. (ed.). 2004. *Caring for American Indian Objects: A Practical and Cultural Guide*. St Paul: Minnesota Historical Society Press.

Peachey, P. 2003. Roman face cream found at London temple site. *The Independent*, 29 July.

Peers, L., Brown, A.K. (eds.). 2003. *Museums and Source Communities*. London: Routledge.

Philippot, P. 1996. Restoration from the perspective of the humanities. In N. Stanley Price, M.K. Talley Jr, and A.M. Vaccaro (eds.), *Historical and Philosophical Issues in the Conservation of Cultural Heritage*. Los Angeles: Getty Conservation Institute, 216–29.

Podany, J.C. 1994. Restoring what wasn't there: Reconsideration of the eighteenth-century restorations to the Lansdowne Herakles in the collection of the J. Paul Getty Museum. In A. Oddy (ed.), *Restoration: Is it Acceptable?* British Museum Occasional Paper 99. London: British Museum, 9–18.

Pye, E. 2006. Authenticity challenged? The plastic house at Çatalhöyük. *Public Archaeology* 5(4): 237–51.

——— 2001. *Caring for the Past: Issues in Conservation for Archaeology and Museums*. London: James and James.

Rowlison, E. 1994. Rules for handling works of art. In S. Knell (ed.), *Care of Collections*. London: Routledge, 202–11.

Royal Collection. 2007. Caravaggio revealed. [http://www.royalcollection.org.uk] (Accessed 15.04.07)

Sale, D. 1995. Standing out like a sore thumb: A damaged sculpture made of three synthetic polymers. In J. Heuman (ed.), *From Marble to Chocolate: The Conservation of Modern Sculpture*. London: Archetype, 98–103.

Sands, R. 1997. *Prehistoric Woodworking: The Analysis and Interpretation of Bronze and Iron Age Toolmarks*. London: UCL Institute of Archaeology.

Stone, T. 1990. Copyright and conservation. In B.A. Ramsay-Jolicoeur and I.N.M. Wainwright (eds.), *Shared Responsibility: Proceedings of a Seminar for Curators and Conservators*, National Gallery of Canada, 26–28 October 1990. Ottawa: National Gallery of Canada, 149–52.

Sully, D. 1992. Humidification: The reshaping of leather skin and gut objects for display In P. Hallebeek, M. Kite, and C. Calnan (eds.), *Conservation of Leathercraft and Related Objects*. London: ICOM-CC, 50–53.

Tate Modern. [http://www.tate.org.uk/modern/exhibitions/raisedaware ness] (accessed 7.04.07)

Thornton, J. 1998. A brief history and review of the early practice and materials of gap-filling in the West. *Journal of the American Institute for Conservation.* 37: 3–22.

Torraca, G. 1996. The scientist's role in historic preservation with particular reference to stone conservation. In N. Stanley Price, M.K. Talley, and A.M. Vaccaro (eds.), *Historical and Philosophical Issues in the Conservation of Cultural Heritage*. Los Angeles: Getty Conservation Institute, 439–44.

Trupin, D. 2001. Patriotism in fabric and stitches: The history of flag conservation/restoration in the United States. In A. Oddy and S. Smith (eds.), *Past Practice, Future Prospects*. British Museum Occasional Paper 145. London: British Museum Press, 189–94.

Tubb, K.W. (ed.). 1995. *Antiquities: Trade or Betrayed?: Legal, Ethical, and Conservation Issues*. London: Archetype Publications.

Van de Wetering, E. 1996. The surface of objects and museum style. In N. Stanley Price, M.K. Talley, and A.M. Vaccaro (eds.), *Historical and Philosophical Issues in the Conservation of Cultural Heritage*. Los Angeles: Getty Conservation Institute, 415–21.

Vaughan, P. 1985 *Use-Wear Analysis of Flaked Stone Tools*. Tucson: University of Arizona Press.

Victoria and Albert Museum. [http://www.vam.ac.uk/vastatic/microsites/1376 touch me/] (accessed 7.04.07)

Villers, C. 2004. Post minimal intervention. *The Conservator* 28: 3–10.

Watkins, S., Scott, R. 2001. Timeless Problems: Reflections on the conservation of archaeological ceramics. In A. Oddy and S. Smith (eds.), *Past practice, Future Prospects*. British Museum Occasional Paper 145. London: British Museum, 195–200.

Wedd, K. 2004. *The Foundling Museum*. London: The Foundling Museum.

Williams, N. 1992. The Sutton Hoo helmet. In A. Oddy, *The Art of the Conservator*. London: British Museum, 73–88.

8

THE ELDERLY AS 'CURATORS' IN NORTH LONDON

Michael Rowlands

Assumptions about the moving of the elderly from domesticity to cared environments or sheltered accommodation—or, more crudely, about their being 'put in a home'—affect us all, directly and indirectly, (and for most of us in a rather guilty fashion). The linearity of the phrase 'from domesticity to care' betrays the assumption that the move to cared environments involves a loss of the capacity to care for oneself and others, as in the frightening words 'taken into care'. Yet the institutionalised provision of care, whatever anxiety it invokes, is widely considered fundamental to a *humane* society.

The fact that the institutional provision of care impinges directly on corporeal needs, conjuring analogues with other institutions of care such as asylums, prisons, and museums, diverts attention from the differences both in terms of choice and relief from the responsibilities of care. Yet the analogy of personal care to that of curatorship, the care for collections, is made starkly poignant by the Oxford English Dictionary (OED) definition of a museum curator: *A person who has charge or oversight /care of a person or a thing—especially the custodian of a museum, art gallery, etc.* A consequence of this tendency to associate care with institutionalisation is to oppose domesticity to care in the various senses of the loss of the ability or the agency of caring, both for oneself and others. To retrieve the value of care as being at the heart of domesticity, we can reverse the institutionalised notion of care as curatorship and examine instead how we are all curators in the personal sense of taking care of ourselves and of things that together constitute our intimate worlds of touch.

To expand the idea that domesticity is a curated personal space, I suggest that we know our personal space principally through touch and, in particular, the *memory* of touch: of touching handles on doors, latches on windows, cutlery in drawers, plates in dark cupboards, and of dusting artefacts on mantelpieces and polishing furniture. If, through caring for objects, we care for ourselves and our intimate others, we do so, I argue, through the faculty of touch. To think of the experience of being at home is to realise how much depends on the familiarity that comes with knowing a space—by walking shoeless, by sleeping, by bathing, by preparing and serving food—and to grasp that domesticity is the sensuality of *being through touch* and *being in touch* with oneself and intimate others.

The research project on which this chapter is based involved architects, town planners, and anthropologists in understanding the material needs of the elderly who are 'in care'.[1] The ethnography involved a study of 18 cases of elderly people moving into cared environments in Harringay in North London. Each person was interviewed about the experience of moving from the autonomy of their own home into 'care'. The results consistently contradicted the assumption that the elderly would feel a loss of care for self and others as they moved to sheltered or cared environments.

If anything, the pattern was often quite the reverse. With increasing age, domesticity had become an unwelcome reminder of their growing incapacity to care, surrounded as they were by the material legacies of previous abilities to care: kitchens used now only in a minimal boiling-an-egg way, or spaces that could no longer be kept clean or functional. Unused spare bedrooms and difficult-to-maintain kitchens were an embarrassment, and caring for furniture and furnishings had become a burden. It was now beyond them to care for these reminders of former days of domestic utility and, perhaps, of grandeur. Among the informants there were, of course, nostalgic glances towards glory days of greater autonomy, and of being in control of their domestic circumstances, but consistently this was offset by statements of satisfaction with being cared for or not having to struggle with caring for oneself.

An example was Mrs S, who had lived in the same three-storey house in Stroud Green for fifty years; she had been married in 1942 and was widowed with three children and seven grandchildren. She was 80 years old and had developed Parkinson's disease, and her GP had arranged for her to move to sheltered accommodation two years earlier. How did Mrs. S feel about the move?

I was a bit upset at first but when I saw this flat it was the best thing that happened to me. Maureen [the warden] is a wonderful woman. But I was anxious. If the children hadn't been on at me, I don't think I would have moved.

Mrs. S explained later that her anxiety related to her frailty as well as a concern that she would no longer remember where things were in her new environment. For instance, she often had to get up during the night to go to the bathroom and she needed to feel her way in what had become an intimate space. When she was asked 'When you came here for the first time, how did you feel?' she replied: 'Well it was warm, the windows look out. . . everything about the flat. . . plenty of cupboard space. . . I just felt free. . . not being cold. . . I felt free.' Which suggests that the old space had become a trial and the new warmer and lighter space allowed her to re-invent a sense of touch.

This discrepancy was not only a surprise to the investigators on the project; equally, it seems to have been a surprise for the elderly. Often, applying for sheltered accommodation had been seen as a humiliating matter, forced by circumstances and/or persuaded by friends and relatives, but, once done and dusted, it led to surprised experiences of renewed gaiety and life. To some extent, this was also a bit of a surprise for sons and daughters who may have been instrumental in the decision to sell the family home and to move mum or dad into a 'home'. They typically felt considerable guilt, and had difficulty accepting their surrender of their own responsibility for care of parents or grandparents because of personal circumstances. They had rationalised on the lines that having to be cared for is inevitable with age and it is the duty of the Council or Housing Association to provide that care.

The researchers had also anticipated a linear movement from a life of self-care and care for others in the domesticity of home (whatever that might mean) to one where the institution takes over and administers care. This may sometimes be the case, particularly with disability, and its implications for human dignity may be in fact, open to abuse. But the fact that the experience of the transition from one state to the other did not match assumptions made both by our informants and the researchers was a paradox to be explained.

I argue that this is because we have not gone deeply enough into the question of care. We do not understand what it means to 'care' for someone or something. It is also important to recognise that, as with any good curator (in contrast to the OED definition), this is done reflexively. Care is curation, and taking this out of the museum and into personal life involves understanding how decisions are made about what to keep and what to discard. Personal acts of curation shape the process of producing a past and projecting a future for the self. Yet, the fact that the future of the elderly in Harringay was often seen by them in the very short term (5 out of 18 were over 90 years old), also meant explicit anxieties about getting that curatable past finally in order. New acquisitions for the future were low in priority but decisions on disposals were a real source of concern—though not in all cases. As we shall see, some cases (mostly male) fiercely resisted recognising a stored past; instead, they anticipated events in their current life (visiting the pub, the betting shop, a friend) and focussed on preserving continued personal access to public space. Either way, it is the metaphor of care as curation that requires further exploration.

Analogues can be drawn between personal acts of curation and the formal curatorial skills of documentation, classification, and conservation of collections. Most of our informants, when asked, could remember the furniture and other objects that they had previously accumulated and in some cases given away or discarded. It's not that they kept a written record but, rather like the art of memory described by Yates (1966), they could remember a piece of furniture by its position in a room or by its use, and also by the person to whom they may have given it. A mental/visual classification of things once belonging to them was reinforced (if not sustained) by a reminiscence of touch—through the memory of having once used or cleaned or polished them. If one of the cardinal rules of the good curator is 'Do Not Touch', the forms displayed by the elderly in Harringay are resolutely about who may touch. Preserving the right to say who can touch or use a thing is one of the more important priorities of disability; to say who can help move you, carry you, or bring things to you helps maintain a sense of self.

As researchers, we had taken the notion of care and caring environments rather for granted, which diverted our attention in the study to the objective circumstances of 'care'; how much space was provided, the functions of space, the use of objects, and the like. The literature on ageing is generally devoid of questions about the nature of care. In retrospect this is surprising, given the central importance of the ontology of care for the development of both phenomenological and existential philosophies in twentieth-century thought. In *Being and Time*, Heidegger recounts an ancient creation myth in which a deity, Cura, shapes human beings from clay (donated by Earth) and infuses them with spirit (donated by Jupiter), whereupon the beings created are named as human by Saturn (Mulhall 2005, 112–13). Heidegger uses this myth of the shaping of Being to argue that care is the basis of being human, i.e. Cura is the creator of *Dasein* (being-in-the-world).

In evoking this tale of human creation through curation, Heidegger made a distinction between *caring for* as anticipatory and future-oriented, and the actions of *taking care of* something or somebody as reflexive and past—or care as intention contrasted to care as disposition. To *care for* something or somebody is anxiety ridden; however much you may care, your caring is contingent upon unpredictable future events.

The human condition is fated to a self and to a world of other selves and objects about which one cannot but choose to be concerned. To *have taken care of* something or somebody is reflexive of past actions, characterized by acts of bringing together to ensure the conditions of collective well being. Whilst both these aspects of care relate to creation (i.e. creation of self), their separation is unified by their temporality; or, rather, as modes of caring they represent experience of different temporalities in the present. As we shall see, the more nostalgic may contrast with the more forward-looking, although both temporal experiences can exist in a personal experience.

With age, the capacity to care for something or somebody in the future runs up against the limiting condition of awareness of one's own death. This makes the elderly's experience of care a more reflexive, past-oriented concern. As persons capable of self-reflection, we are all curators in the general sense of curating a life; in the use of objects, photographs, clothes, souvenirs, and household furnishings as a means of narrating a life story. In this respect, the elderly in Harringay are exemplary curators who reflect on their earlier circumstances of having cared for persons and things and in the process make sense of a life well spent.

Four cases illustrate, with different inflections, this tendency to curate a life reflexively.

Mrs C is a widow with three sons, who came to Britain from Jamaica in the 1950s to take up a nursing career. She still has furniture and crockery inherited from her parents, and what she describes as 'all the things that make a home', waiting in storage in Jamaica for her eventual (as she sees it) return. In fact, she is disabled with rheumatoid arthritis and moved two years ago to sheltered accommodation in Wood Green, where she is visited every week by one of her sons. She tells a sad story of being married to an alcoholic husband who sold all their belongings to feed his habit. She was left with nothing when he died and, now disabled, had relied on others to help furnish her new accommodation.

She described the furniture in her flat in terms of who had given it to her. The settee was the oldest. It was given to her by a nursing friend twenty years ago and, though it is now old, she keeps it for sentimental reasons. Other friends gave her a table and chairs, her nephew bought her a fridge, and her sister-in-law bought her a special recliner chair, around which her day revolves. She eats there off a tray, watches television, keeps the telephone there, and reads borrowed books and a magazine called *Friends* given her by a neighbour upstairs. She keeps a garden chair in the flat to remind her of the days when she had a garden, and likes the flat because it has a sunny sitting room. This gathering in of second-hand furniture and things, she associates with cosiness.

She has a large collection of soft toys about which she says, 'they remind me of gentleness, because they are so cuddly'. They also look after her: 'You see that little monkey on top of the TV, he sits there. I say to him if I am going out, you watch the place while I am away'. She keeps photos of her family, most of which she took herself: 'It just reminds me that I am not alone. I have got a family even though I live alone'. One of the photos is of herself as a nurse 'when I used to be a school nurse. I always keep it to remind me that I used to be helpful to others'. She also stores cushions in two of her cupboards. 'I don't need them myself', she explained, 'but they might be useful to people who fall on hard times'.

It is not surprising to see the home of Mrs C as the summation of a life of a carer curated around the responsibilities of care. Her story, as one of caring for others and others for her, suggests a rather nostalgic present of having once cared for others that her disability now prevents her from doing. However, the cuddly toys are the more active part of her concern for care because they may be both cuddled and touched, and are responsible for keeping order in the flat whilst she is away. As far as she is concerned, the toys care for her as much as she cares for them. In other words, the soft toys have agency, even a therapeutic value, in providing company and allowing themselves to be touched and handled that is reminiscent of 'grooming behaviour' (Figure 8.1).

At the other extreme is Miss G, who lives in a block of sheltered accommodation in Muswell Hill and doesn't appear to care for her things at all. She is in her seventies, unmarried with no children, and with a brother who lives nearby in the same block. She took the accommodation as a furnished flat rented for her by the Council. Most of the furniture belongs to the landlord and, when asked if she saw it as her home, she replied: 'Well, no. It's a place where I live. You make what you can of it, don't you?'. When asked about what she would see as improvements to the flat, however, Miss G provided one of the longest lists of detailed recommendations that we got for the Bartlett architects. She had prepared a written list of recommendations for how to improve the ventilation, for sealed windows to keep the heat in, for better ways of cleaning surfaces, for the priority of a washing machine, and many other recommendations that would, she felt, improve the lot of those in rented sheltered accommodation in general. She was very concerned about the implications of all this for others, and that the research would lead to tangible results.

Figure 8.1   The intimacy of soft toys.

We then asked Miss G about the collection of books and music cassettes that she kept in the flat. They turned out to be the one personal
collection that she was very committed to keeping. This is because she
is involved with a local church that has a club meeting once a week and
she provides the music for the occasion. She not only does the music
programmes for the club members but she also uses her books to devise
quizzes. Amidst all the things belonging to the landlord, the music
system and the bookcase were the items for which she felt a strong
sense of possession.

Although she is in her seventies, through these activities she denies
she is old, speaking about the care she takes of the 'old folk' in the
club and how she likes to see their old photographs and hear their old
stories. This relates to the fact that she was the lastborn following two
brothers and a sister, and that she had stayed at home looking after
her parents until she was well into her forties. When her father died,
Miss G moved with her mother to Blackpool (her mother's birthplace)
where she lived until her mother died. She subsequently moved back
to London to be near her brother.

When asked what had happened to all the furnishings from her
mother's house in Blackpool, she replied that she had just got rid of
it all. This lack of concern for her own things seems to be an attitude

shaped by a life committed to externalising a sense of care to others and their requirements rather than care for herself. Unmarried and un-domesticated, she maintains her freedom to care (or not) and to refuse the burden of possessions that require care.

The study so far suggests that among the elderly informants the institutionalisation of their care has promoted a reflexive concern with the narration of personal histories. Mrs C and Miss G, for example, are both concerned with remembering that they have personal histories of taking care of others, and of this being reciprocated. Mrs C is more subjective in feeling that her own care of others in the past has been recognised and reciprocated in the help she has received more recently in her disabled state. Miss G is more objective, and externalising, in continuing her personal trajectory of taking care of others whilst neither expecting, nor perhaps wanting, this to be reciprocated. This suggests that, by relieving them of the anxiety of care for themselves or others in the future, the institutionalisation of care promotes this reflexive turn that makes the present a sort of summation of their personal pasts, experienced through either active reminiscence about the use and disposal of possessions or a kind of absolute forgetting of the relevance of such memories.

But other case studies suggest that it can be more complicated than personal accounts of well-curated lives. Take for example, Mrs T's concern with her present situation and relative lack of concern with her personal past:

> Well, I've had many lives. Different stages, you know. This is my last phase, this is. I've just got to accept it. It's a bit of a job to accept it, you know. I shall be 90 in May. I mean, that is quite a good age. But I don't like it, I don't like the idea at all. I know that every day could be my last—you know, you only live for one day. You know, like a butterfly.

Yet, for someone living her last day, Mrs T is resolutely 'caring for', and anxious about the future. Her days are spent 'caring for' objects, things, and attached persons, whose well-being directly impinges on her own: 'Every day I do bits and pieces here and there. I do bits of washing—odd bits of washing. I clean some cupboards—something like that—just to keep going, you know.'

The obstacles that prevent her being able to care in the future are resolutely confronted and solutions found, so that she can still act in the world. When we asked her to explain why she had complained about not being able to go out at weekends, we expected a depressing story of the frailty of age. Instead, it was how the ordeal for her to walk from her flat to the laundry had been overcome through the help of a carer, who takes her laundry down and gets it done for her. There is little sign in Mrs T, therefore, of fear of loss of the capacity to care, either with age or her sense of closeness to death. Instead, the daily round is a constant battle of getting things and people in order.

Mrs T has a new chair that cost £200. She has replaced the cover on it from her old chair that had developed a broken leg, so it was still familiar to her. But the acquisition of a new item of furniture has put the arrangement of her living room into question.

> I always sit in my chair, but I'm seriously thinking of changing the room round because I really need another chair here, a comfortable chair. The lady next door has two chairs here, armchairs, but she hasn't got a table. You'll see her furniture is entirely different from mine. It goes all around the room. But I think to myself - what if I put that table there?
> [Interviewer] You mean near the window?
> Yes, I could sort of move the place round and move that chair over here where the table is. I could put the chair over there, and Chris could still watch his TV.

We hadn't heard about Chris up until then, and discover that he is a neighbour's son who comes to visit her and sits watching her TV. But this arrangement would create further problems and, as usual, when one item of furniture is changed it means the whole system is upset, which Mrs T finally realises: 'I might put that chair over there. I could put it anywhere. Actually, I'd rather wait till Margaret comes this afternoon and I am going to ask her what she thinks'.

There is no reason to assume that the more anxious future sense of 'caring for' dissipates either with age or with the security created by living in the conditions of institutionalised care. The principle that you never surrender the wish to remain a carer for people and things in the future asserts a primacy of 'caring for' in the everyday life of Mrs T over the reflexive 'taking care of ' of Mrs C and Miss G. From a personal perspective, whilst we might say in all these cases their 'being in their worlds' is unified by 'care', the differences are experienced as differences in temporality. The more nostalgic experience of Mrs C contrasts with the more resolute past present of Miss G, and both contrast with the present future sense of what is important for Mrs T.

The study could be criticised at this point for promoting a system of 'ideal types' as an analytic model to subsume the detailed particularity of these case studies. But then we come to Mr K. He is 75, unmarried, with no children. He has one sister living in Ireland and another who lives nearby. He was homeless before he came to the refuge, and it was his sister who brought him to where he is now. Yet his response to a question about his sister elicited a series of denials about his need for care:

Yes, she brought me here, but she hasn't got anything to do with me.
[Interviewer] You mean she is not your sister ?
She is my sister but she is nothing to do with me.
[Interviewer] Do you have other relatives?
Yes, but I don't bother with them.
[Interviewer] Does your sister live near?
Oh, yes, at number 32. I see her every day. When I was ill, she cooked for me every day.
[Interviewer] Do you go out?
Well I go out to play music—Irish music.
[Interviewer] Do you play in a group?
I do not. I play on my own. It keeps me busy.
[Interviewer] Can I take some photographs of the flat?
You can, but I don't want to be too long now because I have to go out.

The interview was so short that it is probably inappropriate to say much, except that the image of Mr. K's own personal 'lack of care' inside the flat connects well with his desire to be out of it—in a pub, playing music. What he was concerned with doing was outside, and his irritation with sources of constraint on his mobility was fairly palpable.

Conclusions

I started off with a deconstruction of the 'care' metaphor and its linear trajectory within the modern institutional care setting. The term *care* is so identified with the institutionalisation of care that the everyday concerns of people to care for, and to have had a past of having taken care of others, tends to be obscured. The idea of 'being taken care of' or being put into care, bequeaths images and metaphors of nineteenth-century death, poverty, the workhouse, and urban isolation that, in fact, are not the experience of many in this sample, perhaps precisely because it is these images that have had to be worked against in institutional settings of care.

The examples discussed in this paper suggest that care relates to different temporalities, often within the experience of the same person. Everyone to some extent has to 'care for' and to 'take care of', and expects this of others. Who or what might be the object of care, or who or what cares for you, need not matter. But hard lives can lead to reflections on the past and an increasing emphasis on summing up a past of care for families and others that, in many complicated ways, may help to justify a life and make it complete. The need to do this is no doubt a feature of age and anticipation of one's own death, so that one cannot experience or 'care for' or expect to be 'taken care of' except in a transcendental manner. This may or may not be according to personal religious disposition, but, in the broader sense of 'religion' literally meaning 'to bind', the ethical imperative that insists that it is human to 'care' is strongly metaphysical.

How may a curated life contribute to achieving this? It may be about how the care of objects and images, and the arrangement of soft toys, flowers, photos and candles, turns images and objects into shrines (Figure 8.2). Being cared for in this way may also make up for past lapses and gaps in one's personal biography, considering the inevitable anxiety of care for children, family, and friends in earlier life. Hence a certain amnesia is encouraged with the arrangement of objects and photos into a shrine-like arrangement that reconstitutes the self, with the potential to re-inscribe oneself in people's memory as a more idealised subject.

Marcoux has described this as a process of auto-ancestralisation; reiterating the anthropological point that death is a lengthy process, and later life becomes a process of making oneself a living ancestor (Marcoux 2001, 231). Using the 'journey' metaphor, he describes the whole process of moving (in this case to sheltered accommodation), as a means of reconstructing the self in old age and constructing one's own death. I would attribute the reflexive 'taking care of' in the case of Mrs C to such an ancestralising process, as she is able to surround herself with a memoryscape of things that confirms her continued importance to others. The elaboration of shrines—invariably, the chair in which the incumbent sits much of the time takes a prominent position—has many of the hallmarks of a fetish-like urgency, in which the totality of the

Figure 8.2   A shrine to the intimacy of touch.

image is capable of reaching out and motivating ancestral connections. In a sense, this care for objects is autonomous and self-constitutive, and the curative aspect lies precisely in the creation of a totality that is able to care both for itself and its ancestral being. Miss G with her books and cassettes, is part of the process of doing this for others, the self-sacrifice demanded by ancestors. But others such as Mrs T or Mr K are more resolutely independent and refuse to construct themselves in death. Instead, care for them remains future-oriented. Their concern with objects and people is contingent and relative depending on convenience and use which invariably is about being free to do something or go somewhere, no matter what that might be.

Finally, we can recognise how the institutionalisation of care shapes these personal dispositions. Curating a life as a kind of 'repair job' that serves to forget the failed bits and create a purer narrative of care for others, is facilitated by the cared environment that finally relieves one of the obligation to sacrifice. In the face of one's own death being not far away, the need to reflect on a life well led is a special kind of memory work that places particular value on personal ideas of a successful life. The transformation into a 'living ancestor', venerated as a holder of memory, creates shrines of material culture that family and friends may visit in a state of some reverence. Yet a similar facility of the provision of institutionalised care promotes the continued life of a renouncer, able to break with the past and take advantage of change. Here, the will to be free both rejects the past and also displays irritation with those who wish to ancestralise. One can equally imagine the irritation of children and others who find the elderly irascible and unwilling to play their role. The idea that 'things' do not belong to one, or can be changed or disposed of at will, has the added benefit that visitors may never know quite what to expect. This idea that there is nothing fixed about cared environments, whatever the assumptions behind their provision, aptly summarises this need to care for objects, and the feeling that objects care for us in the curation of personal lives.

Notes

1. The project was entitled *'From Domesticity to Care: A Study of the Mobility of the Elderly in UK'* and was funded by EPSRC. It was carried out at University College London between 1999 and 2001, led by Juliet Hanson of the Bartlett School of Architecture and Town Planning. The study focused specifically on the material provisioning offered by local councils to the elderly in seven different parts of the UK. Whilst the major responsibility lay with the UCL Bartlett School, it is to their credit that they provided for an ethnographic

component. I am grateful to my anthropological colleagues, Leone Kellaher and Jean Sebastian Marcoux, for their help and collaboration in writing up the project report on which this account is based.

References

Marcoux, J.S. 2001. The Casser Maison ritual. *Journal of Material Culture* 6(2): 213–36.
Mulhall, S. 2005. *Heidegger and Being and Time*. London: Routledge.
Yates, F. 1966. *The Art of Memory*. London: Routledge and Kegan Paul.

9

EASING THE TRANSITION: USING MUSEUM OBJECTS WITH ELDERLY PEOPLE

Claire Jacques

Introduction

This chapter is an account of reminiscence work with the elderly in Lincolnshire, written from the perspective of a museum professional employed to lead a team that organises and delivers cultural and learning activities to specific audiences. The chapter focuses first on the apparently therapeutic benefits of the object-based reminiscence work currently taking place in elderly care-homes. Second, it describes how a multi-disciplinary team of care-workers and museum professionals are working together to develop ways of creating visual, tactile, and olfactory representations of residents' life histories that can further improve the relationships among residents, professional carers, and family carers.

The Current Project

As museum professionals, we have been working with a team of care-workers, based in seven local authority–run elderly care homes throughout rural Lincolnshire, to develop some reminiscence resources containing tactile museum objects suitable for use in care-home settings.

Over the year 2006–2007 we have been running a programme of group reminiscence sessions. These sessions take place in each of the seven care-homes, some of which offer intermittent care for the elderly and others of which are specialist units for residents with the onset of dementia. The average age of the participants is 75 and older.

All sessions are jointly facilitated by museum staff and care-workers, who regularly meet to discuss progress and impact. The museum staff and carers involved have been instrumental in the selection of objects and images and have received training from reminiscence specialists from Age Concern[1] in how to encourage reminiscence using museum objects. We have found that groups of up to ten participants are appropriate because this allows objects to be circulated rapidly enough to stimulate discussion. This group size also encourages people to join in the experience and ensures that everyone gets a chance to speak or to be involved.

Working as a team, we have now created two sets of resources containing objects and images chosen to appeal to this age group. Over half of the objects have come from Lincolnshire County Council's museum collections, but only duplicates have been used. We have worked with Collections staff to select the most robust examples available. Conservation has not yet been an issue, but it has been agreed that once any damage occurs to individual objects they will be removed from the resource for examination by a conservator. Because we aim to use relatively recent objects, we have been able find the rest in charity shops.

The resources are based around themes such as 'home life', 'working life', and 'courtship and marriage', and include items aimed at engaging all the senses. For example, we use laundry soap, furniture polish, and other scented products to stimulate the sense of smell; a darning mushroom, a heavy old-fashioned iron, and shaving brushes are included to stimulate the sense of touch (Figure 9.1). It is important not to use too many objects in each session, as this can bombard participants with too much stimulus. For each session we select up to six objects that we feel are most appropriate for the group. The resources act as memory 'triggers' and encourage lively discussion and increased communication amongst participants. We have found that residents who have participated enjoy talking about their lives and that the objects act as positive prompts in this process.

The participants have a range of physical and mental abilities, and in most cases are suffering from early to moderate stages of dementia. Deterioration of other senses can result in touch being one of the only non-verbal types of communication that can be fully perceived. It appears that multi-sensory triggers can help compensate for different cognitive impairments, so objects that can be touched, handled, and passed around are particularly important.

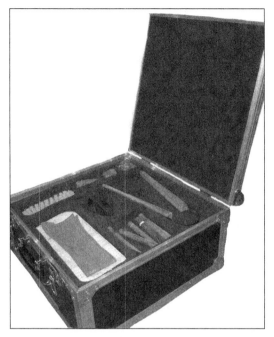

Figure 9.1 The wash-day resource in its carrying case. Objects include: laundry soap, tongs, clothes-pegs, a flat-iron, and an old-fashioned detachable shirt collar. (Courtesy of Lincolnshire County Council © LCC)

We find that the objects work very effectively to get discussion started; we also use images, particularly photographs, that focus on different themes, such as 'seaside' or 'courtship and marriage'. We considered using prepared questions to set things going, but we have found that the sessions are more successful if we adopt a flexible approach.

Evaluation

Our team endeavours to evaluate the majority of the sessions we deliver. In addition to meeting with care-workers regularly to discuss progress, sessions are observed by members of staff. We have designed a simple questionnaire for care-workers to fill out, focusing on the value of using objects in the reminiscence process. Evidence from our initial evaluation clearly demonstrates that objects are powerful tools.

In observing participants' reactions, we have discovered that the objects do awaken their senses and act as effective triggers for the recall of memories. This enables individuals to make connections with the past, to 'make it feel real', and to develop a deeper understanding of what the past was actually like. In many cases, objects gave participants a reason to communicate with others and to share their memories and emotions; this helped to include the silent, and sometimes connected people unexpectedly. Handling and reminiscing about the objects also gave the residents the opportunity to teach their carers, and so to feel of value. The sessions were a distraction in an otherwise monotonous daily routine, they improved social interaction amongst participants, and between carers and those they care for, and generally raised morale.

Other observations suggest that for some participants who were reluctant to talk because they were frightened of making fools of themselves, familiar objects gave them confidence to communicate more freely. For patients with poor vision, objects that have particularly tactile qualities were important (Figure 9.2). Further, we found that things with a distinctive smell are really successful, especially with blind patients.

Are These Sessions Therapeutic?

As a museum practitioner, I am not qualified to say whether the impact we have observed is truly therapeutic. All I know is that the evidence

Figure 9.2   An elderly blind resident (with the author), remembering the introduction of decimal coinage to the UK in 1971. They are handling a 'decimator', which was used to help people convert old pence into new pence. (Courtesy of Lincolnshire County Council © LCC)

we have collected so far, through observations and questionnaires, strongly suggests that these reminiscence sessions do have a profound effect on the behaviour of the elderly people who are taking part. There is widespread belief in this kind of work, as evidenced by the number of guides that have been produced to encourage its use (see, e.g. Gibson 2000, and publications by Age Exchange[2]), but studies published in both general and museum-related literature often refer to anecdotal evidence rather than clinical research. However, I strongly believe that reminiscing using tactile objects encourages older people with dementia to become actively involved in reliving and sharing their past with others. Although reminiscence involves recalling past events, it has an effect in the present because it encourages the elderly to communicate and interact with a listener.

Taking This Further

Reminiscence allows us to relive events from our past. It is a process that focuses on the personal way we experience and remember events rather than on chronological or historical accuracy. When we reminisce, we don't simply recall random events in a cold factual way; we are able to relive the experiences that are personal to us in a way that is vivid and engaging. Reminiscing gives us pleasure and a sense of relatedness and connection with what has gone before. In addition, as a means of psychological support, reminiscence is aimed at generating self-esteem and the expression of individual identity (see, e.g. Webster & Haight 2002).

Alzheimer's disease and other dementias present a growing challenge to an aging population, to families, to community care services, and to health and Social Services professionals. Dementia is an isolating condition. It causes difficulties in communication within families and separates people with dementia and their carers from each other and from others around them. It is important to find effective ways of reducing or postponing this isolation in order to preserve and enrich the quality of life for all concerned. With this in mind, we are now actively working in partnership with social care colleagues to take our reminiscence work with tactile objects one step further.

The C.A.R.E.R Model

Recently we have been discussing with colleagues from Social Services the potential of assisting them in a trial of the C.A.R.E.R (Collaboration and Assessment with Relatives of Elderly Residents) model, originally developed by Suzanne Wightman, Memory and Day Services Manager for South West Yorkshire Mental Health Trust (Wightman 2006). This involves working in partnership with family carers to produce life histories and improve care for elderly residents.

Following admission of an elderly person to a care-home, professional carers can experience difficulties in communicating both with the elderly person and their family, partly because they may know little or nothing about the new resident. The C.A.R.E.R model provides a means for establishing the elderly person's identity through gathering together aspects of their life history, and revealing the unique character of the individual. This offers a new perspective, helping the professional carer to see beyond the dementia and to have increased empathy with the resident. This makes communication more personal and transforms task-oriented care into person-centred care.

Tom Kitwood, in his study 'Dementia Reconsidered: The Person Comes First', states:

> If personhood is to be maintained, it is essential that each individual be appreciated in his or her uniqueness. Where there is empathy without personal knowledge, care will be aimless and unfocused. Where there is personal knowledge without empathy, care will be detached and cold. But when empathy and personal knowledge are brought together, miracles can happen. (Kitwood 1997)

We have developed a modified version of the C.A.R.E.R model. When an elderly person is referred to long-term care, the first thing we do is identify the family carer or the close companion who has acted as carer. We then send them a letter including information about the C.A.R.E.R project, and the team, and enclosing a copy of the life history questionnaire, asking them to fill it in. When we receive the life history information, the project team (consisting of key care-workers, family members, and museum inclusion staff) arranges to see the resident to talk about their life history, using as a prompt the information already gathered. We then decide whether the new resident would benefit from producing a 'life book' and/or a 'memory box' that would eventually be accessible to professional care staff.

Life History Work: What Are Its Functions?

Life history/story work involves looking back on, gathering information about, and recording a person's past, usually on a one-to-one basis. A life history/story book, illustrated with photographs and objects, or a memory box containing objects, provides people with some tangible reminder of their identity that may help them hold onto a positive sense of self.

While not every older adult would be suited to this kind of work, nor wish to be involved with telling their life story, there is increasing evidence to support the view that life story work is an invaluable tool in enabling professionals to provide person-centred care, particularly for those with dementia:

> If care is to be truly personal, we will need to have detailed knowledge about each person for whom we are responsible and to be clear about how we intend to provide care for them. In any group care setting, it is especially important to do this systematically, because it can be so easy to lose the sense that each person is special. (Kitwood & Bredin 1992)

Researchers have discovered a number of ways of using life story work with people with cognitive problems (Murphy 1994; Goldsmith 1996; Mills 1998; Murphy 2000). The life story provides, in written and illustrated form, some sense of the person beyond the illness, and so improves understanding of the person being cared for. It can be used to detail likes and dislikes and to explain past and present behaviour; thus, it provides an illustrated personal profile that can be immediately available to new staff, especially when a person moves between care environments. For the person themselves, using the life story can be a creative activity that engages them as storyteller, with their carer and their wider family and friends, at a stage in their life when they may feel helpless. Significantly, it can enable people living with dementia to feel that their life has been worthwhile and that they are still of interest with something to 'give back'. Also important is its role in helping the family carer to remember the many and varied aspects of the life and character of the individual with dementia, both while that person is alive and after their death.

Using Museum Objects in Life Books and Memory Boxes

Building on the C.A.R.E.R model, I want to explore how we can assist carers in the production of a life book or a memory box using carefully chosen museum objects as well as photographs and cherished personal objects—all of which would help trigger memories.

At the beginning of the life history collecting process, we will work with care-staff and a family carer to design a life history booklet. The booklet will then be used with the resident during carefully planned one-to-one sessions. We will develop a number of questions that can be used to prompt talk about the person's life history. (However, it is important to judge carefully how far to go when working with people with advanced dementia because too much questioning can be inappropriate.)

We will work with family and professional carers to collect a range of personal and non-personal objects for use during the one-to-one life history sessions. In addition, we hope that, as a museum service with vast collections at our disposal, we will be able to supply a range of particularly tactile objects relating to life history themes. With these we aim not just to encourage talk about the past, but to use selected objects to prompt buried memories and help fill gaps in life stories. We aim to select and use the objects one at a time to support each step in the process, and to guide the person out of one memory and into another.

One of the aims of the project is to research whether the use of objects in this way does help to aid the collection of life history information, and whether it encourages positive responses from the residents involved. We are currently at the early stages of the pilot and are going to test the model at one home initially, engaging with up to three residents over a period of, possibly, three months. The residents have been selected by professional care-workers, and have consented to take part with the agreement of their families. Colleagues at the home are enthusiastic and keen to try working in this way. Depending on the results of the trial, we hope to train carers in this use of tactile objects as memory prompts in developing the life stories.

An important aspect of this project is that museum staff will take part in each stage of the trial, including the one-to-one sessions with residents. We have worked hard to build a relationship with the professional carers based on mutual trust and understanding. Without this sound relationship, the development of this initiative would be impossible. This is something we truly value.

Conclusions

We hope that the life history will help to individualise the care of the person with dementia and to maintain their identity. It will also help people caring for the individual to know them and develop stronger relationships with them. Evidence gathered during our group work sessions over the last year clearly indicates that using objects is an important way of stimulating responses and can provide a focus for the recollection of deeply embedded memories. We believe that, if used in a systematic way during one-to-one sessions with elderly people affected by the onset of dementia, significant objects freely handled will aid the life history review process. More important, through this process the people cared for will be recognised as unique individuals with their identity regained and preserved.

Notes

1. Age Concern is a UK charitable organisation concerned with the welfare of elderly people. [http://www.ageconcern.org.uk]
2. Age Exchange is a UK charitable organisation working with elderly people through activities such as drama or reminiscence. [http://www.age-exchange.org.uk]

References

Gibson, F. 2000. *Reminiscence Trainers Pack*. London: Age Concern.

Goldsmith, M. 1996. *Hearing the Voices of People with Dementia: Opportunities and Obstacles*. London: Jessica Kingsley.

Kitwood, T. 1997. *Dementia Reconsidered: The Person Comes First*. Buckingham: Open University Press.

Kitwood, T., Bredin, K. 1992. *Person to Person: A Guide to the Care of Those with Failing Mental Powers*. Loughton, Essex: Gale Centre Publications.

Mills, M. A. 1998. *Narrative Identity and Dementia: A Study of Autobiographical Memories and Emotions*. Aldershot: Ashgate.

Murphy, C.J. 2000. *'Crackin Lives': An Evaluation of a Life Story Book Project to Assist Patients from a Long Stay Psychiatric Hospital in Their Move to Community Care Situations*. Stirling, Scotland, UK: Stirling Dementia Services Development Centre, University of Stirling.

———— 1994. *'It started with a Sea-Shell': Life Story Work and People with Dementia*. Stirling, Scotland, UK: Stirling Dementia Services Development Centre, University of Stirling.

Webster, J., Haight, B. (eds.). 2002. *Critical Advances in Reminiscence Work*. New York: Springer.

Wightman, S. 2006. The C.A.R.E.R. model: A framework for partnership: working with family carers to improve person-centred care for people with dementia in long term care. Paper given at the Fifth National Conference for Mental Health in Older People: Best Practice in Dementia Care, University of Leicester, September 2006. Unpublished.

10

THE TOUCH EXPERIENCE IN MUSEUMS IN THE UK AND JAPAN

Julia Cassim

Origins of the Touch Experience in Museums

Touch exhibitions were the first full expression of a museum or gallery's commitment to the provision of services for their visually impaired visitors. As an exhibition form, they developed from handling sessions, in themselves an outgrowth of the long-standing tradition of loan services to schools first developed in the nineteenth century (Hooper-Greenhill 1991) Thus, the groundwork was laid early for the idea that museum artefacts could be safely handled under controlled conditions, even by children; however, the visually impaired public remained invisible to museums at that time.

Impact of Legislation

Groundbreaking and comprehensive legislation like the 1995 Disability Discrimination Act (DDA 1995) in the UK, and its equivalents elsewhere, was the major driver in enforcing compliance for measures that would meet the needs and aspirations of disabled people. Thus, the early history of initiatives on their behalf in the museum sector is one of dedicated individuals working often in isolation and unsupported by any specific policy or funding. Many initiatives were experimental and proved temporary. The introduction in the UK of the National

163

Curriculum in 1988 (National Curriculum 1988) and the enactment of the DDA changed things dramatically. Programmes and educational materials were tailored to the needs of visitors of varying social and cultural backgrounds, learning styles, and interests.

Early Touch Exhibitions in the UK

Museums and art galleries are institutions founded predominantly on a visual culture, and those who cannot see were assumed to be unlikely to derive benefit from or even be interested in their collections. Attitudes have thankfully changed, matched by a growing body of initiatives since the first touch exhibition at a major venue in the UK, the Tate Gallery's 'Sculpture for the Blind' in 1976 (Pearson 1991, 122). These focused initially on the handling of small-scale sculptures, moving in the 1980s to a broader multisensory approach, and from there to a tie-in with the more interactive style of exhibitions and interpretation in general.

A pioneering and influential example of the idea that an exhibition could be a multisensory installation in its own right was 'It Makes Sense: Art Works to Touch, Smell, See, and Hear' at the Greenwich Citizen's Gallery in London in 1989 (Hunt 1989). Works by five artists were commissioned to appeal to all five senses in order to show that there were other aesthetic and sensory realms besides touch for visually impaired visitors, or vision for their sighted peers. The exhibition ushered in an era of multisensory initiatives with varying degrees of impact, success, and understanding of the possibilities of such an approach.

With 'Dialogue in the Dark' held at the South Bank Centre in 1995 (South Bank Centre 1995), the idea of the exhibition as a multisensory installation in its own right came full circle and the tables were turned on the sighted audience. Organised not by a museum but by the Stiftung Blindenstalt (SBA), a German organisation for the blind, it has travelled worldwide since it first opened in Dusseldorf in 1989 and is due to become a permanent facility in Southwark (see London SE1 Community Website 2007). Pitch-black and soundproofed, the installation consists of four specially constructed rooms in which scents, sounds, wind, temperatures, and textures convey the characteristics of everyday environments. The sighted visitor is led through them by a visually impaired guide, with their visit culminating in the bar at the exit. Here they are invited to order drinks served by their guide, who rarely gets their order wrong. The purpose of the installation is to raise awareness of issues relating to visual impairment.

Issues in the Choice of Handling Materials

Contemporary artists have continued to explore the possibilities of sensory vocabularies in their work, and museums and galleries in the UK have shown creativity and innovation in the interpretative measures they have adopted for non-traditional audiences. Yet the conservation hurdle remains wherever touch is made central to the visitor experience. How can museums reconcile their duty to preserve often-fragile objects in optimum condition for posterity with the needs of a population for whom touch is of such importance? As Jim Druzik of the Getty Conservation Institute notes: 'Things that have existed for half a millennium have very little residual instability, so when they begin to deteriorate, it's purely an environmental effect' (Knell 1994, 84).

Then there is the issue of suitability. Many modern sculptures have to be ruled out not only on conservation grounds but also because their scale and composition renders their overall logic difficult to grasp through touch alone. They may be too big or too fragmented to understand even where whole-body touch techniques are employed. Their materials and construction may present hazards in terms of toxicity and general safety.

What is left may represent a fraction of any museum's collection. A smaller museum or gallery may have few suitable three-dimensional works in their collection, and what there is may be of scant tactile interest. One could argue that in the normal course of a day a visually impaired person will come into contact with a far richer set of tactile and other sensory experiences than can be provided by the limited range of works on offer at most art museums. An artwork that may be seductive visually and of importance in art historical terms may be uninteresting or incomprehensible as a tactile experience for a visually impaired visitor unfamiliar with its significance.

There is also the question of whether touch should be the sole means by which art and artefacts can be made accessible to visually impaired audiences. Most works in art museums and galleries are two-dimensional in nature; paintings, prints, photographs, and drawings outnumber those in three dimensions, and touch does little to reveal their mysteries. This is even the case for low-relief works or those with thick impasto, which may have some surface interest but whose content cannot be deciphered through touch alone. If all these are ruled out, then a one-sided view of art is presented. The challenge lies in interpreting such works effectively to an audience for whom vision has never been, or is no longer, their primary information gathering sense.

Access, Education, and the Japanese Museum Sector

Such questions were central to a set of initiatives undertaken by the author in Japan between 1994 and 1998.They centred on the design and curation of exhibitions and the creation of interpretative materials for visually impaired audiences alongside work with Access Vision (the core group with whom the author was associated during this period). Many of the findings published by others working with visually impaired museum visitors relate to single museum visits. In contrast, Access Vision afforded the opportunity to observe the developing relationship of the group with artworks over a period of three years. It enabled an interpretative methodology to be developed, tested, and refined, and led to the design and testing of a new form of raised image: one that could be used in conjunction with audio description and one that eliminated some of the design issues of the standard versions on microcapsule paper commonly used in museums and schools for the blind.

The situation facing those interested in expanding provision for visually impaired museum visitors in Japan is in many ways the reverse of the West. The youth of its museum culture and buildings has guaranteed that Japan's museums boast superb physical access, unlike many of their historic Western counterparts. Between 1960 and 1992, 5495 museums of every type were constructed in Japan, including 2793 constructed after the International Year of Disabled People (IYDP) in 1981, when physical access became mandatory for public buildings (*AERA*, 1993). Even those built before this date are modern structures with elevators, ramps, and other access features that have been retrofitted to comply with access regulations. However, they suffer universally from poor cognitive access, and this is particularly so for art museums. Museum education in Japan tends to be an event-based, summer-holiday affair for children that ends when they return to school (Cassim 1991, 1993a, 1993b, 1994a, 1996a). Art museums routinely organise curatorial lectures, symposia, and occasional concerts to accompany temporary exhibitions, yet few have specialist education officers or conservators on their staff.

This educational vacuum has hampered the growth of initiatives on behalf of the visually impaired population. Where they do happen, they tend to be ad hoc affairs. Since 1989, the Hyogo Prefecture Art Museum has organised an annual summer touch exhibition and from 1989 to 1996 the Nagoya City Art Museum held a biannual exhibition for visually impaired visitors (Cassim, 1992). These are not backed, however, by any regular services. An exception is the Mie Prefecture Museum of Art. For over 15 years, it has had a thriving and active volunteer body; visitors of all types are encouraged and services are provided for them. This demonstrates the influence of the former chief curator, Takeshi Morimoto, his belief in the community-based function of a museum, and the educational policies he encouraged and funded (Cassim 1998). As was the case prior to the 1970s in the West, initiatives in Japan tend to depend upon the interest of individual curators working in isolation. Even where ongoing programmes for visually impaired audiences are part of the museum calendar, lessons learned from these events do not influence the museum's general practice. The print on the labels remains small, the contrast poor, and the lighting insufficient.

Early Touch Exhibitions in Japan

The history of the museum access movement for visually impaired visitors in Japan began with the work of the private Gallery TOM in Tokyo that was founded in 1984 by Harue Murayama, whose son was blind. Its motto is 'We, the blind, we too have the right to enjoy Rodin'. From its inception, the gallery has carried out wide-ranging activities in addition to its regular tactile exhibition programme (Cassim 1995, 1997a, 1997b). It has also functioned as central clearing house for information and advice in this area. Many of the inaugural touch shows in Japan were inspired, aided, or organised by the gallery. Murayama, a designer in her own right, has an extensive network of contacts in the arts and disability worlds. In 1986 the Gallery created the TOM prize, which aims to encourage creative activity within the seventy schools and institutions for the blind in Japan. The resulting artworks, predominantly in clay, are exhibited in the gallery and have been included in numerous museum shows (Cassim 1996b). The high quality of many, especially those by children working with the sculptor Yohei Nishimura at the Chiba School for the Blind, has attracted widespread curatorial interest in Japan and abroad. This has been a major factor in encouraging their showing outside the welfare context and within the mainstream art world, thus encouraging debate on the aesthetics of blindness and their influence on creative expression. They have also created a precedent for the idea that touch shows are an effective way of engaging the sighted and unsighted public, are a valid genre in exhibition terms, and can evolve into new iterations where the idea of 'touch' is open to broader interpretations.

A multisensory approach is also evident in the pioneering annual exhibitions held since 1989 at the Hyogo Prefectural Museum of Art, whose aim has been to explore ways in which all the senses can be engaged. In 2005, for example, the artist Takao Sugiura installed two interactive pieces: one, named 'Ganmen Basamiki' (Sandwich the Face), invited the visitor to enclose their head in a trap-like wooden box and physically enter another spatial and sensory reality; the other was a room filled to shoulder height with tiny expanded polystyrene beads in which bronze sculptures were buried but with their tops just visible above a sea of white. Visitors were invited to wade through the polystyrene and handle the works in a whole-body version of the lucky dip.

However, with no history of handling sessions and few museum educators to devise programmes, the best opportunity for the tactile exploration of artworks remains outside museums. Since the 1980s, Japan's urban landscape has played host to an army of new public sculptures. This has provided an opportunity for visually impaired people to explore sculpture beyond the confines of museums. The best example is at Faret Tachikawa, just outside Tokyo, which has a contemporary collection of 109 works by 92 artists from 36 countries (Cassim 1994a, 1994b, 2000). Part of an urban redevelopment project, the sculptures are at ground level, close to each other and, importantly, are exceptionally good examples of contemporary work. Curated by Fram Kitagawa of the Art Front Gallery in Tokyo, it is—unintentionally—Japan's best touch trail.

'Art & the Inner Eye #1' and Access Vision

Access Vision came into being against this background. In October 1994, I was co-curator with Minako Tsunoda of 'Art & the Inner Eye #1', an exhibition of contemporary art held at the Nagoya City Art Museum and the third in a series of biannual touch exhibitions. Two hundred and twenty visually impaired and 4,082 sighted people visited it during its three-week duration. We ignored the orthodox format of small-scale sculptures in wood, metal, or stone and chose instead two- and three-dimensional works by contemporary artists, including figurative and non-figurative works selected for their strong imagery or textural interest. The sculptures were chosen for their tactile complexity, the polysensory qualities of their materials, and the simplicity and coherence of their overall form, while the exhibition itself was designed to ensure access for different audiences on a physical and cognitive level (Figure 10.1). The catalogue contained Braille and raised monochrome images on 'Swell' paper. The catalogue also included colour photographs and interpretative descriptions and the audio guide included interviews with the artists.

The positive response to the exhibition, plus the fact that the College Women's Association of Japan gave the author the *20th Anniversary Volunteers for Blind Students Award* in the shape of a bursary, led to the formation of Access Vision with Yoshimi Harada, head of the Visual

**Figure 10.1 Blind child and sound sculpture at 'Art & the Inner Eye #1',
Nagoya City Art Museum, 1994.**

Impairment Section at the Nagoya Sports and Rehabilitation Centre
(NCSRC). Access Vision was composed of 26 visually impaired people
of different ages who were partially sighted, or adventitiously or
congenitally blind, most of them graduates of, or currently attending,
Harada's training courses in independent living at the NCSRC. For
some, their vision loss had been gradual and was complicated by other
impairments such as hearing loss or mobility difficulties; for others,
it had been sudden and traumatic. Thus the group was a representa-
tive cross-section of the visually impaired population anywhere.

A monthly visit to an exhibition or cultural event was organised to
maintain the momentum of 'Art & the Inner Eye #1', develop interest
among participants, and exert pressure on museums to introduce services for disabled visitors and develop effective methodologies
and interpretative materials. Where the visit involved paintings,
microcapsule-paper raised images were prepared and a newsletter
Access Art News was produced monthly in Braille and large-print

from January 1996 onwards. The newsletter presented details of visits as well as events of interest. Members contributed essays on the exhibitions and the workshops organised by the author that they had attended. From 1996, the group was awarded an annual grant from the Fuji Xerox Corporation.

The first six-month period centred on creating a guide to the permanent collection of the Aichi Prefectural Museum of Art. Built in the 1950s, the museum's collection was qualitatively mixed and lacking in coherence, having been acquired piecemeal through purchase or gifts. It reopened in a new building in October 1992 with professional curatorial staff under the new director Toru Asano, previously of the National Museum of Modern Art, Tokyo. Asano fleshed out the permanent collection with works of Western-style painting, sculpture, and prints and Japanese 'nihonga' painting from the Meiji Period (1867–1912) onwards. However, it had no handling collection, few examples of sculpture suitable for tactile exploration, and no workshop space. Overall, the range of tactile experiences offered was extremely limited, with figurative works in bronze and hard stone predominating—a situation typical of art museums everywhere. It was a major factor in turning my attention away from three-dimensional works to the possibilities inherent in two-dimensional ones.

To help Access Vision members develop a broader tactile vocabulary, monthly visits were organised to collections of objects of many kinds. Workshops were organised to teach handling techniques and object and material identification methods, culminating in ones where participants created low-relief artworks of their own to enable them to expand their understanding of the terminology and concepts of art.

The Visually Impaired Audience

Tactile Literacy and Visual Memory

Most Access Vision members had experienced vision loss in mid-life and had not developed compensatory tactile skills; they had been unable to master Braille with any fluency and remained in the information limbo characterising so many late blind who are unable to access the tactile, auditory, and other information crucial to their ability to make sense of the world. Touch is a learned faculty and, like any other sense, develops through practice. For John Hull, who lost his sight at 35, it took approximately five years to look for 'weight, texture, shape, temperature, and the sounds things make' (Hull 1990, 2). The late-blind Access Vision members proved as tactilely 'illiterate' as the sighted population. Many, however, retained vivid visual memories and understood the complexity of the visual world, which gave them a basis for understanding figurative works in two dimensions. They became increasingly interested in paintings, prints, and photographs. For the late-blind, descriptions of the two-dimensional works stimulated their rapidly fading visual memory, whereas for the congenitally blind such works provided vital information about the visual world. Thus emphasis shifted from three-dimensional works to the more complex, untapped area of two-dimensional artworks, which threw up a fresh set of challenges regarding interpretation and the design and use of raised images.

Few of the adventitiously blind members were able to read Braille, and the condition of their hands was poor due to age; however, they were aware of the diagrammatic rendering of three-dimensional forms, had experience of drawing, could follow a linear diagram, and were familiar with the visual conventions of common pictograms. In contrast, the congenitally blind members had a high degree of tactile literacy but were unfamiliar with two-dimensional symbolic renditions of the visual world and had no drawing experience.

Visual Literacy

In 1986 the education department of the Museum of Modern Art, New York, undertook a survey of 150 randomly selected visitors to ascertain their knowledge of modern art (Housen 1992). The results were surprising. They found that this sophisticated audience had definitions of art too narrow to embrace much modern art, were ignorant of specialised vocabulary, misused stylistic terms, and displayed a minimal grasp of the concepts underlying modern art. They could only recognise the work of prominent artists but could not interpret their meaning and had difficulty in discerning exhibition themes or chronologies. The museum commissioned the cognitive psychologist Abigail Housen to find ways to better serve their audience.

Since the late 1970s, Housen has studied the aesthetic reactions to two-dimensional works of art of audiences aged between 14 and 80 in the United States. From this she developed a theoretical model mapping the five primary stages of aesthetic development leading to visual literacy (Housen & Miller 1992, 3; Yenawine 1997, 12):

- **Stage 1**: Accountive viewers or storytellers whose reading of painting is subjective
- **Stage 2**: Constructive viewers who view a work through the filter of their values and life experience
- **Stage 3**: Classifying viewers who 'adopt the analytical and critical stance of the art historian'

- **Stage 4**: Interpretive viewers who 'seek a personal encounter with a work of art'
- **Stage 5:** Re-creative viewers who 'know the ecology of a work— its time, its history, its questions, its travels, its intricacies'

Housen's survey indicates that while children are in Stage 1, most adults fall within Stage 2 with a minority between this and Stage 3. Few have reached Stages 4 or 5.

Visual Memory and Visual Impairment

Housen's research is also relevant to visually impaired visitors. In 1991 in Japan, 67.1% of the visually impaired population was aged over 60, and even where they were classified as 'legally" with (i.e. registered) blind, roughly 90% had some residual vision (Ministry of Health and Welfare 1991). The statistics are similar to other countries, and mean that, in any group of visually impaired adult museum visitors, the majority will have a visual memory. The strength of it will depend upon the age at which they lost their sight and how long ago it happened. The earlier their sight loss, the more tenuous their visual memory, since it fades with time and lack of stimuli.

Those interested in art before their sight loss, who could be termed visually literate, will be in a minority. They are likely to fall into Housen's Stages 1 or 2, as will those who are congenitally blind and likely to be ignorant of the concepts and vocabulary of art. Their concepts will be highly individual, based on non-visual constructs formed through their individual experience. As John Hull notes: 'The ... memories of the blind adult ... focus upon what the body experienced, or underwent. This is quite different from visual memory because your body does not feel what your eye sees' (Hull 1990, 105).

Trevor-Roper reports the difficulties of those who regain their sight through surgery: 'Colours were always a problem because the emotional tones that had previously been developed to give them "labels" were difficult to adjust to the reality.' He gives the example of a woman for whom scarlet signified 'something like the sound of a trumpet', a non-visual concept that is difficult to transfer to a visual image (Trevor-Roper 1990, 176).

By far the most important factor is what Naughton describes as the 'subtlety' of visual impairment:

> The effects are determined not only by the eye condition or combination of conditions but also the person's outlook on life and the type of experience to which they have been exposed. An inquiring mind and visual or sensory stimulation, while clinically not improving the person's sight, might in

fact create a better awareness and understanding of their surroundings (Naughton 1993, 16).

One cannot assume that a person is visually literate, even though they once saw. What is common knowledge to a sighted person familiar with the vocabulary of art may be alien to someone who cannot see. Everett and Blagden cite the example of their blind students:

> So many words have been learned in school ... are stored in the memory, without real knowledge ... such as 'transparent, silver, glimpse, distance, fog, photograph, and shine.... It is fascinating to hold a conversation without using visual language, it enables one to use the language of the other senses: 'Can you sound like the feel of silk?' 'Can you describe the resilience of freshly wedged clay?' (Blagden & Everett 1992, 25)

In devising a descriptive method for the paintings studied with Access Vision members, the language had to be lively and evocative, with an extensive use of similies linked to a tactile or sensory experience but prefaced by detailed description to establish the visual structure of the work. Achieving a workable mental image or 'map' of the physical attributes of the artwork required intense concentration. A balance had to be struck between the group's attention and tiredness levels and their need for physical description as well as interpretation. To avoid information overload, descriptions followed a set order, with information relating to the physical reality of the work linked to navigation of the tactile graphic, preceding the interpretative content.

Mental Maps

One had to be aware of the way information was sequenced so that a coherent mental map could be formed in tandem with the tactile graphic. As Oliver Sacks has noted:

> . . . the blind build their worlds from sequences of impressions (tactile, auditory, olfactory) and are not capable, as sighted people are, of simultaneous visual perception, the making of an instantaneous visual scene. (Sacks 1995a, 117)

Sighted people arrive at an unconscious series of conclusions drawn from visual evidence, achieved by scanning a set of visual clues in a painting without necessarily scrutinising each element. A tree will be 'read' as a tree, not as an independent form examined anew in its individual complexity, unless it is the single subject of the painting. Similarly a figure will be 'read' according to its portrayed character, based on the visual evidence supplied by the painter and the viewer's pre-existing knowledge of character types or social and cultural history.

The rest of the painting will be decoded in similar fashion, drawing on a series of pre-existing visual 'mental maps'.

Sacks describes this in an article written on Edelman's research in the area:

> A 'map', as he (Edelman) muses the term, is not a representation in the ordinary sense, but an interconnected series of neuronal groups that responds selectively to certain elemental categories: for example, to movements and colours in the visual world. The perception of a grand-mother or, say, of a chair depends on the synchronization of a number of scattered mappings throughout the visual cortex: mappings relating to many different perceptual aspects of the chair (its size, its shape, its colour, its 'leggedness', its relation to other sorts of chairs—armchairs, kneeling chairs, baby chairs, etc.); and perhaps in other parts of the cortex as well (relating to the feel of sitting in a chair, the actions needed to do it, etc.). In this way the brain, the creature, achieves a rich and flexible precept of 'chairhood', which allows the recognition of innumerable sorts of chairs as chairs (computers, by contrast, with their need for unambiguous definitions and criteria, are quite unable to achieve this). (Sacks 1995a, 106–07)

This making of 'mental maps' is true for a blind person but will depend on an alternative set of sensory information. Thus the sighted world's representational 'maps' will be difficult to decipher for those with no visual memory or knowledge of visual conventions. Edman describes the inherent difficulties of creating tactile graphics:

> The classic picture of a house—a slanted roof, two windows, and a door—quickly produces in a sighted child an association with many different houses. But what does this picture do for a blind child who has never physically experienced the proportions of a house as a whole and who, at best, can barely put together his or her individual experiences of it, one at a time, to make the complete form? Naturally, blind children can learn to recognize a house if they often come in contact with pictures of a house. But change the form and position of the house and the young blind child may have difficulty, because the symbol representing the house is not the same. (Edman 1992, 26)

An example of this was a photograph of a rectangular box shown in recession in an exhibition catalogue. The raised image produced to accompany it was 'read' tactilely by a congenitally blind Access Vision member, unfamiliar with the rules of perspective, as an object that became progressively slimmer.

Cheselden, Sacks and Perception

The perceptual difficulties in deciphering the visual world were noted by William Cheselden, the eighteenth-century eye surgeon. He was the first to suggest that perception does not automatically accompany sight, and that shapes, colours, lines, forms, objects, and their meaning must be recognised and learned before they become part of an unconscious mental map. Writing of a congenitally blind boy whose cataracts were removed in 1728 when he was 'thirteen or fourteen years of age', Cheselden describes how the boy first perceived pictures and the difficulties he experienced in making connections between the two-dimensional portrayal of a shape and its three-dimensional reality:

> We thought he soon knew what pictures represented, which were shew'd to him, but we found afterwards we were mistaken; for about two months after he was couch'd, he discovered at once they represented solid bodies, when to that time he considered them only as party-colour'd [partly coloured] planes, or surfaces diversified with a variety of paint; but even then he was no less surprised, expecting the pictures would feel like the things they represented ... and asked which was the lying sense, feeling or seeing? (Cheselden 1728, 447)

Cheselden's patient was quick to construct a new series of mental maps, to help him decipher the visual world. Others have not been so fortunate, finding the task of adjusting their long-term perceptual worlds to a different reality emotionally devastating. Two centuries after Cheselden, Sacks describes how difficult it was for 'Virgil', a man who regained his sight in mid-life, to gain a 'sense of unitary objecthood' through vision alone.

> 'Virgil' was taken to the zoo but could only make sense of the gorilla that he could see by exploring through touch a life-size bronze statue of one in the enclosure. His face seemed to light up with comprehension as he felt the statue. 'It's not like a man at all,' he murmured. The statue examined, he opened his eyes and turned around to the real gorilla standing before him in the enclosure. And now, in a way that would have been impossible before, he described the ape's posture, the way the knuckles touched the ground, the little bandy legs, the great canines, the huge ridge of the head, pointing to each feature as he did so. (Sacks 1995b, 126–27)

Awareness of the different perceptual understanding of congenitally blind people to that of adventitiously blind people proved essential both in the creation of tactile graphics and in the verbal descriptions created for Access Vision members.

Images in Tactile Formats

Melanie de Salignac

Perhaps the earliest reported use of tactile images was that by the resourceful and accomplished Frenchwoman Melanie de Salignac, who was born blind in 1741 (Ross 1951, 82–84). Long before the invention of

Braille in 1829, Melanie taught herself to read using cut-out cardboard letters. She wrote in pencil with a ruler as a guide, friends pricked out their replies to her letters with a pin and she read these tiny marks with sensitive fingers. She could play the violin and guitar; reading the score first in relief, she would memorise the composition, pinpricking the music to aid her memory. To learn geography, she used relief maps with raised features fashioned from wire, silk threads, pinheads, and blobs of sealing wax.

Tactile images became generally available only after reform ensured that education of blind children was compulsory and specialist schools were established. The resulting need for tactile aids led to research into methods that would permit mass production for educational purposes.

In the gallery sector, one-off interpretative artworks have been produced such as James O'Hanlon's imaginative interpretation of 'Wall Street Journal' by Conrad Atkinson in the permanent collection of the Wolverhampton Art Gallery. O'Hanlon's version includes audio, textural, and other elements. The different qualities of its brushstrokes have been rendered in thick paint, tubular steel, steel springs, wire, copper strips, and lacquered plaster of Paris; small doors can be opened to activate audio interpretation. Its many features have proved popular with visitors of all types and extend the appreciation of the original work. Such an approach is clearly not feasible for large collections, thus tactile images that are capable of cheap mass production are crucial.

Thermoforms, Microcapsule Images and the 'Muse' Print

A tactile image is a highly simplified, diagrammatic representation of the artwork, analogous to a map, used with detailed verbal description. The raised image does not give enough information about the original for it to be used alone.

Such images fall into two main generic types—thermoforms, and raised images on microcapsule or 'Swell' paper (sometimes referred to as 'Minoltas' in the UK, after the Japanese company that manufactures the copying machine used in their production). Swell paper is coated with a styrene emulsion composed of millions of microcapsules that swell in response to heat. A diagram of the work is photocopied onto microcapsule paper, then passed through an infrared heater. The blackened areas absorb heat faster and the microcapsules beneath the ink expand, producing a raised, textured image. Thermoforms have been developed by the Living Paintings Trust (LPT), which works ex-clusively in this format (Cassim 1997a) while microcapsule images have been used extensively in the United States by Art Education for the Blind, Inc. (AEB 1996).

While their production, aesthetics, durability, and cost differ, raised images on microcapsule paper and the 'Muse' print developed by the author are equivalent conceptually. Both are based on linear illustration and both require that the user decipher information through a tactile process resembling the act of drawing, with the outline of the shape traced with the finger in response to audio description. This type seems to be preferred by many adventitiously blind people with visual memories and experience of drawing or writing. In contrast, the thermoform describes volume and mass rather than line. It is 'read' as a three-dimensional or low-relief shape and is dependent on the tactile literacy more common in congenitally blind people who read form rather than line. While a thermoform is an excellent means of depicting form and proportion in a painting, it is less successful at conveying linear qualities, which a raised image on microcapsule paper or 'Muse' print can do well. In working with Access Vision, it was not possible to produce thermoforms because I had no access to the specialist equipment or skills required to produce the three-dimensional model from which thermoforms are pressed.

Microcapsule images, based on a drawing of the original artwork, are more flexible, can be easily adapted and altered, and are less time-consuming and expensive to produce (Figure 10.2). Their major disadvantages are their lack of colour information, while some users find their texture and 'temperature' unpleasant; made of styrene, they are slightly warm to the touch and degrade quickly with use. They cannot

Figure 10.2　Examples of microcapsule images

successfully convey a fine line or variation in texture and are disliked by exhibition designers for their 'special needs' appearance, which makes them unsuitable for display or inclusion in catalogues. They also require a coloured reproduction of the original to provide full information about the original work. For these reasons I looked for an alternative.

The 'Muse' print is based on a process in which raised lines or Braille are silk-screened over a blank page or an existing graphic or photograph. The inks used have an acrylic resin or cellulose base and can be either transparent or coloured. Since 1994, Mediamuse the Tokyo company that developed this format has experimented with use of transparent inks as a Braille overlay on guidebooks, calendars, and books for blind children with the help of Sanichi Kogeisha, a specialist printing company. The ink's transparency and durability made it perfect for use as a replacement for microcapsule images, for the following reasons:

- It was possible to overlay diagrammatic lines on an existing coloured reproduction of a painting with no visual disturbance.
- The format was durable and attractive.
- It was approved by designers and curators.
- It could be used independently by a visually impaired person in conjunction with an audio guide.
- It was not bulky and could be included in an exhibition catalogue.
- The height of the raised line could be tailored precisely for ease of reading.

'Muse' prints were used in 1997 for the catalogue produced for 'Dialogue of the Spirit, Able Art '97', an exhibition, on which I worked, of paintings by artists with learning disabilities that was held at the Tokyo Metropolitan Museum of Art (Figure 10.3) (Able Art '97 Tokyo 1997). Budgetary limitations determined their use as an overlay on only four of the works in the catalogue—three paintings and one sculpture, chosen for their pictorial simplicity. To minimise visual disturbance, the 'Muse'-print overlay was registered exactly over the image and not on a different part of the page. With regular geometric forms, exact registration is relatively simple but it is more difficult where the forms are irregular or sharply cursive. The raised line can be printed between 0.25 mm and 0.40 mm high, but the higher the line the more uncomfortable it is for extensive reading. We used a 0.25-mm line with a Braille dot 0.35 mm high for the Braille text overlay, which was deemed the most comfortable. Reactions to the 'Muse' prints were

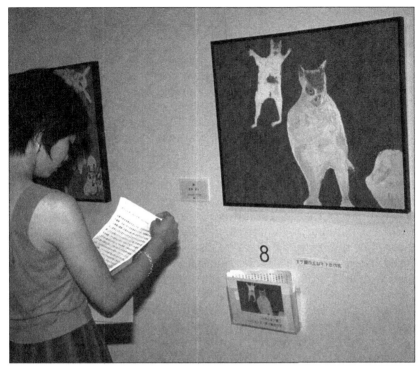

Figure 10.3 'Muse' print for use with work by Shoji Mori for 'Dialogue of the Spirit' at the Tokyo Metropolitan Museum of Art, 1997. The Muse prints were stored in a box below each work. In this photograph, a sighted visitor is reading the large-print text that accompanied the Muse print, and there was also an audio guide.

universally encouraging but, until the technique becomes more widespread, production costs will remain prohibitive.

Selection of Works

Piecing together a mental image of a two-dimensional artwork based on verbal description and a raised image is time-consuming and can be exhausting and frustrating for someone with impaired vision. However, figurative works containing familiar narrative elements can yield profound insights and prompt discussion. This was the case for the work of the Japanese painter Tamiji Kitagawa (1894–1989), who tackled major social and political problems in a direct and critical way. The subjects of his paintings, the events and struggles of his life, and his humanist thinking had many resonances for members of Access Vision. Older members had lived through the same turbulent political times that inspired his paintings. Thus, the power of the subject overcame the need to provide a tactile experience beyond that of the raised image because the context was known.

Where, the cultural context was unfamiliar, problems could arise. *L'Echo*, by Paul Delvaux, was the least successful of the works introduced to Access Vision. At first sight, the painting is straightforward, with clear structural elements allowing it to be examined in sections without losing the visual or narrative thread. The nature of the composition, and the opportunity to use it as a textbook example of the rules of Western perspective, seemed to make it a suitable choice. However, while the group could visualise the composition clearly with the help of the microcapsule image and verbal description, they remained puzzled by the painter's conceptual intention. The myth on which it was based was not part of their cultural experience, nor were they familiar with Surrealist thinking. 'Why are they walking down the street naked in the middle of the night?' and 'Are they sleepwalking?' were questions asked. There was even a joking suggestion that they may have been on their way back from the public bath, a popular community facility in Japan.

Abstract works, while easier to render diagrammatically as raised images, may be problematic in interpretational terms, but there are exceptions. Miro's 'Painting, 1928', in the collection of the Aichi Prefectural Museum of Art, excited a great deal of interest from Access Vision members, even though it was abstract and despite their unfamiliarity with such work. On a swirling azure ground, we see a tiny black dot, a pair of red lips, a patch of white like a fluffy dandelion tuft, a curly patch of indigo fleece, and three forked lines with a drooping tail. They are linked by a sprightly thin line that is whipped around like a kite string in a high wind. It was described thus, evoking strong images of the cold but sunny kite-flying days of the Japanese New Year and of summer picnics in the mountains. The simplicity of the image liberated Access Vision members to make their own free associations about its meaning and start imaginative journeys in response to its creative stimulus.

Conclusion

Tactile images are an extremely effective way of enabling visually impaired people to access the beauties of two-dimensional artworks. One challenge will remain: however spare and effective the raised image produced, the original artwork on which it is based was neither a diagram, a plan, nor a working drawing. It was a creative work in which the artist used a specific vocabulary of line, volume, form, colour, texture, and material to express a visual experience. The tactile image can only hint at this richness. Thus good verbal description is crucial if the interpretation is to succeed. There has been a tendency to view tactile images as 'magic bullets' to the understanding of two-dimensional works of art. They are one tool among many, and are difficult to decipher by touch alone, even for a blind person with a high level of tactile literacy. Members of Access Vision found them baffling initially. Over time, and with critical input, those produced by the author were edited severely. They became an essential tool in the interpretative process, helping Access Vision members to construct mental images of the works under study and to have access once again to the visual world now beyond their reach.

References

Able Art '97 Tokyo. 1997. *Dialogue of the Spirit: Mizunoki Workshop + Chuichi Nishigaki, Chiba School for the Blind + Yohei Nishimura* exhibition catalogue (in Japanese), Tokyo Metropolitan Museum of Art, July 31 to August 13, 1997.

AEB (Art Education for the Blind). 1996. *Making Visual Art Accessible to People Who Are Blind and Visually Impaired.* New York: New Education for the Blind, Inc.

AERA. 1993. Tansei Sogo Kenkyujo statistics, quoted in 'Cultural Coffins', *AERA,* February 2, 1993 (in Japanese), Tokyo: Asahi Shimbun Group.

Blagden, S., Everett, J. 1992. *What Colour Is the Wind?* Corsham: National Society of Education in Art & Design.

Cassim, J. 1991. Letting kids get a feel for art. Tokyo: *The Japan Times,* July 21.

——— 1992. Art for hands-on experience. Tokyo: *The Japan Times,* September 20.

——— 1993a. Toyama Museum constructed with care. Tokyo: *The Japan Times,* February 21.

——— 1993b. Summer programs keep kids busy. Tokyo: *The Japan Times,* August 1.

——— 1994a. Open-air, public-art project in full bloom. Tokyo: *The Japan Times,* December 17.

——— 1994b. Fiction functional in open-air sculpture. Tokyo: *The Japan Times,* December 24.

——— 1995. Tactile art challenges imagination. Tokyo: *The Japan Times,* May 28.

——— 1996a. Keep the kids off the streets with summer art workshops. Tokyo: *The Japan Times,* July 14.

——— 1997a. Tactile landscapes of the soul. Tokyo: *The Japan Times,* June 15.

——— 1997b. Intangible presence in wood and copper. Tokyo: *The Japan Times,* August 30.

——— 1998. Beyond stuffing envelopes: Museums energized by volunteer spirit. Tokyo: *The Japan Times,* May 24.

Cassim, J. 2000. Public spaces, public art. *Insight, Japan* 8(4): London.

Cheselden, W. 1728. An account of observations made by a young gentleman. *Philosoph Trans* 7: 402.

Disability Discrimination Act (DDA) 1995. [http://www.opsi.gov.uk/acts/acts1995/1995050.htm]

Edman, P.K. 1992. *Tactile Graphics.* New York: American Foundation for the Blind.

Hooper-Greenhill, E. 1991. *Museum and Gallery Education.* London and New York: Routledge.

Housen, A. 1992. Validating a measure of aesthetic development for museums and schools. *ILVS Review, A Journal of Visitor Behavior,* 2. New York: Exhibit Communications Research, Inc., The International Laboratory for Visitor Studies.

Housen, A., Miller, N.L. 1992. Spring. *MOMA School Program Evaluation Study, Report II,* 3. New York: Museum of Modern Art.

Hull, J.M. 1990. *Touching the Rock: An Experience of Blindness.* London: SPCK.

Hunt, B. 1989. *It Makes Sense! Artworks to Touch, Smell, See and Hear: New Challenges in Contemporary Art.* London: BP re-Vision and Greenwich Citizen's Gallery.

Knell, S. 1994. *Care of Collections.* London and New York: Routledge.

London SE1 Community Website 2007. [http://www.london-se1.co.uk/news/view/1602]

Ministry of Health and Welfare. 1991. *Official Survey of the Disabled Population of Japan* (in Japanese). Tokyo.

Nagoya City Art Museum. 1996. *Art & the Inner Eye: Sculpture for Walking, Sculpture for Listening* (in Japanese). Nagoya.

National Curriculum. 1988. The regulations on content, and assessment, of what is taught, in UK schools [online]. [http://www.nc.uk.net] (Accessed 27.04.07)

Naughton, P. 1993. *Babies Teach Their Mothers What They Need to Know: An Inquiry into the Art of the Registered Blind.* Dublin: National College of Art & Design.

Pearson, A. 1991. Touch exhibitions in the United Kingdom. In *Museums without Barriers: A New Deal for Disabled People,* Fondation de France and ICOM. London and New York: Routledge.

Ross, I. 1951. *Journey into Light.* New York: Appleton-Century-Crofts, Inc.

Sacks, O. 1995a. A new vision of the mind. In J. Cornwell (ed.), *Nature's Imagination: The Frontiers of Scientific Vision.* Oxford: Oxford University Press.

—— 1995b. *An Anthropologist on Mars.* London: Picador.

South Bank Centre. 1995. *Darklight: BT dialogue in the dark.* London: BT & Royal Festival Hall.

Trevor-Roper, P. 1990. *The World through Blunted Sight,* 2nd edn. London: Penguin.

Worts, D. 1995. Extending the frame: Forging a new partnership with the public. In S. Pearce (ed.), *Art in Museums.* London: Athlone.

Yenawine, P. 1997. *Writing for Adult Museum Visitors.* New York: Visual Understanding in Education.

11

TOUCHING ART, TOUCHING YOU: BLINDART, SENSE & SENSUALITY

Sharareh Khayami

BlindArt is a charity, founded in the UK in 2004, to promote contemporary artwork that can be explored through all five senses, especially touch. It promotes the works of sighted and visually impaired artists side by side, challenging the public to distinguish the difference, and demonstrating that sight is not essential for artistic ability either in its creation or appreciation. Thus it aims to shift the established rules of art appreciation from the dominance of sight to the inclusion of touch.

Touch is often regarded as a supplement or alternative to sight, providing an aid for the visual sense. This approach, however, is limited in that it regards touch as a substitute for sight rather than as an end in itself. It assumes that the visually impaired person's experience of cultural artefacts and artworks is a partial experience compared to the sighted person's. BlindArt confronts this head-on with its **Sense** & Sensuality projects: annual art competitions and exhibitions showing work by a cross-section of artists—both visually impaired and sighted— providing a multisensory interactive art experience for a diverse audience. At these events, visitors are actively encouraged to explore the works through touch.

The Exhibitions

Exhibited works are drawn from a nationwide open art competition with the brief to create works that are specifically suitable for a visually impaired audience. The terms of this brief are non-prescriptive; the only stipulation BlindArt makes is that all works must be allowed to be touched. Selected works are exhibited utilising a variety of access measures to enable all visitors to experience the works. These include, for example: large-print and Braille labels and catalogues, sans serif typefaces with contrast on all printed material, multi-layered descriptive audio guides, tactile representations of selected works, raised floor plans, and works hung at low level for ease of visual access and to facilitate exploration through touch.

Throughout the competition, selection, and exhibition process, BlindArt refuses to announce to the panel of judges, the visitors, or the press whether an artist is sighted or visually impaired. Works are selected for exhibition on the strength of artistic merit alone, yet many works of art by partially sighted and, indeed, blind artists have been selected over the works of their sighted colleagues. This ensures that the exhibited works can be experienced without preconceptions concerning visual and artistic ability. When asked, visitors to **Sense &** Sensuality have rarely been able to distinguish between the works by sighted and visually impaired artists.

The inaugural exhibition, **Sense** & Sensuality 2005, at the Henry Moore Gallery, Royal College of Art, London, was an overwhelming success, receiving unprecedented broadcast and print media coverage for a six-day exhibition. This and the exhibition the following year at the Bankside Gallery are estimated to have reached, directly or indirectly, a very wide audience.

Artists and Their Works

Sense & Sensuality's brief has inspired artists to achieve a fresh perspective by considering the nature and possibilities of artworks that can be touched, and to innovate and adjust their artistic vision and practice accordingly. Specifically, the requirement that works be experienced through touch has encouraged artists to make their works robust, sensorially diverse, and in most cases to create works where shape, form, scale, texture, and the capacity to interact are all utilised to achieve their artistic aims. Artists are attempting to develop innovative ways to utilise touch and physical interaction: works that produce or change sound when touched or moved through; screen-printed raised text that can be read by touch as well as by sight; tactile etching; fabric that releases scent when touched; sign systems created from knotted cord; musical furniture; and tactile light boxes (Figure 11.1).

In her textile sculpture 'Eden 1', Anna Zakis has created an artistic interpretation of the Eden Project eco-centre in Cornwall. Formed from

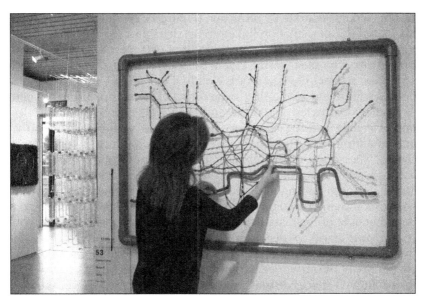

Figure 11.1 Visitor exploring Andrew Senior 'Quipu II', a map of the
London tube system in knotted cord. (Sense & Sensuality 2006,
© BlindArt)

fabric stretched over a series of semicircular metal curves, the large
sculpture stretches from wall to floor at an angle of about 45 degrees.
While its natural-cotton fabric, autumnal colours, and branch-like
shape recall plant-forms found in the Eden Project's greenhouses, the
sculpture's metal framework echoes the famous domes of the centre's
biospheres. The soft medium and sensual curves of the sculpture in-
vite touch, and touch triggers scent. Zakis has inserted pierced plastic
tubes into the fabric containing aromatherapy oils. Touching the
sculpture causes oils to leak into the fabric and release their natural
fragrances. As the oils are warmed through contact they increase in
intensity. The sculpture therefore represents the smells as well as the
forms of the Eden Project and draws attention to the first sensation that
would be experienced as an unsighted person entered the verdurous
greenhouses.

Nick Ball's sculptural installation, 'Black Cube', is a work that addresses the senses physically and conceptually, involving the visitors'
senses of sight, touch, and hearing, and exploring ideas of sensorial
confusion. The work is made out of 462 two-litre plastic bottles sus-
pended on wire from a grid in a 6-foot (1.83 metres) cube formation.
The bottles on the outside of the sculpture are translucent, while the
ones in the centre are green, blue, red, and yellow. When viewed from
the outside, this mimics the effect of light travelling through glass,

where colours separate by refraction (Figure 11.2). Ball is playing with his materials (a fascination linked to his dedication to recycling waste through art), and thwarting our expectations of those materials' inherent properties. The clear outer layers of bottles, with their scuffs and scratches, also act like a cataract, clouding our picture of the coloured bottles within and replicating some forms of visual impairment. Sight is further obstructed when the audience walks through the bottles and is veiled in a fog of watery light. In fact, walking through the bottles sculpture creates a number of unexpected effects involving our senses. The sound of the air-filled bottles clattering together creates a thunderous, buoyant sound that reminds one of diving into water, and the smooth parting of the columns of bottles further reinforces the notion of moving through water or a sort of viscous air. Emerging on the other side of the installation is like returning to the surface as you regain your clarity of vision (for the sighted), the thunder stops, and the air thins. For sighted and visually impaired audiences alike, the experience of the artwork confounds sensorial expectations, narrowing the traditional space between aesthetic and bodily experience.

Responses to the Exhibitions

Sense & Sensuality exhibitions set out to be mainstream, stimulating and inviting events for all lovers of art while remaining truly accessible

Figure 11.2 Visitor in Nick Ball's installation 'Black Cube,' 2-litre plastic bottles and wire. (Sense & Sensuality 2006, © BlindArt)

to people with disabilities. The invitation to touch artworks also removes cultural as well as sensorial barriers and so attracts people that tend not to visit art exhibitions.

The exhibitions offer a unique experience for sighted visitors as well. A consideration of how sighted people use touch can open the possibilities of the sense of touch as a primary method to interact and engage with art, and therefore as a direct rather than a secondary method of experience and appreciation. The traditional 'Do Not Touch' sign in a museum or gallery excludes not only visually impaired people who need to use touch to access most works, but also many people who feel put off by the character of the institution that has such rules. 'Do Not Touch' implies snobbery, elitism, and restriction of the art experience. This intellectual and cultural barrier deters people who are not used to visiting museums and art galleries. Objects that cannot be touched appear exclusive and forbidden. By allowing visitors to touch artworks, they become tangible, accessible, and intimate (Figure 11.3). Apart from urging people not to mishandle artworks, BlindArt does not instruct visitors how to touch art, just as they are not told how to look at art.

BlindArt has conducted surveys (using questionnaires) of people's responses to **Sense** & Sensuality exhibitions and the experience of touching art. The following quotes are taken from questionnaires completed by artists and visitors and give an impression of reactions to the exhibitions:

Figure 11.3 Visitor touching detail of painting by Peter Clossick, 'Egyptian Princess,' oil on canvas. (Sense & Sensuality 2006, © BlindArt)

Artists

I suddenly realised how entrenched my taboos about touching paintings were. Watching people stroking and touching my painting gave me strange feelings; I wasn't quite prepared for it. To actually touch other people's work in a gallery situation had a similar effect upon me. In the end it gave me a great feeling of liberation. **Sense** & Sensuality was a growing experience for me. (Pete Flowers)

The piece is only completed when the viewer touches, sees, and smells the piece; it then begins to work on all levels, and to see this happening is amazing. Personally, textiles and touch have always been inseparable for me, so this exhibition was a fantastic opportunity. The idea was inspiring. (Anna Zakis)

It was wonderful as an artist to be able to touch other artists' work and understand their energy in making the works. We are so used to listening or seeing things in such an instant fashion, that I found the actual touching ... slowed down my response, and gave me a much deeper understanding of the work. (Linda Lieberman)

For me the fundamental contrast with **Sense** & Sensuality was the people who came to see were as much part of the exhibition as the art on show. The very audibility of people enjoying their interaction through the exhilaration of being hands-on transformed a traditionally solemn space into an extra-sensory playground. (Steve Farley)

Visitors

'Fantastic! Really liberating. I will really remember this exhibition'.
'Felt nervous and excited touching the art. Taboo/freedom/liberating'.
'Overthrowing years of not being allowed to touch art. Quite mind-bending'.
'A privilege to be trusted by the artist to touch'.
'Reminds me how evocative and sensual touch can be—a lovely exhibition.'

Art Professionals

The following are quotes from correspondence.

Having been in the visual arts all my working life, I never appreciated that blind or partially sighted people could experience the pleasures of the visual arts by touch. I was surprised and very moved by this experience. (Marian Stone, former director, Waddington and Flowers East Gallery)

As a young sculptor I always extolled the idea of touching sculpture; it was a romantic idea for any sculptor enamoured with the likes of Brancusci. It was only more recently that I realised the changing effect that touching has on materials. There is, in the long term, at worst a risk of erosion or at best a subtle temporal patina. Many artists, galleries, museums, collectors, and conservators want and need to have a fixed and static state for a work of art. The visually impaired, the participating viewer, children, etc., all eagerly want to feel and touch, to get physically involved. It is a current debate that has surfaced with particular reference to the BlindArt exhibitions, and will go on into the future. (Glynn Williams, Head of Fine Art, Royal College of Art)

People who have been blind for even a short time are used to making the sense of touch stand in for their eyes and thereby comprehend a surprising amount about the objects in front of them. Watching their hands run expertly over the various surfaces made me realise how much more attuned they were to tactile signals, how natural an activity it was for them to grasp something and let fingers do the job which I would instinctively assign to my sight. Moreover, their method of enjoying sculpture seemed a more appropriate response to three-dimensional artefacts than the usual keep-your-distance relationship fostered by museums, whether at the Tate or anywhere else. Looking round the show, I saw everyone feeling, probing, stroking, prodding, and playing with the exhibits in a spirit of eagerness which contrasted well with the alienated way we normally survey sculpture, our hands held in absurd abeyance. These blind visitors, many of whom had probably never been inside an art gallery before because of the innate futility involved, were questioning and testing the works with an enviable sense of discovery. (Richard Cork, art critic; and see Cork 2003)

I feel that I have been very lucky because in my work (I am a photographer) I have always had to touch and handle works of art, sometimes very special and valuable pieces. This has given me a very fortunate position. Placing a sculpture on a background table or a painting onto an easel is still an amazing experience, especially when the work is beautiful. I get to turn them over and examine them properly. There is still nervousness around touching art; like forbidden fruit, it can't be done. It's a difficult situation, as clearly some art is not meant to be touched, or could not stand up to constant physical pressure, but surely it is possible to allow some access to appreciate the solidity and structure of artworks properly. Isn't it? (Fraser Marr, photographer)

BlindArt's Development

BlindArt was conceived as a small project but it quickly developed an unexpected avalanche effect. Alongside the **Sense** & Sensuality exhibitions, innovative education and outreach work is being undertaken focused on encouraging the interaction of sighted, visually impaired, and disabled people in the cultural realm through the 4Senses project (BlindArt 2006a, 2006b; Hayhoe 2005). Artists are supported through sales of their works at BlindArt exhibitions, and through other sales opportunities such as art fairs and the Internet.

BlindArt promotes its projects by publishing papers on the 'Think!' section of our website, and by taking part in conferences, and seminars on touch, art, and access. The BlindArt Permanent Collection continues to grow, with works purchased through the BlindArt Purchase Prize and donations from artists and the public. BlindArt works with galleries, art fairs, and a variety of institutions in the UK and abroad so that the permanent collection can reach and touch as many people as possible. In the longer term it is the charity's aim to find a permanent home for the collection in the UK.

References

BlindArt website: [http://www.blindart.net/]

BlindArt 2006a. 4Senses Education Project Report [http://www.blindart.net/events/display?contentId=3639]

BlindArt 2006b. Sense2Sense Education [http://www.blindart.net/events/display?contentId=3629] (Accessed 23.04.06)

Cork, R. 2003. *Everything Seemed Possible: Art in the 1970s*. New Haven and London: Yale University Press.

Hayhoe, S. 2005. 4Senses Installation Project, unpublished paper [http://www.blindart.net/events/display?contentId=3010] (Accessed 23.04.07)

12

LEARNING THROUGH TOUCH

Tara Trewinnard-Boyle and Emily Tabassi

The Nottingham Loans Collection has had a varied history since it was first developed in the 1940s. After a period of declining use and several years in storage, it was resurrected in 2004 to respond to enthusiasm in schools and community groups for the opportunity to use 'real museum artefacts'. The handling collection complements the formal education programmes and community outreach projects run by the museums.

Bringing the Collection Back to Life

The decision to bring the collection out of storage was a response to increased government funding for regional museums, resulting from the Renaissance in the Regions report (MLA 2001). Impetus for the reawakening of the collection as a functioning loans service also came from the *Childwise Report* (ChildWise 2004). The report was based on extensive consultation with teachers across the region, who remembered and missed their loans collection. Asked to rate a list of possible museum services, 79% of Nottingham Schools cited 'object loans box' as the service they would most like to use (this was the top-ranked answer). When asked about barriers to schools visiting museums, 82% of schools responded that the most significant barrier was the cost of transport. All these factors culminated in the resuscitation of the loans collection in 2004 (Tabassi & Holmes 2006).

Role of Handling Collections

The aim of loan boxes and handling collections is to give pupils the opportunity to explore objects linked to the theme of a lesson and to make the past more vivid. For example, actually holding an unfamiliar object such as a Victorian flat iron, and imagining what it would be like to use it, may prompt deeper understanding of what domestic work was like in the days before electricity. Community groups may use the loans to extend their particular interests, and as a focus for mutual support and socialising. The collections also break the 'Do Not Touch' taboo which can make museums off-putting to many audiences.

The Organisation of the Collection

Most of the objects in the collection are unprovenanced, although with some there is brief information, including details of the donor and, occasionally, the circumstances of acquisition (Cooper & King 2005a). After rationalisation in 2004, the collection consisted of 8,000 handling artefacts, with around 1,500 items in Perspex cases.

The loans collection team consists of a Schools and Community Loans Officer responsible for planning and managing the loans service, consultation with users, and development of new loans resources; a Collections Access Assistant responsible for collections care and management; and, at various times, a freelance project co-ordinator who leads a team of freelance community workers. A member of staff from the children's services department was also temporarily seconded to the project; having worked with the collection for many years, he was passionate about seeing it in use once again. A large team of committed volunteers and Museum and Heritage Management postgraduate students from Nottingham Trent University has also been crucial to the success of the project.

Consultation

In July 2005, a history teachers' discussion group was formed. Members of the group were initially recruited through a city-wide questionnaire and information leaflet sent to all schools. All city teachers were invited to attend an initial meeting, and from this a smaller group of teachers has become committed to the project and meets with us every term.

Through the discussion group we have formed close partnerships with twelve schools, and looser links with a further nine schools. These partner schools are given the opportunity to participate in our free pilot sessions for new resource boxes, and to become part of the decision-making process. Many of these schools are based in deprived areas of Nottingham and the teachers' experience is vital in helping us to create appropriate resources that are also relevant to the National Curriculum – regulations on content, and assessment, of what is taught in UK schools (UK National Curriculum).

Our resources for community groups are produced in conjunction with the groups themselves. During the first phase of the project (2004–2006), we worked with a library book group, an art and literature group for inmates at Nottingham prison, an English for speakers of other languages (ESOL) group based at the University of Nottingham, and a group focused on giving up smoking.

Collections used in the resource boxes are not selected only for their aesthetic or particularly tactile nature; it is also important that they fit the theme of the box. For example the 'Toys' box contains nineteenth- and twentieth-century jigsaws, dolls, models, board games, books, skipping ropes, constructional games, and card games that can be looked at and handled. The aim is to use a variety of toys from different time periods; the only restrictions are the contents of the collections. It also includes a range of modern replica toys that can be actively played with. If there are many examples of the same type of object in the collection, then the best or most complete will usually be chosen for a resource box. Objects are not rejected because they are delicate; it is accepted that every object will be used. Great care is taken to prevent damage, but it is inevitable that some objects will be lost in this way. Appropriate training and the best efforts of staff, teachers, and community group leaders are relied on to minimise the risk.

Making the Collection Accessible

The collection is made available in a variety of ways:

Themed Resource Boxes for Schools

These are handling boxes usually containing between fifteen and twenty artefacts, a comprehensive teacher's pack, and additional items such as tablecloths and 'feely bags'. The boxes are created around specific themes that are often linked to the National Curriculum, and to popular topics taught at primary and secondary levels, although extracurricular and skills-based resources are also developed. Current resource boxes include: 'Victorian Kitchen', 'World War One', '1950s, 1960s, 1970s', 'Romans in Britain' (Figure 12.1), and 'Africa Inspires!'. The 1950s, 1960s, 1970s re-source box includes domestic and children's items such as roller skates, hair slides, a women's magazine, an original

Figure 12.1 Using the Romans in Britain resource box with a class at Firbeck Primary and Nursery School. (Courtesy of Nottingham City Museums and Galleries)

newspaper, a coronation tin, and a jubilee flag. These boxes are available both to schools and to community groups.

The 'feely bags' included in our resources are calico drawstring bags that can be used for artefact investigation. The teacher chooses an object from the box and puts it into the bag before the class begins. The object chosen for this activity should be robust and safe to handle without being seen. The bag is then passed around the class and children have a chance to feel the object and describe what they experience. Often the object is something that they will never have seen before and the aim is the exploration of the object using senses other than sight. Many activities can be developed from using these bags, and piloting the resources has demonstrated that their use is successful from nursery age to adults.

Themed Resource Boxes for Communities

These are also boxes containing around 15 to 20 artefacts and a comprehensive pack written especially for community use, including guidance on suggested activities (Figure 12.2). Themed boxes include 'Storytelling', 'Illuminated Books', and 'Personal Treasures'. The artefacts for the Storytelling box are drawn from different world

**Figure 12.2   Members of the Bulwell Library Group investigating a book
from the *Illuminations* community loans resource. (Courtesy of
Nottingham City Museums and Galleries)**

cultures, and can be used as the basis for telling stories from those
cultures – examples are part of a North American Indian peace pipe, a
Pacific Island fish hook, a Jamaican measuring tankard.

The Cased Collection

The large cased collection was inherited from an earlier period. A
variety of objects had been put in Perspex cases in order to display
sets such as toys. Some objects have now been removed from cases but
others, such the models, have been kept in the cases to protect them
from breakage; the taxidermy specimens particularly need to remain
enclosed to prevent handling for health and safety reasons. These
cased objects are lent out in sets that can be created specifically for
each teacher or community group leader. This resource is under-used,
however, so sets of themed boxes such as 'Food Chains' or 'African Art'
are being developed and publicised.

Health and Safety

Potentially dangerous items are not usually chosen. However, exceptions are made when an artefact would be central to a theme, for example, a Lee Enfield rifle from the First World War forms part of our World War One resource. It has been disarmed, and a special lockable case has been made to house it when it is sent out to schools. The gun can be handled carefully under supervision by the teacher. Other hazards must be considered, such as the asbestos in World War One and World War Two gas masks. These masks are evocative objects so, rather than disposing of them, we consulted our health and safety department who advised sealing the filters and attaching warning labels. The masks can still be handled, but users are alerted to the potential hazards and it is stressed that they should not to be worn under any circumstances.

Handling guidelines are provided, together with a comprehensive risk assessment for each resource. In most cases, objects are handled without the use of gloves but in certain cases—lead toys for example—gloves are provided and their use is strongly recommended.

Safety of the Objects

The user takes responsibility for the safe handling of the items. Basic advice given in the guidelines (e.g. 'hold the object with two hands and always assume it is more fragile that it looks') has undoubtedly prevented breakages. In fact, no losses or breakages have occurred during the first year of the project. More detailed training is also provided for teachers, showing them how to handle the collections and also giving ideas on how to get the most out of the resources in the classroom. This training will soon be extended to community groups.

Creating Resource Boxes for Schools

The project staff, with the museums education officer, choose about eight themes before the termly teachers' meeting, and suitable artefacts are selected from the collection to provide a flavour of the possibilities. The teachers' group can choose from these themes or suggest further themes for the resource boxes. In the current phase, themes chosen for teachers to consider will include: prehistory and the local area; North American Indians; medieval Britain; the life of Jesse Boot (the Nottingham founder of Boots the Chemists); and Victorian laundry. So far, this has been a successful and open way to ensure that the resources will meet the needs and interests of the users, and to encourage schools to borrow the boxes once they become available.

Each object is researched individually. The resulting information is presented in the form of a series of simple questions: What am I? How old am I? What am I made of? Who would have made me and why? Who owned me or used me and what for? What stories can I tell? The questions are intended to present relevant information quickly, easily, and in a consistent format. So that teachers can get maximum use out of the loan box, the printed information is limited to two sides of paper for each object; this may seem arbitrary, but it is important that the resources are easy for the teachers to use.

Piloting New Resources

The piloting of new loan boxes starts with the Schools and Community Loans Officer, who takes the objects and activities into our partner schools to lead a session with a group of pupils. This gives an idea of what works and what does not, it shows which artefacts spark pupils' imagination, and reveals practical issues arising from working in a classroom. At this stage, teachers and pupils are asked to give their evaluation. The next stage is to gather additional information and write the teachers' packs, including suggested activities. The partner teachers are then given the opportunity to borrow the resources once again for a week in school and provide further evaluation. During this trial, the Loans Officer observes the resources being used in the classroom.

It is important for the Loans Officer to visit local schools in order to try activities and resources. For example, the 'feely bags' were found to be particularly successful and are now included in many resource boxes—though not where the artefacts are not robust enough, as in the 'Romans in Britain' resource, which consists mainly of ceramics, or for a theme such as 'World War One', where the objects are intended to encourage pupils to consider the experience at the front and at home during the conflict. The teachers that participate in the pilot are usually the teachers who regularly attend the termly teachers' meeting, and they say that they appreciate seeing another professional lead a session. As these are the teachers who commit their time and energy to the project, they are the natural recipients of the free pilot sessions.

The community loans boxes are developed in a rather more flexible way. Themes are chosen, then the Outreach Officer, who has close contacts with many community groups in the city, asks groups if they would like to become involved with the development of a resource.

At the end of the piloting process, the artefacts for both schools and community loans resources are packed safely in 'flight-style' cases padded with Plastazote (polythene) foam. The resources are then available for loan—free to community groups and for a small charge for schools.

Managing the Collection

A collections policy was written in 2004 that details the history and content of the collection, as well as acquisition and disposals procedures. This now forms part of the Nottingham City Museums and Galleries main collections policy document (Tabassi 2004).

The collections are not formally accessioned, for a variety of reasons. In most cases, transfer of title is not possible because there is no record of the previous owner. Active collecting is not currently a part of the collection management plan unless an object becomes available that is vital to the resources. The collections remain as a separate handling collection but accepted standards of collection care and documentation are applied to their management (see SPECTRUM, the UK standard for museum documentation).

Rationalisation was needed when the collection was initially brought out of storage in 2004. Many objects had become damaged by water and pests, and breakages had occurred through the repeated moving of the collections. Some objects were of no use as part of a handling collection, either because they were dangerous (such as knives) or their content or language was inappropriate for the audiences that would be using the collections. Storage space was also a major issue, so large groups of similar objects were thinned out in consultation with the curatorial staff in the city, and notification of any collections for disposal was published in the *Museums Journal*. Some objects, such as tools, were donated to charities so they could be reconditioned for use in developing countries.

Some dangerous items, such as spears, have been retained, and teachers have worked with us to consider ways of packaging and interpreting those artefacts sensibly so that they can be used in the classroom. Some of the original historical objects, such as books, include stories, images, or wording that would not be considered appropriate in today's world. In consultation with teachers, it was decided that these should nevertheless be included in the resource boxes because they represent examples of historical attitudes. Teachers can decide whether and how to use them with their classes.

Evaluation of the Project

As a Renaissance in the Regions–funded project, evaluation was built in from the beginning. At the end of the first phase a major evaluation report was produced (Tabassi & Holmes 2006). Evaluation in this first phase (2004–2006) was based on the 'Inspiring Learning for All' framework of the Museums Libraries and Archives Council (MLA), using the framework's generic learning outcomes (GLOs) (MLA 2007):

Increase in knowledge and understanding
Increase in skills
Evidence of enjoyment, inspiration and creativity
Evidence of activity, modified behaviour and progression
Change in attitudes and values

A range of evaluation methods is used including teachers', pupils', and community participants' questionnaires, drawings, photographs, observations, interviews, and informal discussions. The aim of the evaluation was to discover to what extent seeing and handling 'real' objects had helped to bring the past to life, thus enhancing understanding and learning.

Comments taken from the report on the first phase (Tabassi & Holmes 2006) include:

[It provided a way of] developing their ability to question, hypothesise, suggest, and justify their opinions .... The atmosphere felt supportive to joining in and having a go.... (Karen Woollard, history co-ordinator, Brocklewood Infant School, Nottingham)

It has taught them to look carefully, [to] analyse evidence. (Jane Ridley, history co-ordinator, Welbeck Primary School, Nottingham)

Using the loans boxes is already part of a major project on the life of a soldier in the trenches. (Louise K. Place, head of history, Fernwood Comprehensive School, Nottingham)

[I have been] learning new things that I would probably not have understood if I had just been told them. (Year 6 pupil, age 10–11, Welbeck Primary School, Nottingham)

It helped me learn a lot of things while I was having fun. . . . If I wasn't having as much fun I probably wouldn't have learnt as much. (Year 5 pupil, age 9–10, Heathfield Primary School, Nottingham)

It made me appreciate the harshness and brutality ... which cannot be conveyed by statistics and pictures. (Sixth form student, age 17–18, Bilborough Sixth Form College, Nottingham)

The response has been overwhelmingly positive, with teachers already keen to borrow resource boxes and items from the cased collection. In just the first year of our new service, more than 9,500 participants from 51 schools and 7 community groups have enjoyed our loans resources. The piloting of our newest resource boxes has involved 11 schools and more than 425 pupils. Community resource boxes take longer to pilot than the school ones because each needs to be appropriate for a variety of groups, but community groups can borrow our schools resources during holidays, so they have already been keen to get involved.

References

ChildWise. 2004. *East Midlands Museums, Teacher Research*. [http://www. emms.org.uk/EM-Hub/Phase%201%20and%202%20Report.doc] (Accessed 14.03.07)

Cooper, M. 2007. *Natural History Register* (unpublished NCMG internal database).

Cooper, M., King, A. 2005a. *A History of the Nottingham Natural History Museum 1867–2000*. Nottingham City Museums and Galleries [NCMG] internal report.

———— 2005b. *Report on the Natural History Register Project, 1999–2005*. Unpublished NCMG internal report.

MLA 2007. [online] Inspiring Learning for All. [http://www.inspiringlearning forall.gov.uk] (Accessed 27.04.07)

MLA (Council for Museums Libraries and Archives) 2001. *Renaissance in the Regions: A New Vision for England's Museums* [online]. [http://www.mla.gov. uk] (Accessed 27.04.07)

Renaissance East Midlands. 2006. *Business Plan document 2006–2008*. Renaissance East Midlands Programme Board. Unpublished.

SPECTRUM [online]. [http://www.mda.org.uk] (Accessed 27.04.07)

Tabassi, E. 2004. *Collections Policy*. Nottingham: Nottingham City Museums and Galleries, Education Loans Collection.

Tabassi, E., Holmes, C. 2006. *The 'Lazarus' Project': A Collection Reawakened for Nottingham City Schools and Communities: Evaluating the Development of an Artefact Loans Service*. [www.mlaeastmidlands.org.uk/document.rm?id=508] (Accessed 14.03.07)

UK National Curriculum [online]. [http://www.nc.uk.net] (Accessed 27.04.07)

13

TO PLAY OR NOT TO PLAY: MAKING A COLLECTION OF MUSICAL INSTRUMENTS ACCESSIBLE

Andrew Lamb

The Bate Collection of Musical Instruments is part of the faculty of music at the University of Oxford. Opening in 1970, it originated with the gift of Philip Bate of three hundred European orchestral wind instruments. Bate was a leading organologist and one of the founder members of the Galpin Society, an international institution dedicated to the study of musical instruments (Arnold-Foster & La Rue 1993; Montagu 2000). One of the conditions of the gift was that the collection should be made available for judicious use by scholars. Bate was the author of a definitive volume on the history of orchestral musical instruments, and many of the instruments in the gift had been used as examples in his work. It was considered important that future researchers should have access to this primary source material.

Of equal importance, in Bate's view, was that musicians should be able play historical instruments in order to compare them with modern instruments. For example, modern flutes differ enormously from their Baroque equivalent of the early eighteenth century. The modern flute has been designed to be played in a large orchestra. It has a comparatively loud volume and an evenness of tonal quality across the scale. The baroque flute has a softer tone and, while it can play with brilliant clarity in its own major scale, it has subtler, softer qualities when using chromatic notes far removed from its home key. Additionally it was not played in anything larger than a small chamber orchestra. These differences were so marked that it was felt that playing period music using modern instruments and a modern style of musicianship was inappropriate and misled the modern audience, whereas playing music on the instruments of the period illuminated knowledge of the composers' intentions. Similar differences applied to other types of musical instruments. For example, when composing the *Symphony Fantastique,* Berlioz originally scored for an old brass instrument, the ophicleide, during the movement incorporating the 'March to the Scaffold'. The modern symphony orchestra seldom has an ophicleide in its brass section and substitutes a modern 'equivalent' such as a euphonium. However, when comparing a performance using modern instruments with a performance using the original score, the original provides an utterly different soundscape and the emotional effects of the composition are completely changed.

The authorities of the university accepted that access to the collection would have to be greater than that normally associated with collections of musical objects (for discussion of levels of access to musical instruments in museums, see CIMCIM 1985; Odell & Karp 1997; Barclay 2004). It was agreed that the Bate should have a specialist curator who would not only lecture on subjects connected to the collection but also assess the needs of researchers and visiting scholars and maintain an appropriate level of access to the instruments. This would necessitate auditing the condition of the collection and assessing the users to ensure that objects were not placed under threat. These have become, in effect, the crucial factors in managing the collection.

Types of Access

There are now about 1800 instruments in the collection, mainly from the European orchestral tradition, and all can be made available to some extent. Some are in sufficiently robust condition to allow visiting members of the public to handle them with minimal supervision, and about a quarter of the instruments are playable to some degree. Most of the keyboard instruments are kept in fully playing order, but, as many of them are nearly three hundred years old and have been maintained and repaired during their lives, they are not in original condition.

The instruments are categorised according to permitted levels of use. The categories are influenced both by the rarity of the instrument and by issues of conservation.

Faculty of Music Instruments

Modern instruments bought by the faculty for student use (e.g. contrabassoon, bass clarinet, alto flute) that are used by the student orchestras and lent for rehearsals and concerts. Occasionally they are used by musicians from outside the university.

Modern Copies

Replicas of historic instruments (e.g. viols, crumhorns, cornetts, natural trumpets) which are available, on long- or short-term loan, to students interested in studying period music.

Historic Instruments

Old instruments which depending on the suitability of instrument and player, are sometimes borrowed from the Collection. If the borrower has demonstrated a genuine interest and commitment to working with the Bate, a programme is arranged that involves the musician coming into the Bate over an extended period to handle as wide a selection of the type of instrument as possible. This gives the musician the opportunity to decide which musical period, and which instrument, they wish to study and ultimately take away on loan. At the same time, it enables the Bate staff to observe and assess the musician's handling technique.

In-House Historic Instruments

Other old instruments which may not be borrowed but may be played under supervision at the Bate (e.g. keyboard instruments). Some instruments are kept in full playing condition but moving them away from the Bate gallery would place an unacceptable strain on their structure and would be likely to cause traumatic damage. Musicians are encouraged to arrange to come and use the instruments and demonstrate their use to others (Figure 13.1).

Other Instruments

Other instruments are made available for casual visitors to play without making special arrangements; for example, a modern copy of an early keyboard instrument and a modern copy of a serpent are available for people to try out simply to hear how they sound. There are also several folk instruments available for children to try out. The gallery attendant supervises and ensures the instruments are not mishandled.

Figure 13.1 Playing a tenor/bass trombone by Boosey & Co dated about 1920.

Some are available for visitors to try, but under slightly higher levels of supervision. These can be used by visiting education groups, or family groups on special opening days, and include modern copies of historical instruments such as crumhorns, cornets, baroque trumpets, and rebecs. Some historical instruments are considered robust enough to be handled and played by non-experts, under supervision, and have been acquired specifically for that purpose. There is also a collection of modern copies of mediaeval and renaissance instruments available for loan for special events. These are playable and may be used under limited supervision by non-specialists. The Bate also owns a Javanese Gamelan Orchestra, housed in a separate building and used by the Oxford Gamelan Society. This is also available to groups booking a workshop or visit.

The mouthpieces of wind instruments are cleaned with disinfectant during use by visiting groups and again after they have departed. Visitors are not expected to wear gloves when handling the objects; however, the instruments are swabbed with white spirit to remove grease and other deposits.

These are broad descriptions of levels of access. Other uses range from instruments displayed in a glass case, allowing viewing and photography by visitors, to objects that may not be played but are available for study, measurement, and analysis by researchers, Then there are different levels of playability, right up to a skilled musician's being allowed to borrow an instrument to play in a concert to a large audience. With this last form of use, the number of people who may benefit is potentially very large, starting with the musician, followed by the rest of the orchestra, and then the audience. Finally, if the concert is recorded or broadcast, thousands of people may hear the instrument. An example occurred in 2006 when an eighteenth-century orchestral hand horn was borrowed by Anneka Scott of the Orchestra of the Age of Enlightenment. She used it in a performance of Handel's *Hercules* in the Sheldonian Theatre, Oxford, to an audience of over 300 people. The performance was recorded and subsequently played on the radio. When the rest of the orchestra heard the instrument for the first time during the final rehearsal, they burst into spontaneous applause.

Decision-Making Protocol

The question of which instruments might be borrowed and by whom was in the hands of the curators during the early period of the Bate's existence. Since then, and following a number of negative experiences, procedures have been tightened so that there is now a solid protocol for deciding which instruments may be borrowed. This was necessary not only for good management but also to make it clear to potential borrowers that there was no favouritism.

Before we can sanction the playing of a historic instrument we must ensure that its entire context has been explored. Its position in the collection and its relationship with similar instruments in other collections must be evaluated. Its state of originality must be assessed and any changes analysed. Finally, the risks of using the instrument must be explored in terms of the materials of fabrication and their condition.

Instrument Categories

Following a survey of the Bate Collection in 1997, Robert Barclay of the Canadian Conservation Institute proposed a set of standard matrices that could be used to categorise instruments and aid decisions about whether they could be played (Barclay 1997).

The first stage is to assign values to the instruments according to three separate criteria: rarity, risk of damage, and state (Table 13.1). In order to assign the appropriate values to each object, it is essential for documentation to be as complete as possible and for categorisation to be determined in an impartial way and reviewed at regular intervals. Assessing risk of damage also relies on experience with handling instruments, as well as knowledge of materials and their degradation.

Table 13.1 Instrument Categories

Rarity	Risk	State
Unique	Highest	Perfect
Rare	High	Excellent
Historic	Medium	Good
Common	Low	Mediocre
Replaceable	Lowest	Poor

The following indicates the types of instrument that might be included in each category.

Rarity

- **Unique**: The only example of its type. An example from a famed maker. Well-documented association with a particular historic event or person.
- **Rare**: One of the few examples of its type. Associated with a particular historic event or person.
- **Historic**: Relatively scarce. Having some documentary value but not associated with a particular historic event or person.
- **Common**: One of many extant. No longer in production.
- **Replaceable**: One of many extant. Still in production.

Risk of Damage

Many of the older historic instruments are made predominantly of organic materials such as wood or ivory and this makes them particularly vulnerable to changes in humidity (e.g. caused by blowing down a woodwind instrument) or to the tensions created by stringing. Instruments are ranked according to risks of damage in the following way.

- **Highest**: The instrument will certainly be damaged by use. Includes ivory, glass, and ebonite wind instruments; stringed instruments with deteriorated structures; instruments made of brass or other metal in which the crystalline microstructure has deteriorated and become embrittled.
- **High**: This category includes most woodwind instruments, especially if they are not played regularly; fragile finishes such as lacquers and varnishes; corroded metals, mechanically unsound structures.
- **Medium**: This includes metal instruments in sound mechanical and chemical condition with movable parts such as slides and valves plus all old wooden instruments.
- **Low**: This encompasses metal instruments in sound mechanical condition with no movable parts; more recent wooden instruments of solid construction.
- **Lowest**: This category comprises recently made instruments in sound condition.

State

This category is a measure of the information value of playing a historic instrument. It is a combination of two independent features—physical condition and degree of replacement. It would be quite legitimate to designate an instrument as 'poor' even if it is in good working condition but contains many replacement parts. Thus, an instrument that has been repeatedly restored to working condition and has a long tradition of use will score low.

- **Perfect**: No traces of use. No damages. No repairs. All components in place. All parts original.
- **Excellent**: No damages. No repairs. All components in place. All parts original. Obviously used but well maintained.
- **Good**: Obviously used and with traces of repair and maintenance. Some parts not original but consistent with earlier state.
- **Mediocre**: Essentially fulfilling its function but with evidence of heavy use. Significant number of replaced parts.
- **Poor**: Functioning but in bad condition. The lowest playable state. Many parts replaced including those that contribute to sound production.

The Matrices

The first matrix plots the values for rarity against risk of damage and is shown in Table 13.2.

Table 13.2 Matrix 1

Risk	Highest	High	Medium	Low	Lowest
Rarity					
Unique	1	2	3	4	5
Rare	2	3	4	5	6
Historical	3	4	5	6	7
Common	4	5	6	7	8

Once the value for Risk/Rarity is identified from this first matrix it is then compared with the object's Condition using the second matrix shown in Table 13.3.

Table 13.3 Matrix 2

Condition	Perfect	Excellent	Good	Mediocre	Poor
Risk/Rarity					
1	1	2	3	4	5
2	2	3	4	5	6
3	3	4	5	6	7
4	4	5	6	7	8
5	5	6	7	8	9
6	6	7	8	9	10
7	7	8	9	10	11
8	8	9	10	11	12
9	9	10	11	12	13

Key to Scores

The score derived from comparing the two matrices provides a key to the amount of use an instrument can sustain. The scores and their effects are as follows:

1. There are no circumstances under which the instrument should be played or used.
2. The instrument may be played or used only under exceptional circumstances, for a limited time, only under close supervision, and after expert assessment of its condition and the information likely to be gained from its use. The player/user must be able to demonstrate familiarity with the instrument. A high-quality recording should be made of the session.
3. The instrument may be played or used only under exceptional circumstances but for a longer duration than under 2, under supervision, and after expert assessment of its condition and the information to be gained from its use. The player must demonstrate familiarity with the instrument. A high-quality recording should be made.
4. The instrument may be played or used more frequently than under 3, under supervision, although duration should still be

limited. Such limitation to be decided on an individual basis and relying on accurate and complete documentation of condition before and after use.

5. The instrument may be demonstrated or used more frequently, and with sessions of longer duration. Familiarity with the instrument is still necessary.

6. The requirements above may be relaxed slightly. Expert assessment of the information to be gained through function is still desirable but not essential.

7. The instrument can be demonstrated or used frequently, and for fairly extended periods. There is less need to establish the value of information gained.

8. Regular demonstration and use of the instrument can be maintained, although it should still be played under supervision. Players should still be required to demonstrate expertise on the type of instrument.

9. As for 8, but use need not be supervised.

10. Unsupervised use is the norm, although regular monitoring is still required.

11. The user does not need to be an expert in the instrument, but must demonstrate a familiarity with historic material.

12. The instrument may be used unsupervised by museum visitors unfamiliar with its capabilities.

13. Objects with this score tend to be useful for interactive purposes, and are essentially disposable. They cannot be considered as heritage material. (Barclay 1997)

Categorisation according to these matrices is not the only factor used in reaching a decision; there is a continual process of assessment as further information about the history of an object and its material condition become available. It is also necessary to balance the score with other policy factors; so, for example, it may be decided that certain instruments may not be taken from the Bate on extended loan regardless of the score.

Conditions of Loan

The conditions of loan for the Bate Collection were drawn up by La Rue in 1996. These conditions might apply, in modified form, to any kind of museum object. The current conditions are:

1. To care for the instrument with as much attention as though it were your own;

2. Not to lend, nor allow the instrument to be played by anyone else;

3. Not to leave the instrument unattended;
4. To return the instrument on the agreed date and time to the Bate Collection;
5. Not to give the instrument to a third party for return to the Bate Collection;
6. Not to carry out or have carried out any repairs of any nature: especially not to replace nor disturb any pads or lappings nor to stick Bluetack [adhesive putty] or Sellotape [adhesive tape] on any part of the instrument;
7. Not to take the instrument out of the United Kingdom mainland without first informing the Bate Collection and subsequently arranging for the instrument to be insured to our specifications;
8. Where the instrument is being played in an Oxford University orchestra (or equivalent), to provide the Bate Collection with 1 or 2 tickets for the performance.

The person who will be playing the instrument *must* be the person who collects it and signs the required form. They *must* also be the person who returns the instrument at the end of the loan period. We assume that the person signing the form has accepted complete liability for its care.

Persons wishing to borrow instruments from the collection are required to provide a letter of reference from a senior member of the university. They are also required to provide a deposit in the form of a cheque for £100 and to pay an administrative fee (La Rue 1996).

These conditions were originally framed to apply to the loan of modern instruments for orchestral use. However, it was found that, with small amendments, they applied equally well to all types of loan. The conditions are explained to each person borrowing instruments, and the underlying reasons for the conditions are also explained so that there can be no doubt about the implications. Borrowers are told that if they breach any of the conditions they will forfeit the deposit and will not be allowed to borrow instruments in the future. Additionally, students of the university are reported to their senior tutor for possible disciplinary action. It is hoped that these sanctions will prevent negligent use of the collection.

Preparation for Loan

Some of the instruments in the collection are of robust construction and are in good enough condition that they may be taken out on loan without any special preparation. However, some of the woodwind instruments may not have been used for some time and need gradual 'warming-up' to increase the moisture content of the microstructure of the wood. The fear is that playing the instruments for any length of time will introduce moisture to the structure too quickly, causing traumatic damage at a microstructural level that results in splits and cracks in the wood. To avoid this, a programme of acclimatisation is developed during which the instrument is warmed up gradually until it is considered that the threat of damage is reduced to a low level. This involves requiring the musician to come to the Bate every day. First they hold the instrument against the body to warm it up and then blow warm, moist air into it for a period of about five minutes. This is repeated every day for a period of up to two months, with the time of warming and blowing increasing up to about fifteen minutes. The musician may then be allowed to take the instrument away.

This procedure serves three purposes. First, it prepares the instrument so that the risk of damage is reduced. Second, it allows the museum staff an opportunity to observe how the potential borrower handles the instrument, and last, it prepares the borrower and impresses on them the fact that they are engaging with a historical object that requires special handling and attention. Again, it is hoped that this will prevent negligent handling.

Repairs, Restoration and Conservation

When instruments in the collection become damaged through negligence or fair wear and tear, decisions have to be made about their future use. Some can be sent to specialist repairers and brought back into use as playing instruments (particularly the instruments currently available for orchestral use). Others may not be treated so easily; for example, a historical recorder on which the ivory beak has become split may not be repaired, as this would require replacement of the original historical part. In this case the instrument would be removed from the category of playable instruments to the category of unplayable instruments because to continue playing it would certainly propagate the damage. While the instrument would have lost use as a playing instrument it would still maintain its value as a rare or historical instrument and the technical information it contains will still be extant. Even the worst-damaged instruments contain elements of historical or technical information that give them value to researchers as 'informative wrecks'.

For all instruments, a programme of care exists in line with main-stream museum policy. Environmental conditions are monitored and maintained at acceptable levels for mixed organic objects. Any new acquisitions are examined for possible deterioration and a rolling pro-gramme of inspections aims to identify possible threats; for example, there are annual bug hunts to identify any signs of insect infestation.

All of these measures would be familiar to conservators responsible for a collection that maintained those levels of access within a mainstream museum. However, there is an additional requirement to gauge whether objects may be classed as playable or unplayable; this requires a breadth of specialist knowledge that may not be within the scope of any one individual. Thus, it can be necessary to seek technical expertise from specialist consultants and other sources.

Feedback

There are several ways, both formal and informal, in which information and experiences can be reported back to the Bate. Casual visitors occasionally send a thank-you letter, which is kept on file. The leaders of visiting school groups are asked to complete a feedback form and their observations are used to improve the education programme. Researchers who examine and measure instruments are required to provide full copies of their reports and diagrams, and these are made available to other researchers and musical instrument makers. Students who have used modern instruments are asked to report if any repairs are necessary.

Musicians who have borrowed historical instruments are involved in a much more profound process, and the feedback starts when they first come in to select a suitable instrument. Using standard forms, records are kept of the amount of use the instrument receives along with observations about its playability, tonal qualities, and other subtler musical qualities. This is a difficult process because some researchers may have already read texts on this type of instrument and their opinions may be influenced by the observations of other researchers; therefore, the forms are regularly reviewed in order to avoid 'leading' the musician. This feedback continues throughout the loan period. At some point, when the musician feels comfortable with the instrument and has had a chance to make some objective observations, they are asked to give a public presentation on the subject that includes a musical recital. Some researchers use this as an opportunity to express their own observations about the differences between the historical instruments and their modern copies.

Historical instruments are not always recorded in use; this is done only when the player has had a chance to become familiar with the playing qualities of the instrument. Very occasionally, borrowers use the instruments to make commercial recordings.

Here are some examples of feedback from some users of the collection:

Thank you very much for showing us around your collection of instruments. You have improved our knowledge immensely and made it a very enjoyable experience. We enjoyed playing the instruments and discovering more about the history of them. Our favourite instruments were the spinet, also the serpent, and not forgetting the steel drum. (Leckford Place School, December 2006)

The timbre of these instruments is unforgettable. This experience has definitely enhanced my style and knowledge as a performer. (Rachel Hatton, Royal Academy of Music, March 2007)

The opportunity to play these instruments is of vital importance to anybody involved in early music. By bringing students here again and again it is an essential opportunity to be in touch with the objects of their study. (Professor Peter Holtslag, March 2007)

Often the information gained from playing the instruments is intensely personal and cannot be expressed easily in words or diagrams; for example, the way, when playing a historical recorder, the instrument seems to 'blow back far harder than the modern copy'. These observations may mean little to non-specialist museum staff but may describe subtle playing qualities of the instruments, and this kind of information finds its way into academic journals and articles in other publications. A document file is maintained for each instrument that has been studied so that reports from different researchers can be compared.

Conclusion

The difficulties associated with maintaining a collection of objects with extended public access should not be underestimated. The risks and costs may be considered too high to be acceptable in a public collection. It requires an extensive commitment of time on the part of the museum staff and an element of moral courage when dealing with 'specialists in the field'. However, the benefits of extended access also should not be underestimated. There is still a need to provide first-hand source material and information to researchers and musicians. The Bate can provide this in a controlled way under supervision of specialist staff. This ensures that the information gained, no matter how obscure or intangible, is recorded, and that the technical information and the instruments continue as far as possible in an uncompromised form for the use of future researchers.

References

Arnold-Foster, K., La Rue, H. 1993. *Museums of Music: A review of Musical Collections in the United Kingdom*. London: HMSO, in Association with the Museums and Galleries Commission.

Barclay, R. 1997. *Recommendations for the Bate Collection*. Unpublished report, Canadian Conservation Institute.

Barclay, R. 2004. *Preservation and Use of Historic Musical Instruments: Display Case or Concert Hall?* London: Earthscan Publications.

CIMCIM. 1985. *Recommendations for Regulating the Access to Musical Instruments in Public Collections*. CIMCIM: The International Committee for Musical Instrument Collections of the International Council of Museums. [http://www.music.ed.ac.uk/euchmi/cimcim/irt/irte.html] (Accessed 10.01.06)

La Rue, H. 1996. Conditions of loan. In *Conditions for the Use of Instruments on Loan from the Bate Collection*. Unpublished, University of Oxford.

Montagu, J. 2000. Philip Argal Turner Bate, 1909–1999. *Galpin Society Journal* LII:6–8.

Odell, J., Karp, C. 1997. Ethics and the use of instruments. In R.L. Barclay (ed.), *The Care of Historic Musical Instruments*. Edinburgh: Museums and Galleries Commission, Canadian Conservation Institute and the Museums and Galleries Commission; The International Committee for Musical Instrument Collections of the International Council of Museums, 1–7.

14

COLLABORATIVE TOUCH: WORKING WITH A COMMUNITY ARTIST TO RESTORE A KWAKWAKA'WAKW MASK

Jessica Johnson

Introduction

This chapter reviews the philosophy of the Smithsonian's National Museum of the American Indian (NMAI), Washington, D.C., then explores a case study that illustrates how this philosophy is used to guide conservation treatment. The philosophy at NMAI is to allow maximum access to the collections by the descendants of the Native American communities from which the objects originally came. In practice, this attitude is expressed by consulting community representatives about the care and interpretation of the collections, allowing objects to be handled and used in ceremony (also involving touching and handling), and returning objects to the communities on long-term loan.

The mission of the NMAI reflects this consultation approach:

The National Museum of the American Indian is committed to advancing knowledge and understanding of the Native cultures of the Western Hemisphere—past, present, and future—through partnership with Native peoples and others. The Museum works to support the continuance of culture, traditional values, and transitions in contemporary Native life. (NMAI 2005)

This approach represents a fundamental and conscious reversal of the traditional museum practice, which allowed only the professionals to touch and handle the collections, leaving visitors to view them at a distance.

Access to Objects in the NMAI

Finding ways to give Native people physical access to our collections has been part of the ethos of the museum since the beginning. The Cultural Resources Center (CRC), which opened in 1989 outside of Washington, D.C., in Suitland, Maryland, was designed to welcome Native communities and show respect to the material culture housed within. The building reflects:

> . . . Native American cultural and design principles. The design inspires respect for the collections the building holds and the cultures it represents, and at the same time, it creates a welcoming atmosphere. The CRC's design also represents a Native approach to architecture and landscape that emphasizes a connection to the environment. Carefully placed windows and skylights introduce natural light, and many elements of the building, beginning with the east-facing entry, are oriented toward one of the four cardinal directions. . . . The building also includes indoor and outdoor spaces where Native visitors may use objects in the collection for traditional ceremonies. (NMAI 2007, paragraph 2)

Conservation and collections management staff use the layout of the building to continue this approach in the physical and day-to-day workings of the museum. For example, storage spaces are arranged geographically and by community. Ethnographic items collected from communities who live in the north of the continent are located in the north end of the collections storage. Items stored in the central area are from the United States, and the south end contains items from Mexico. Other levels are arranged similarly.

Workrooms set aside as flexible spaces allow groups of items to be taken from the stored collections and placed in a private workspace during consultations and other visits from communities. This privacy is intended to help make visitors feel more comfortable and to foster relationships as items are handled, examined, and discussed. Often during visits for conservation consultations (and at many other times), community members carry out a ceremony in which staff are invited to participate.

Handling by Visitors

The basic attitude towards access is that these items belong to the source and descendent communities and NMAI is just the steward of the collections—that it would be inappropriate to limit intimate contact by the descendents of the makers. The NMAI presents an official handling-guidelines document to all researchers who want to use the collection, though it is not used for groups who visit as part of a guided tour. This document includes a warning about what is known about pesticide contamination of the collection (many collections of this kind were routinely treated with pesticides in the last century). Because most items have an individual storage mount, objects can be picked up for closer examination without being physically touched. Individuals are asked to wear gloves if they want to touch an item; however, collections staff who are working directly with the individuals do facilitate more intimate contact if it is appropriate. There is no prescribed standard approach, and all staff find ways to facilitate access to the objects while still ensuring long-term preservation. Damage happens only rarely during these visits (it is much more common during more typical museum practices such as packing, shipping, mount making, and exhibit installation) and if it occurs it is documented in a standard manner.

Access and Handling during the Conservation Process

The NMAI conservation department also uses community consultation to develop approaches to treatment. Projects that include consultation as part of the process are some of the most satisfying parts of our work. Over the years, a number of projects have been carried out where community members handle the objects and carry out repairs and refurbishment of items alongside the conservators at the NMAI (Johnson et al. 2006). The consultation process affirms that Native people are important contributors to the care and conservation of the collections.

Listening to Our Ancestors

The exhibit 'Listening to Our Ancestors: The Art of Native Life along the North Pacific Coast' opened at the Smithsonian Institution's National Museum of the American Indian Mall Museum, Washington, D.C., in the fall of 2006 (NMAI 2005). Items from eleven indigenous communities who live along the northern Pacific Coast of the United States and Canada were selected by community representatives to tell a story about each community. Consultation and the development of long-term relationships with Native communities is a priority of the Museum and guides the way work is carried out. The practicalities of consultation are always evolving and expanding (Pepper Henry 2004, 106).

As part of the process of preparing for the 'Listening to Our Ancestors' exhibit, two members of the Kwakwaka'wakw community,

Barb Cranmer and William Wasden, came to the NMAI Cultural Resources Center to advise NMAI conservators on how the items should look when they went on display. Barb Cranmer had previously selected the items for the exhibit from the NMAI collections, with advice from other community members. During the conservation consultation, all the items that had been selected were laid out on tables and available for review and handling. Objects were often picked up to show how they worked or how they were used in the community. Participants often handled the objects to show how they should be positioned while on display.

One of the items selected by representatives of the Kwakwaka'wakw community was a large (approximately 1 x 2 m) mask of 'Namxxelagayu', attributed to Charlie James or Chief Mungo Martin and created ca. 1910. The mask represents the Kwakwaka'wakw first ancestor riding on the back of a sea monster. The mask is made of painted fabric stretched over a wooden frame and nailed into place. A large painted wooden head and a hinged tail are attached at opposite ends of the frame. A cord runs along the top of the spine and would be used to make the tail move up and down when the mask is danced. Some time after the item was collected by the Museum of the American Indian, Heye Foundation (the precursor to the Smithsonian's National Museum of the American Indian), the first ancestor figure was lost from the back of the mask.

Kevin Cranmer was identified by Barb Cranmer as an artist who would have the knowledge and experience to make a replacement ancestor figure. Kevin Cranmer is a working artist who lives in Victoria, British Columbia, Canada. He gained experience while working with renowned masters such as the Kwakwaka'wakw artist Tony Hunt Sr. and Nuu-Chah-Nulth artist Tim Paul. He has been initiated as a Hamatsa, the most important of the complex dance societies of the Kwakwaka'wakw, and his grandfather had owned the mask.

According to Kevin Cranmer, 'There are many legends amongst our people of sea monsters, but this mask is a specific sea monster, "Namxxelagiyu". The sea monster "Namxxelagiyu" is an ancestor of the Namgis tribe.' The legend of this mask was described in detail by Kevin's aunt, Gloria Cranmer, for the catalogue *Chiefly Feasts* (Jonaitis 2001).

Conserving the Mask

Kevin Cranmer was contracted by the museum to carve a replacement figure and travel to the NMAI Cultural Resources Center (CRC), which houses the NMAI collections and conservation laboratories, to work with NMAI conservators to replace the figure on the mask.

In order to make the replacement figure, Kevin Cranmer was provided with a historic photograph that showed the old ancestor figure in place on the mask, and photographs of the current condition of the mask, as well as measurements of the gap on the object where the new piece would fit. Based on this information, he created a new figure. He carved the replacement figure from yellow cedar and painted it with latex house paint, materials he chose and that he uses for his own art.

The original object had collected grime and dust over its years of storage in the museum and had several small areas of aesthetically ir- ritating damage. Fabric wrapped around a wooden frame to create the body of the sea monster had torn and come loose from its attach- ment. There was a small loss in one of the pointed appendages attached to the face of the figure and a large chip out of one ear. Before Kevin Cranmer arrived, conservators treated the sea monster portion of the mask to improve the aesthetics and stabilise a fragile portion of the mask. This part of the treatment was developed through earlier discussions with Barb Cranmer and William Wasden during the con- servation consultation.

Attaching the new figure to the old part of the mask was not straight- forward. Once he arrived at the CRC, Kevin Cranmer worked closely with conservators for two days to develop a method to attach the replacement figure and to adjust the surface colour and texture of the figure to more closely match the older sea monster. Working in partner- ship, the artist and the conservators touched and handled the object as necessary (Figure 14.1). Everyone working on the project, including the artist, had the same access, and gloves were not worn during the treatment process.

Working together, the conservators and the artist came up with a strategy for attaching the new figure. The area on the sea monster's spine where the original figure was located still had nails protruding, probably from the attachment of the original figure. In the end it was decided that these nails would be trimmed. The new figure was then attached by drilling holes in the spine of the original piece and the bot- tom of the new figure, and inserting wooden dowels to connect the two. The dowels were held in place with a stable adhesive. The colour of the new piece was adjusted with paint and sanding to more closely match the older part of the mask (Figure 14.2). All steps in the process were carefully recorded using written and photographic documentation.

During the writing of this paper, Kevin Cranmer was asked to com- ment on what the experience meant to him. To paraphrase what he shared, 'I enjoyed seeing the piece that had been put away and neg- lected for so long brought back to something close to its original state. Now the mask has a purpose again, to educate people about who we

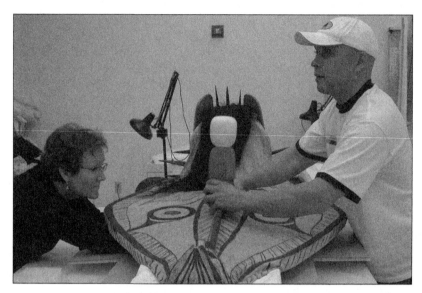

Figure 14.1 Artist Kevin Cranmer (Kwakwa̱ka'wakw) and conservator Kim Cobb assessing how to attach the newly created ancestor figure to the original mask. (Courtesy of Conservation Department National Museum of the American Indian, Smithsonian Institution)

Figure 14.2 Kevin Cranmer adjusting the surface finish of the new figure so that it will be more aesthetically integrated with the older, original mask. (Courtesy of Conservation Department National Museum of the American Indian, Smithsonian Institution)

are and where we come from'. He said he was honoured, knowing that the mask had belonged to his grandfather, to be chosen to make the little figure. Kevin also noted that it was an honour for him and others from the Kwakwaka'wakw tribe to attend the opening of the exhibit and perform, so that the piece on display, which had always been used in ceremonies, could hear the songs again.

'Listening to Our Ancestors' closed in Washington in January 2007. It is being exhibited at the NMAI George Gustave Heye Center in New York City from August 2007 to May 2008. After that, the exhibit will be separated into its eleven component community sections, and many of the items will travel back to the North Pacific Coast to be put on display, where they may be used in ceremonies by the communities who are descendents of the original creators. The items are being lent to the communities through NMAI's regular loan procedures and will return to the NMAI at the end of the loan period.

The refurbished 'Namxxelagayu' mask (Figure 14.3) will travel back to the U'mista Cultural Center in Alert Bay, British Columbia, Canada. The mandate of the U'mista Cultural Center is to ensure the survival of all aspects of the cultural heritage of the Kwakwaka'wakw (U'mista Cultural Center 2007). The way it will be displayed and used by the community while it is in Alert Bay is currently being planned.

Figure 14.3 The Kwakwaka'wakw 'Namxxelagayu' mask after conservation. (Courtesy of National Museum of the American Indian, Smithsonian Institution)

It was a great joy and pleasure to work with Kevin Cranmer. He gave generously of his time, his knowledge and his great sense of humour during the course of this project, and is continuing his support of NMAI's conservation department as we present our reflections on the experience to our professional colleagues.

Note

Thanks to Barb Cranmer, William Wasden, and Kevin Cranmer for participating in the project and sharing their knowledge. Many NMAI conservators and students worked on this project, including Lauren Chang (the first conservation liaison for the exhibit), Marian Kaminitz (head of conservation, NMAI), Anne Murray, Kim Cobb, Megan Emery, Elizabeth Nunan, Steve Tamayo (Lakota), and Renata Peters.

References

Johnson, J.S., Heald, S., McHugh, K., Brown, E., Kaminitz, M. 2005. Practical aspects of consultation with communities. *Journal of the American Institute for Conservation* 44(3): 203–15.

Jonaitis, A. (ed.). 2001. *Chiefly Feasts: The Enduring Kwakiutl Potlatch.* Seattle: University of Washington Press.

NMAI (National Museum of the American Indian) 2005a. *Listening to Our Ancestors: The Art of Native Life Along the North Pacific Coast.* Washington D.C.,: The National Geographic Society.

NMAI (National Museum of the American Indian) 2005b. *Strategic Plan for the Period Fiscal Year 2006–Fiscal Year 2008.* Unpublished internal document.

NMAI (National Museum of the American Indian) 2007. Cultural Resources Center (CRC) Frequently Asked Questions: How Was the Museum Designed? [http://www.nmai.si.edu/subpage.cfm?subpage=visitor&second=md&third=cfaqs#three] (Accessed 18.04.07)

Pepper Henry, J. 2004. Challenges in managing culturally sensitive collections at the National Museum of the American Indian. In L.E. Sullivan and A. Edwards (eds.), *Stewards of the Sacred.* Washington D.C.,: American Association of Museums in cooperation with the Center for the Study of World Religions, Harvard University, 105–12.

U'mista Cultural Society. 2007. *About Us: The U'mista Cultural Center.* [http://www.umista.org/home/index.php] (Accessed 26.04.07)

15

TOUCHING GHOSTS: HAPTIC TECHNOLOGIES IN MUSEUMS

David Prytherch and Marie Jefsioutine

Introduction

New technology is becoming increasingly commonplace in public institutions, and the use of additional sensory experiences, including touch communicated through simulations, is developing rapidly. Techniques from the area of virtual reality (VR) that provide force feedback through hand-held devices, are becoming small and cheap enough to be incorporated into museum exhibitions. What remains unexplored is whether these techniques can add value to visitor experiences.

The development of technology itself often depends on a 'suck it and see' approach, where playing with applications stimulates an appetite and generates ideas for innovation. Other motivations may be market-led, in that visibly keeping up with the state of the art in displays helps woo visitors in search of the 'wow factor'. A more sustainable, and perhaps more ethical, approach involves careful consideration of the value of such technology to the visitor. Arguably, such a consideration begins with a reflection on the purposes of museums and the nature of the visitor experience. An analysis of the technology can then address the question of whether it can support or enhance the museum experience.

Museums and Haptic Experiences

Holden and Jones (2006) argue that museums have shifted from a passive repository role to one of creating cultural value, empowering individuals, and stimulating creativity and fresh interpretations of the world.

As well as being accountable at the social and economic level, museums need to offer personal value to individuals if they are to maintain visitor numbers. In Britain in 2005–2006, 43% of the adult population visited a museum or gallery (Department of Culture, Media, and Sport 2006). The most commonly cited reasons for visits were general interest in the subject of the museum/collection and to see a particular display or exhibition. Underlying motives may include seeking escapism and contemplation, stimulating creativity, aesthetic pleasure, awe and wonder, a sense of personal relevance, cultural identity, and nostalgia (Morris Hargraves McIntyre 2003).

Sensory Interactions with Objects

Sensory interaction with objects in the museum has traditionally been visual (Hetherington 2002). The prevailing policy in museums is 'hands off', for which there are many good reasons, such as the fragility of exhibits and their subsequent degradation as a result of inexpert handling. Candlin (2004, and Chapter 5 in this volume) argues that the prohibition of touch for museum visitors is more than a pragmatic concern for conservation and has roots in status and a belief that true aesthetic appreciation transcends the haptic senses.

> Sight is privileged to the extent that, despite the various sensory attributes of art objects, they become synonymous with the visual, and curators work within a paradigm where touch is not only an antithesis, but is quite literally repellent to the conjecture of vision, aesthetics, and knowledge. (Candlin 2004, 84)

Hetherington (2002) argues that to acknowledge the haptic experience as being a legitimate and fundamental part of the museum experience would threaten the very idea of the museum itself.

> It is the Otherness of touch that poses that threat. Not just a threat to the object but to the idea of the museum itself and the kind of scopic regime it helps to constitute. (Hetherington 2002, 202)

Increasingly, however, museums are under pressure to provide tactile access to visitors (Candlin 2004). Whilst this pressure comes largely from directives to meet the needs of visually impaired or blind visitors, there is evidence that haptic experience is an important, if neglected, aspect of understanding objects for everyone. The meaning of an object relies on a complex network of mediation (Hooper-Greenhill 1999), although very little is known about how people interact with artefacts (vom Lehn et al. 2001a, 2001b). Sonneveld (2004) observes that tactile information can convey attributes of an object, such as its personality and quality, and that the tactile experience is strongly individual. Jonas (1982) claims that touch is the only sense to bring an experience of reality of an object, evidenced by the perception of resistance and impact, and states that 'Through the kinaesthetic accompaniment of voluntary motion the whole perception is raised to a higher order: the touch qualities become arranged in a spatial scheme, they fall into the pattern of surface, and become elements of form' (Jonas 1982, 141).

Davidson et al. (1999) argue that given the option to explore tactile aspects of objects, museum visitors favour this interaction. Tests of children's attitudes towards computer displays with associated tactile experiences in a museum environment have shown that they 'found it very engaging' (Brewster 2005, 279) and considered it contributed significantly to their visit. In this situation, the virtual display was positioned close to an exhibit of Egyptian hieroglyphics that could not be touched and 'the children really wanted to know what the hieroglyphics felt like and the virtual exhibit allowed them to find out' (Brewster 2005, 279).

In addition, Davidson et al. (1999) found that designing exhibits for sensory impaired visitors by increasing opportunities for multisensory interaction, particularly touch, improved enjoyment of learning for all visitors. During handling sessions, Ciolfi and Bannon (2002) observed that visitors derived great pleasure from exploring surfaces and materials, feeling weight, looking at hidden surfaces, and feeling inside cavities. Handling the objects stimulated social interaction and discussion, and there was a high degree of excitement about handling 'real' artefacts.

The Role of Touch in Learning

The nature and impact of learning in museums is considered under-researched (Hooper-Greenhill 2004) and appears to be influenced by many different factors. For example, adult learning in museums seems to focus on sociocultural aspects, while children's learning tends to be concrete, devoted to recognising the size, shape, and peculiar features of objects (Falk & Dierking 1992).

The importance of multisensory involvement in learning is extensively documented (Piaget 1952; Falk & Dierking 1992; Davidson et al. 1999; Ward & Holtham 2000). Kolb (1984) suggests a model of four distinct learning preference styles, and a four-stage cycle of learning, in which touch and active examination play a fundamental role (Smith & Kolb 1986; Mainemelis et al. 2002).

The value of handling objects to enhance learning has long been recognised by museums (Caulton 1998). The use of museum artefacts in schools and small museums was common in the nineteenth century (Hooper-Greenhill 1992), although this approach was superseded by a shift in focus from objects to subjects or themes (Butler 1992). The role of touch is now becoming more popular through interactive exhibits, particularly in science and technology museums (Caulton 1998) and this is often justified in terms of learning theory and constructivist learning approaches. Davies (1994) found that the ability to interact with exhibits was identified as one of the key factors that encouraged people to visit museums.

Museums and Haptic Technology

The deployment of haptic interfaces to digital objects in museums offers the potential to transform our relationships with museums and their collections. Haptic interfaces may be any hardware computer-interface device capable of providing the illusion of touch feedback in relation to a digital 3D object. Such devices can be used to consolidate the experiences gained from other senses and help to create a more lasting impression of an artefact. They may contribute on a number of levels: attracting attention, stimulating interest in those with a kinaesthetic learning style or prior interest, providing the opportunity for haptic involvement; and by challenge and skill development. The devices have a range of uses; for example, researchers accessing fragile objects, visitors seeing and feeling virtual objects located at other institutions, museums exhibiting artefacts in storage, and visually impaired people being enabled to touch exhibits.

In this context, 'haptics' includes a range of related perceptions:
- Proprioception: sensing of body parts in relation to each other
- Vestibular: sensing the motion of the head
- Kinaesthetic: relating to body motion
- Cutaneous: sense through the skin
- Tactile: pressure sense through the skin
- Force feedback: Mechanical reproduction of information sensed by the human kinaesthetic system.
(adapted from Brewster 2005, 274).

Seeking new ways to attract and communicate with museum visitors is securely on the cultural and political agenda both nationally and internationally (Hooper-Greenhill, 1994). Opportunities offered by new technology have been outlined in the European Union Information

Society Technologies (IST) research programme, DigiCult, which proposed that 'future developments should also lead to a more immersive experience....' and '"Haptics" play a major role in this' (Geser & Pereira 2004, 30). The report also expresses a desire for 'more intuitive user interfaces that render to the user the notion of "what the source knows"' (Geser & Pereira 2004, 38).

Increasing varieties of technologies address the complex problems of haptic simulation, and many are now commercially available; there are several useful taxonomic classifications and reviews of computational approaches and design issues (Srinivasani & Bastogani 1997; Kirkpatrick & Douglas 2002; Benali-Khoudja et al. 2004). Unfortunately, the complexities of haptic perception mean it is difficult to envisage a single solution appropriate in all circumstances. Aspirations for high fidelity inevitably result in high cost, and more affordable solutions suffer from low resolution. Most available devices are based on 'force feedback' systems that address the perception of form and shape. Less common are devices that stimulate tactile responses concerning texture and material surface properties, and it seems that the only commercially available device capable of addressing both of these distinct but closely related sensory systems is the 'Cyber-touch, Cyber-grasp' family of interfaces from Immersion Corporation (http://www.immersion.com/3d/). Unfortunately, the high prices of these devices make them an unrealistic proposition for publicly funded museums and galleries. Important investment decisions are likely to be influenced by accountability, requiring evidence that the implementation of such systems would generate additional income to offset initial investment, as well as demanding rigorous concept testing and proof of application usability, usefulness, and robustness.

Investing in the latest group of technologies may prove particularly problematic for smaller institutions due to the cost of infrastructure. Geser and Pereira (2004, 73) express 'the expectation that, over the next six years, only the large cultural heritage "players" will adopt the latest group of technologies.' Further complications include selecting a specification and development environment, creating an appropriate technological infrastructure, and assessing the impacts on staffing and museum policy, security, maintenance, and hygiene. Economic viability will depend on large numbers of visitors using such installed technology (Donnelly et al. 2004). For smaller institutions, there is a pressing need to find ways of attracting more and younger visitors, to which the introduction of appropriate technology might contribute. Yet these are the very institutions that are worst-placed to adopt complex and expensive technologies. Within this growing and culturally significant sector, the development of pragmatic, low-cost systems and applications would create a foothold for the increasing adoption of haptic technologies. There is a range of emergent technologies that may be deployed that are collectively known as virtual reality (VR) systems. These could include aspects of telepresence (where the physical object can be sensed and experienced remotely) and haptic systems that employ 'force feedback' and related technology. It is timely to review some of the technical options available, how they are currently put to use, and the balance of problems, pitfalls, and cost issues against potential benefits involved in their adoption.

Requirement for a Three-Dimensional Virtual Model

The introduction of haptic technology into museums presupposes the satisfactory construction of a virtual 3D model, either by direct scanning of an existing object or by software construction, using industry-standard 3D modelling programs such as '3D Studio Max' (www.autodesk.com), 'Rhino' (www.rhino3d.com), or 'Maya' (www.autodesk.com). A number of studies have examined problems of model construction in the context of the virtual re-construction of archaeological sites (Terras 1999; Shiode & Grajetzki 2000; Kim et al. 2003). The role and validity of technology is debatable; for example, Grajetzki et al. (2000, online) question whether 3D constructions are an 'impetus or obstacle to learning' and raise such questions as: 'Is the 3D model in VRML (virtual reality modelling language) format too persuasive? Does it instil a belief in its created object, rather than encourage the learner to look at the evidence? How much effort needs to be devoted to reminding the user that this is just one among many possible pasts, and that reality is never quite as tidy as the VR environment?'

Technology for 3D scanning is now commercially available and is being widely used as a method of 'digital conservation', i.e. a means of limiting access to the real thing. This raises a number of issues, including how the images themselves should be stored, since they must remain usable despite future changes of technology. It has also been found that aspirations to reduce handling of originals may backfire because 'it is often found that digitisation can increase usage of the original by publicising the collection's existence' (TASI 2006).

The National Museums in Liverpool have adopted 3D scanning as an effective way of assisting conservation, and offer a bureau service to other institutions via their Conservation Centre (http://www.liverpoolmuseums.org.uk/conservation/). Insight, a British Museum pilot project, has digitised a variety of objects from their collections and used active optical triangulation scanning (one of the most common commercially available methods of laser scanning) successfully to reconstruct a virtual model of one of the largest statues ever built by the ancient Egyptians, a colossus of Rameses II (Cain et al. 2003). The Digital Michelangelo Project (2000) applied similar technologies to digitising Michelangelo's famous statue of David in the Galleria dell' Accademia in Florence (Levoy et al. 2000).

There are few significant examples of research projects bringing haptic display systems into a museum context. The University of Southern California Interactive Art Museum Project based in the Fisher Gallery (McLaughlin et al. 2000) is a well-documented American study that has yet to reach a conclusion. Noteworthy studies have taken place in Japan, though their focus is mainly on the possibility of creating a distributed virtual museum environment (a single virtual environment based in more than one location and linked through a network) (Asano & Ishibashi 2004; Asano et al. 2005). The most significant European example is the Museum of Pure Form, which was designed to enable visitors to several museums to interact with digital models of 3D art forms and sculptures (Bergamasco et al. 2000, 2001; Loscos et al. 2004).

This touring display used two different haptic devices. The first was an exoskeleton device consisting of two sub-systems—an afferent-efferent (input-output) robotic arm worn by the user coupled with another exoskeleton device to exert forces on the index finger and thumb to simulate gripping. The second was a grounded (fixed) desktop device consisting of two robot arms, each with a single thimble mounted on it. These were designed to be used either with a thimble on each hand or both on one hand (generally the thumb and index finger). The aim of these devices was to provide a virtual workspace of sufficient size to allow full, unrestricted arm movement for the users, where the touch feedback would occur wherever the users could physically reach with their arm, making it possible to feel very large virtual objects.

An acknowledged problem with 3D models for haptic rendering is the computational load that models of sufficient detail place on the rendering processor of the computer's visual display. The Museum of Pure Form approached this problem by having two sets of models loaded: models of high resolution for the haptics rendering, and models of reduced complexity that were simplified by bump-mapping techniques for the graphic display, which, in the museum, measured 2 metres wide by 1.5 metres high. The bump-mapping technique used in this instance produced a visual depiction of a texture superimposed on a model of simpler geometry, creating the visual illusion of the more complex object that was being felt via the haptic device. This system allows the haptic and visual displays to be dealt with separately by different processing modules of the computer.

The project was evaluated on the basis of a questionnaire survey of visitors to the exhibition. Some 400 users responded and the overall reaction to the event appears to have been positive, with particular value placed on the instructiveness of the experience (Frisoli et al. 2005). The same authors noted that training or practice considerably improved the discrimination experience of the users of the haptic device. This effect has also been observed by Jansson and Ivas (2000) and Prytherch and Jerrard (2001), and is a fundamental element of the notion of 'craft' and dextrous skill development (Dormer 1994; McCullough 1996; Wolek 1999), which, although related to the *making* of objects rather than their subsequent examination, is considered highly relevant in this context.

Informal observations (Frisoli et al. 2005) indicated that co-location, the mapping of haptic and visual displays in the same physical space, was very important. This realisation is likely to influence future installations and developments. (The concept of co-location is not relevant in the real world, since the object you feel is always in the same place as the object you see; however, with virtual objects, it is perfectly possible to feel an object in a different place from where it is seen. Indeed, many current displays work this way, with the user holding the haptic force feedback 'pen' used to manipulate the object in one space whilst simultaneously watching the interaction on a computer monitor situated a little distance away from the haptic space.) See Figure 15.1.

Other research has demonstrated that the effect of co-location for discrimination of form and manipulation of 3D objects is critical to

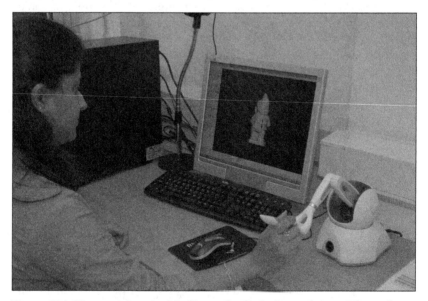

Figure 15.1 Phantom Omni with Claytools 3D design software. Through an industrial-strength 3D CAD system, the carefully thought out haptic implementation reduces project development time and speeds up learning operations.

enhancing the overall effectiveness of the illusion of reality. Shillito et al. (2004, 6) contend that 'the user is presented with an interaction space coherent with their spatial awareness' and tasks that involve 3D rotation result in improved performance (Ware & Rose 1999). Jansson and Öström (2004, 516) also observed that 'Co-location had a significant effect on the Z dimension under Stereo conditions', demonstrating that depth perception of object form was improved. They also noted that performance tasks were 'more difficult in the Not Co-location conditions. This may be still more important for more complex shape perception tasks' (Jansson & Öström 518). Currently, only two companies offer commercially available systems employing co-located displays—Reachin Technologies (http://www.reachin.se/) and SenseGraphics (http://www.sensegraphics.com/), the latter offering open source solutions. See Figure 15.2.

Within the Museum of Pure Form project, aesthetic experiences were not evaluated, though Frisoli et al. (2005) stress the need for this aspect of study in the future. In the context of museum learning, this would seem to be a fundamental, and it would be a desirable aspect of any future studies.

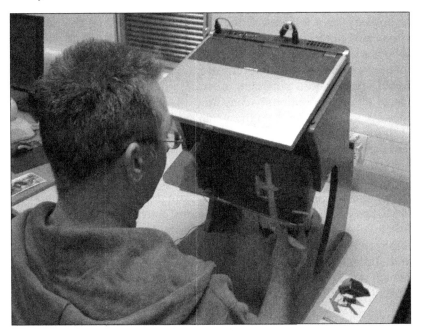

Figure 15.2 SenseGraphics 3D-MIW co-located mobile haptic Immersive Workbench. This places the visual display in the same physical space as the haptic display, perhaps bringing us a step nearer realistic engagement.

Research has shown the value of a stereoscopic 3D display, particularly for processes that involve the manipulation and judgement of 3D objects where a sense of depth, the z axis, is significant. There is evidence that 'subjects estimated depth of 3D objects far more accurately when objects were displayed with binocular disparity than when only monocular cues were provided' (Gaggioli & Breining 2001, 75) and stereopsis has been found to be particularly effective in the placing and positioning of tools during complex 3D manipulations (Davis & Hodges 1994). Experiments conducted by Gaggioli and Breining (2001, 85) also indicated that the use of advanced rendering techniques such as Gouraud shading (a method to simulate effects of light and colour on an object's surface) 'enhanced the user's ability to visualise and mentally manipulate the structure of 3d objects'. Wall et al.(2002) have demonstrated that the combination of haptic feedback and stereoscopic visual display significantly improves the ability of users to navigate and perform tasks.

As long ago as 1992, Lenny Lipton reviewed the possibilities for autostereoscopic (glasses free) displays and affirmed that 'autostereoscopic displays are the holy grail for designers of three-dimensional systems' (Lipton 1992, 156). Recent developments in this type of 3D display technology have introduced the possibility of avoiding the need for specialised (and potentially costly) display accessories such as headsets or shutter glasses (a method of projecting alternate frames of an image to each eye at a high-refresh rate using glass lenses containing liquid crystal and a polarising filter). Within a museum context, the use of these might not only constitute a psychological barrier because they separate the user from the actual environment but also raise other issues such as staffing and technical support, increased unreliability and therefore maintenance costs, security issues of ancillary equipment being lost, damaged, or stolen, and hygiene issues. A 'glasses free' autostereoscopic display would resolve these problems.

The research reviewed in this chapter suggests that haptic technology has the potential to contribute to museums' activities through increased user involvement, stimulation, and sensorimotor learning. The potential implementation of haptic technologies however, has profound financial and strategic implications for museums and a number of questions remain unanswered regarding the viability and validity of introducing currently affordable technology.

Towards a Research Agenda

Research agendas in this field tend to be driven either by the ambitions of technology developers, whose objective appears to be to realise absolute fidelity to our perception of the real world, or by museum managers, who are focused on the impact of new technology on visitor numbers. The nature of experience itself receives less attention (Goulding 2000). The aspirations of museums and their visitors may be better served by a more fundamental approach to the introduction of appropriate haptic technology; thus, our proposed research agenda adopts a pragmatic and user-centred approach.

Consideration of the value of haptic technology to the museum visitor requires examination of the experience as a whole, rather than attention to interface attributes. Hassenzhal and Tractinsky (2006, 95) point out that a user's experience is subjective, situated, complex, and dynamic, and 'is a consequence of a user's internal state…, the characteristics of the designed system…, and the context (or the environment) within which the interaction occurs'.

Jefsioutine and Knight (2006) argue that four qualities central to evaluation are whether a product is usable, accessible, engaging, and beneficial. Their 'experience design framework' suggests a collection of research methods for a multi-dimensional approach to evaluation. Such an approach would seem appropriate to the introduction of haptic technology in the museum, where the visitors' experiences, including learning and aesthetic appreciation, are as important as usability of the interface. Significant questions remain to be answered.

Can Force Feedback Devices Provide a Meaningful Haptic Experience?

An idealised interface might allow the user to interact with a variety of processes and applications through many senses at high resolution, but technological development is far from mature, even with the most advanced equipment currently available. There is the assumption that full-hand haptic gloves are the only type of haptic interface technology appropriate to museums. Current affordable force feedback technology may provide an experience more akin to prodding objects with a pen than touching. How sophisticated must a device be to enrich the visitor experience, and what is the nature of the enrichment? What other benefits may emerge from these devices? Are some artefacts more suited to force feedback devices? What are the aspects of haptics relevant to understanding works of art, e.g. shape, texture, thermal feedback?

How Relevant Is 'Immersion'?

How relevant is 'immersion' (when a user is isolated from external stimuli and fed information from a computer)? Or, is a 'sense of presence' (feeling as if one is in proximity in time or space) or simple 'engagement' (being able to be absorbed in the activity) more important?

In the multidisciplinary domain of VR, definitions of these terms tend to vary and the terms often seem to be interchangeable, which can lead to confusion; however, we would argue that they *are* different and that the differences, whilst perhaps subtle, are highly significant for a clear understanding of how computer-generated simulations might impact on our perceptual systems and of the potential value of such simulations in a museum environment. Donnelly et al. (2004, 247) argue: 'Affordable full-hand haptic gloves are some distance into the future, but it is only through these that a real sense of complete haptic interaction and immersion can be obtained using this type of device.' This seems to assume that complete immersion is a prerequisite for any effective use of the technology. It can certainly be argued that some immersive qualities are desirable because a system should intrude as little as possible between the user and the object being examined, allowing 'transparency' (freedom from the need to think about the technology).

However, there seems to be little real evidence that 'immersion' (which we have suggested is not the same as 'presence') is vital to this effectiveness. Slater et al. (1996, para 1) define the difference between the terms as 'immersion is a description of a technology, whereas presence is concerned with the concomitant behavioural and psychological responses of people', or to put it more simply, 'presence' refers to an internal sensation of the user who is involved with the experience, whilst 'immersion' refers to both the perception of the user and to the nature of the specific technologies used to achieve this impression of reality.

Is Haptic Technology Appropriate for Museums?

Is haptic technology the most appropriate way to address the need for haptic experiences in museums? What is unclear, and worthy of further study, is the role haptics can have in the general experience of museum users. Haptics raise the problem of the often-negative attitudes of museums towards handling artefacts, which may make them question the value of the technology. This, coupled with a tendency to see new technology displays as peripheral and 'dumbing down', may mean there is a danger that haptic interfaces will be treated by curators as trivial and transitory devices. The corollary is that, if touch is regarded as valuable, museums have the capacity to reintroduce the haptic experience with real objects instead of interactive exhibits.

Will Machine Haptics Suffice?

Will machine haptics (mediated haptics) rather than human haptics (direct haptics) suffice? The value of a mediated virtual-touch experience compared to the real experience has yet to be explored and evaluated. Barbara Kirshenblatt-Gimblett has observed that 'digital objects are not so much different from tangible objects, in so far as digital objects are collected, studied, displayed, and interpreted. These operations make digital objects into something new, something different from what they once were, because these operations change our relationship to these digital objects. It is the nature of the knowing and the value we accord objects of all kinds that make them what they are' (Frey & Kirshenblatt-Gimblett 2002, 63).

What Is the Future of Haptics in Museums?

How is this field going to expand? What is the future of haptics in museums? Whilst there can be no absolute certainty of the directions that researchers will follow, it is certain that technological potential will increase. Scientists and engineers are developing solutions to technological problems at an increasing rate, such that we might almost see examples of solutions seeking problems. In the development of haptic technologies, however, we still have much to learn about how our haptic perceptual system operates. Considerable fundamental research remains to be done to measure the sensitivity of our touch perception and how this influences our understanding and experience of the world. As yet, our haptic technologies can simulate only a very small part of our perception. Progress in this area is slow, and current technologies are frequently awkward, inefficient, and expensive. However, having observed the remarkable development of this technology over the last ten years, it seems certain that the next ten years will begin to satisfy many of our current criticisms, and inexpensive devices such as the newly marketed 'Novint Falcon'—advertised as producing forces of 2 pounds [1 kg] within a workspace of 4 × 4 × 4 inches [10 × 10 × 10 cm])—may provide pragmatic and engaging solutions when deployed alongside an actual museum object, though this is currently untested.

As more and more museum collections become digitised and archive management systems become more sophisticated, we can be certain, too, that the addition of haptic properties to visually perceived 3D models will become more widespread. The handling of our cultural objects has always been significant and an important way of learning who we are and where we come from.

Conclusion

Museums are under increasing pressure to find new ways of attracting visitors and to develop new forms of communication and learning experiences. As haptic and associated display technologies improve and become more economically viable, and our understanding of our human perceptual needs expands, haptic displays may become much more prevalent and a fundamental way for museums all over the world to share and display their unique resources.

Research that explores the value of such technology for the museum visitor is needed, both to inform museum strategy and financial planning and to direct the focus of interface development in areas that will enrich visitor experiences.

References

Asano, T., Ishibashi, Y. 2004. Guidance services for a haptic museum in distributed virtual environments. *ICAT '04 Workshop on VR Applications and Entertainment Technology*, 39–42 [http://www.vrsj.org/ic-at/papers/2004/Workshop_2/W2-4.pdf] (Accessed 26.03.07)

Asano, T., Ishibashi, Y., Minezawa, S., Fujimoto, M. 2005. Surveys of exhibition planners and visitors about a distributed haptic museum. *ACM SIGCHI International Conference on Advances in Computer Entertainment Technology*, 246–49.

Benali-Khoudja, M., Hafez, M., Alexandre, J.M., Kheddar, A. 2004. Tactile interfaces: A state-of-the-art survey. *ISR 2004, 35th International Symposium on Robotics*, 721–26.

Bergamasco, M., Avizzano, C.A., Barbagli, F., Frisoli, A. 2000. The museum of pure form: Preliminary considerations. *Proceedings of Photonics East SPIE*, The International Society for Optical Engineering. Boston, 292–99.

Bergamasco, M., Avizzano, C., Di Pietro, G., Barbagli, F., Frisoli, A. 2001. The museum of pure form: system architecture. *Proceedings, Tenth IEEE International Workshop on Robot and Human Interactive Communication*, Bordeaux and Paris, France, 112–17.

Brewster, S.A. 2005. The impact of haptic 'touching' technology on cultural applications. In J. Hemsley, V. Cappellini, and G. Stanke (eds.), *Digital Applications for Cultural Heritage Institutions*. Aldershot, England: Ashgate, 273–84. Available at http://eprints.gla.ac.uk/3280/01/E2VA2001.pdf. (Accessed 30.03.07)

Butler, S. 1992. *Science and Technology Museums*. Leicester: Leicester University Press.

Cain, K., Sobieralski, C., Martinez, P. 2003. Reconstructing a colossus of ramesses ii from laser scan data. *Proceedings of ACM Siggraph, 2003*, San Diego, 1–1.

Candlin, F. 2004. Don't touch! Hands off! Art, blindness and the conservation of expertise. *Body & Society* 10(1): 71–90.

Caulton, T. 1998. *Hands-on Exhibitions: Managing Interactive Museums and Science Centres*. London: Routledge.

Ciolfi, L., Bannon, L. 2002. Observing, analysing, designing: Towards enhanced interactive museum exhibits. In T. Gallwey, T. Waldmann, and L. O'Sullivan (eds.), *Irish Ergonomics Review*. Proceedings, Irish Ergonomics Society Annual Conference, University of Limerick. [http://richie.idc.ul.ie/luigina/PapersPDFs/IES.pdf] (Accessed 26.03.07)

Davidson, B., Heald, C., Hein, G. 1999. Increased exhibit accessibility through multisensory interaction. In E. Hooper-Greenhill (ed.), *The Educational Role of the Museum*, 2nd ed. London: Routledge, 223–38.

Davies, S. 1994. *By Popular Demand: A Strategic Analysis of the Market Potential for Museums and Galleries in the UK*. London: Museums and Galleries Commission, 76–80 [cited in Caulton 1998, 11].

Davis, E.T., Hodges, L.F. 1994. Human stereopsis, fusion, and stereoscopic virtual environment. In W. Barfield and T. Furness (eds.), *Virtual Environments and Advanced Interface Design*. Oxford and New York: Oxford University Press, 145–74.

Department of Culture, Media, and Sport. 2006. *Taking Part: the National Survey of Culture, Leisure and Sport—Provisional Results from the First Nine Months of the 2005/2006 Survey*. London: DCMS Release, 2. [http://www.culture.gov.uk/global/research/taking_part_survey/survey_ouputs.htm] (Accessed 17.05.06)

Donnelly, M., Dobreva, M., Ross, S. 2004. *DigiCULT Technology Watch Briefing 13: Telepresence, Haptics, Robotics*. [http://www.digicult.info/downloads/TWR3-highres.pdf] (Accessed 23.04.04)

Dormer, P. 1994. *The Art of the Maker*. London: Thames & Hudson.

Falk, J.H., Dierking, L.D. 1992. *The Museum Experience*. Washington, D.C.: Whalesback Books.

Frey, B.S., Kirshenblatt-Gimblett, B. 2002. Current debate: The dematerialisation of culture and the de-accessioning of museum collections. *Museum International* 54(4): 58–63.

Frisoli, A., Jansson, G., Bergamasco, M., Loscos, C. 2005. Evaluation of the pure-form haptic displays used for exploration of works of art at museums. *Proceedings, World Haptics 2005* (First Joint Eurohaptics/Symposium on Haptic Interfaces for Virtual Environment and Teleoperator Systems), IEEE Computer Society. [https://www.enactivenetwork.org/download.php?id=117] (Accessed 30.03.07)

Gaggioli, A. Breining, R. 2001. Perception and cognition in immersive virtual reality. In G. Riva and F. Davide (eds.), *Communications through Virtual Technology: Identity, Community, and Technology in the Internet Age*. Amsterdam: IOS Press, 71–86.

Geser, G., Pereira, J. 2004. *The Future Digital Heritage Space, an Expedition Report*. DigiCult: Thematic Issue 7. Information Society Technologies (IST) priority of the European Union's Fifth Framework Programme for Research and Technological Development. [http://www.digicult.info/downloads/dc_thematic_issue7.pdf] (Accessed 23.03.07)

Goulding, C. 2000. The museum environment and the visitor experience. *European Journal of Marketing* 34(3/4): 261–78.

Hansen, M. 2001. Embodying virtual reality: Touch and self-movement in the work of Char Davies. *Critical Matrix: The Princeton Journal of Women, Gender, and Culture* 12(1–2): 112–47.

Hassenzahl, M., Tractinsky, N. 2006. User experience, a research agenda [editorial]. *Empirical Studies of the User Experience* (special issue of *Behaviour & Information Technology*) 25(2): 91–97.

Hetherington, K. 2002. The unsightly: Touching the Parthenon frieze. *Theory, Culture, and Society* 19(5/6): 187–205.

Holden, J. and Jones, S. 2006. *Knowledge and Inspiration, the Democratic Face of Culture: Evidence in Making the Case for Museums, Libraries and Archives.* London: Museums, Libraries, and Archives Council (MLA).

Hooper-Greenhill, E. 1992. *Museums and the Shaping of Knowledge.* London and New York: Routledge.

——— 1994. *Museums and Their Visitors.* London: Routledge.

——— 1999. *Museums and Interpretive Communities.* 'Musing on Learning' seminar, Australian Museum. [http://www.amonline.net.au/amarc/pdf/research/paper2.pdf] (Accessed 21.07.05)

——— 2004. Measuring learning outcomes in museums, archives and libraries: The Learning Impact Research Project (LIRP). *International Journal of Heritage Studies* 10(2): 151–74.

Jansson, G., Ivas, A. 2000. *Can the Efficiency of a Haptic Display Be Increased by Short-Time Practice in Exploration?* Proceedings, First Workshop on Haptic Human Computer Interaction. Glasgow, Scotland: 22–27.

Jansson, G., Öström, M. 2004. The effects of co-location of visual and haptic space on judgements of form. *Proceedings of Eurohaptics 2004*, Munich, 516–19.

Jefsioutine, M., Knight, J. 2006. Design methods for experience design. In P.Z. Kurniawan (ed.), *Human Computer Interaction Research in Web Design and Evaluation.* London: Idea Group, 130–47.

Jonas, H. 1982. *The Phenomenon of Life.* Chicago: University of Chicago Press [cited in Hansen (2001)].

Kim, Y., Kesavadas, T., Paley, S.M. 2003. *The UBVSM: Real-time interactive museum for the northwest palace in Iraq. VSMM 2003. Proceedings, Ninth International Conference on Virtual Systems and MultiMedia, 'Hybrid Reality: Art, Technology, and the Human Factor'*, 54–61.

Kirkpatrick, A.E., Douglas, S.A. 2002. *Application-Based Evaluation of Haptic Interfaces.* Proceedings, Tenth Symposium on Haptic Interfaces for Virtual Environment and Teleoperator Systems. Washington, D.C.: IEEE Computer Society, 32.

Kolb, D.A. 1984. *Experiential Learning: Experience as the Source of Learning and Development.* Englewood Cliffs, NJ: Prentice-Hall.

Levoy, M., Pulli, K., Curless, B., Rusinkiewicz, S., Koller, D., Pereira, L., Ginzton, M., Anderson, S., Davis, J., Ginsberg, J., Shade, J., Fulk, D. 2000. The digital Michelangelo project: 3D scanning of large statues. *Proceedings, ACM SIGGRAPH 2000.* New Orleans, LA: ACM SIGGRAPH, 131–44.

Lipton, L. 1992. The future of autostereoscopic electronic displays. *Proceedings, SPIE Vol. 1669, Stereoscopic Displays and Applications III*, 156–62.

Loscos, C., Tecchia, F., Frisoli, A., Carrozzino, M., Ritter Widenfeld, H., Swapp, D., Bergamasco, M. 2004. The museum of pure form: Touching real statues in an immersive virtual museum. *Proceedings, 5th International Symposium on Virtual Reality, Archaeology, and Cultural Heritage (VAST 2004)*. Oudenaarde, Belgium: Eurographics Association, 271–79.

Mainemelis, C., Boyatzis, R., Kolb, D.A. 2002. Learning styles and adaptive flexibility: Testing the experiential learning theory of development. *Management* 33(1): 5–33.

McCullough, M. 1996. *Abstracting Craft: The Practiced Digital Hand*. Cambridge, MA: MIT Press.

McLaughlin, M.L., Sukhatme, G., Shahabi, C., Medioni, G. and Jaskowiak, J. 2000. The haptic museum. *Proceedings, EVA Conference on Electronic Imaging and the Visual Arts*, Florence, Italy. [http://infolab.usc.edu/Docs Demos/eva2000.pdf] (Accessed 26.03.07)

Morris Hargreaves McIntyre (research consultants). 2003. *Creating Engaging Exhibitions. A Report for Wolverhampton Art Gallery and Birmingham Museum and Art Gallery*. Internal report [unpublished].

Piaget, J. 1952. *The Origins of Intelligence in Children* (M. Cook, trans.). New York: International Universities Press.

Prytherch, D., Jerrard, R. 2001. The visualisation and making of sculpture and its potential implications for computer interfaces and three-dimensional modelling. In C. Baber, M. Faint, M.S. Wall, and A.M. Wing (eds.), *Proceedings Eurohaptics 2001*. Birmingham: Eurohaptics, 135–37.

Shillito, A.M., Gauldie, D., Wright, M. 2004. *Spatial Interaction: Six Degrees of Freedom for Computer Aided Design. Challenging Craft*. Aberdeen: Gray's School of Art. [http://www.eca.ac.uk/hands_on/Papers/spatialInteractPaper.pdf] (Accessed 27.03.07)

Shiode, N., Grajetzki, W. 2000. *A Virtual Exploration of the Lost Labyrinth: Developing a Reconstructive Model of Hawara Labyrinth Pyramid Complex*. CASA. London: University College London (UCL). [http://www.casa.ucl.ac.uk] (Accessed 17.05.06)

Slater, M., Linakis,V., Usoh, M., Kooper, R. 1996. Immersion, presence, and performance in virtual environments: An experiment with tri-dimensional chess. In M. Green (ed.), *ACM Virtual Reality Software and Technology (VRST)*, 163–72. [http://www.cs.ucl.ac.uk/staff/m.slater/Papers/Chess/conclusions_5.html] (Accessed 26.03.07)

Smith, D., Kolb, D. 1986. *User's Guide for the Learning Style Inventory: A Manual for Teachers and Trainers*. Boston: McBer.

Sonneveld, M. 2004. Dreamy hands: Exploring tactile aesthetics in design. In D. McDonagh, P. Hekkert, J. van Erp, and D. Gyi (eds.), *Design and Emotion: The Experience of Everyday Things*. London: Taylor & Francis, 228–32.

Srinivasani, M., Bastogani, C. 1997. Haptic displays in virtual environments: Taxonomy, research status, and challenges. *Computers & Graphics* 21(4): 393–404.

TASI 2006. Technical advisory services for images (home page). [http://www. tasi.ac.uk/advice/delivering/digital.html] (Accessed 26.03.07)

Terras, M.M. 1999. A virtual tomb for kelvingrove. Virtual reality, archaeology and education, *Internet Archaeology*. [http://intarch.ac.uk/journal/issue7/terras_index.html] (Accessed 26.03.07)

The Digital Michelangelo Project 2000 [online]. [http://graphics.stanford.edu/projects/mich/] (Accessed 26.03.07)

The Encyclopaedia of Virtual Environments 1993 [online]. [http://www.hitl. washington.edu/scivw/EVE/IV.Definitions.html] (Accessed 26.03.07)

vom Lehn, D., Heath, C., Hindmarsh, J. 2001. Exhibiting interaction: Conduct and collaboration in museums and galleries. *Symbolic Interaction* 24(2): 189–216.

vom Lehn, D., Heath, C., Knoblauch, H. 2001. Configuring exhibits: The interactional production of experience in museums and galleries. In H. Knoblauch and H. Kothoff (eds.), *Verbal Art across Cultures. The Aesthetics and Proto-Aesthetics of Communication*. Tübingen: Gunter Narr Verlag, 281–97.

Ward, V., Holtham, C. 2000. *Experimenting with Learning about Knowledge: The Art Exhibition and the Garden Shed*. Spark Knowledge Ltd. [online]. [http:// www.staff.city.ac.uk/~sf329/exhibition.pdf] (Accessed 26.03.07)

Wall, S.A., Paynter, K., Shillito, A.M., Wright, M., Scali, S. 2002. The effect of haptic feedback and stereo graphics in a 3D target acquisition task. In S.A. Wall, B. Riedel, A. Crossan, and M.R. McGee (eds.), *Proceedings Eurohaptics 2002*, Edinburgh. [online] [http://www.eurohaptics.vision.ee.ethz.ch/2002/ wall2.pdf] (Accessed 27.03.07)

Ware, C., Rose, J. 1999. Rotating virtual objects with real handles. *ACM Transactions on Computer-Human Interaction (TOCHI)* 6 (2): 162–80.

Wolek, F.W. 1999. The skill development processes of apprenticeship. *International Journal of Lifelong Education* 18(5): 395–406.

16

EXPLORING VIRTUAL TOUCH IN THE CREATIVE ARTS AND CONSERVATION

Angela Geary

Introduction

Haptic interaction devices provide computer users with the physical sensation of touch. Typically, they simulate the force-feedback aspect of haptic sensation by exerting a mechanical response to user actions. This response allows virtual objects to be manipulated—touched as if they occupied real space. Force feedback, experienced in conjunction with visual 3D computer models, can provide a highly realistic simulation of materials and objects.

The first haptic devices to appear, e.g. the Phantom (Massie & Salisbury 1994) developed at MIT in the late 1990s, were based on hand-held stylus control, with force being delivered via a motorised, articulated arm. Such devices provide a convincing interactive experience, particularly when simulating activities that normally involve a tool, like a knife or pencil.

The projects discussed in this chapter use stylus-based haptic interaction; however, this approach has its limitations. Haptic feedback is provided as a single point of interaction. The use of multiple devices can increase the degree of feedback, but this solution quickly becomes cumbersome and demands an inordinate amount of computer processing power. Likewise, the physical reach of the device restricts working space, and locating it in relation to the user's view of the computer display is also somewhat problematic. Positioning a haptic device near the side of the screen, in the area traditionally occupied by a mouse, isolates the visual experience from manual interaction. The result can be uncomfortable and diminish the user's sense of immersion in the virtual environment. This has been resolved in some systems, such as the Reachin Display (Reachin Technologies AB 2007) and the Immersive Workbench made by SenseGraphics (SenseGraphics AB 2007) by co-locating the user's actual hand position and the virtual scene, through the use of a transmissive visual display.

Intense research has been conducted in the field of haptic interaction technology and its application since the early 1990s. The most significant advances in haptics have taken place in the area of applied science and in industries where clear, real-world benefits have been identified and pursued. In particular, medical research has driven the early development and design of haptic interaction tools, with a focus on surgical training and, more recently, remote consulting. Haptic technology has also been exploited in areas such as nuclear power and military applications, where force feedback can enhance the usability and operator accuracy of remotely controlled robotic systems (Lee et al. 2006).

In recent years, however, rapid improvements in lower-cost computing power and the commercial availability of devices such as SensAble's Omni (SensAble Technologies Inc. 2007) have introduced haptics to a wider community. By citing two recent projects, this chapter will provide an overview of current haptic-driven research in the arts and cultural heritage.

Haptics and Art Practice

The development of skill and style are usually highly dependent on touch-based interaction and the physical manipulation of materials. Today, artists routinely use digital tools in the creation and production of their work. They do so, however, in full view of current technological limitations. An artist's ability to interact physically with traditional media—despite their natural constraints—remains a valued aspect of practice that conventional digital tools have previously been unable to offer. The increasing use of haptic interfaces offers the possibility for tremendous innovation within the digital applications used by designers and artists.

Haptics can return the tactile physicality to creative processes that take place in the digital realm. In three-dimensional (3D) digital environments, haptics offers particular advantages where direct spatial manipulation is far more intuitively, and rapidly, achieved by touch as opposed to menu-driven commands (Scali et al. 2003). This fact has resulted in the integration of haptic interaction modes in computer-aided design (CAD) and 3D computer modelling, with several well-known packages including FreeForm (SensAble Technologies Inc. 2007), a stand-alone, haptic-based CAD application that has since been adopted into the workflow of coin design and manufacture at the national mint in the United States (Worden 2006), indicating that haptics is beginning to have an impact on mainstream design practice.

These new and sophisticated tools are aimed principally at CAD specialists and industrial designers; unfortunately, the specific needs of fine artists are not addressed in the interface design or the application features. Although artists can certainly learn to use CAD-oriented tools and adapt them to their objectives, the specialist emphasis and steep learning curves associated with those applications often present significant barriers to immediate user productivity.

A Virtual Haptic Interface for Printmaking (VHIP)

The aims of this project were to prototype a straightforward haptic software application targeting engraved printmaking techniques (VHIP) and to advance the design of haptic software for artists in a field that has been dominated by CAD-oriented applications. Significant motivations were the desire to promote the integration of haptic interface technologies into artistic practice and to explore how such tools might evolve the nature of those practices. Although the use of digital printing techniques is commonplace, artists still crave the unique qualities that accompany prints made using traditional methods.

The physical process of preparing a printmaking plate can be laborious, requiring considerable amounts of time and skill. Using engraving as an example, a metal plate is incised with a burin, a cutting tool with a narrow metal shaft with a V-shaped profile at its cutting edge. The shaft is fixed in a rounded wooden handle, which the engraver holds in the heel of his hand and guides with the thumb and forefinger. Through substantial physical effort, the engraver drives the burin into the metal, cutting a groove in the plate. Simultaneously, he must manoeuvre the plate with his opposite hand to control the direction of the groove.

The VHIP application provides an interim creative platform that allows free experimentation facilitated by a 'soft' virtual metallic simulation (Geary et al. 2006) The application serves as an additional tool, thus forming a hybrid creative process that involves traditional analogue and digital procedures. The virtual plates can be output as data suitable for production of physical plates by computer-aided manufacturing (CAM) technologies, to include computer numeric-control milling or laser engraving (Figure 16.1). The manufactured plate may then be used in the artist's production of the final print (Figure 16.2).

In conjunction with the standard benefits of working digitally, such as saving, undoing, and layering, a haptic virtual environment offers advantages as an additional stage in the printmaking process. Prototyping a plate virtually prior to its manufacture avoids the physical difficulty of engraving a metal plate. Engraving tolerates very few errors: a mark, once made, is permanent. An artist working virtually, however, has unlimited scope to explore ideas before committing to a physical plate.

Haptic technology is changing not only the techniques used in intaglio printmaking but also its very nature. The range of plate materials available to the printmaker has been broadened by the integration of CAM processes, including the availability of non-traditional media such as synthetic resins. Moreover, a single plate design can be used

Figure 16.1 A relief-printing synthetic resin plate developed in a virtual, haptic environment and manufactured by computer numeric control milling.

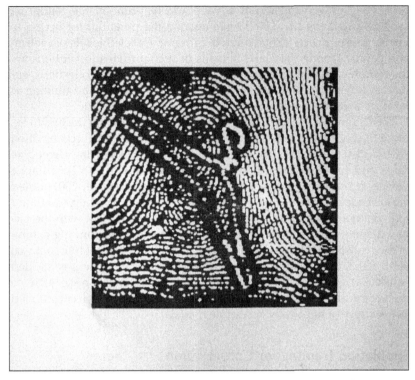

Figure 16.2 'Coat Hanger', a relief-print produced via haptic computer interaction, by Paul Coldwell. Reproduced by kind permission of the artist.

in the production of multiple physical output formats. There are also intangible benefits to be derived from these technological advances; for example, haptic-based processes can enable disabled artists, who might otherwise be unduly challenged by traditional processes, to resume their practice.

Haptic Interaction Applications in Cultural Heritage

We acquire much of our information about the texture, form, and weight of materials through touch. But touching is neither universally practical nor acceptable, e.g. in museums where preservation concerns necessarily restrict touch access. Technology can provide a means of replacing this 'missing' aspect of a museum experience.

Models derived from 3D digitisation technologies, such as laser scanning, can be used to create highly realistic, virtual facsimiles suitable for visual and haptic representation. The availability of greater computer processing power and recent advances in real-time visual rendering systems (3D Labs Inc. 2007) have created the potential for access to virtual museum artefacts rendered with unparalleled levels of realism and detail. Among the many benefits of such virtual substitutions are the remote study of objects, virtual handling of fragile collections, enhanced access for blind and visually impaired visitors, and training in heritage professions such as conservation and art handling.

The Digimuse project (Goldberg et al. 1998) was among the first to explore the haptic presentation of virtual museum objects in combination with a visual display. The project digitised embossed daguerreotype cases and presented the digital models using the PHANToM haptic device. A similar project at Glasgow University (Brewster 2001) tested various haptic virtual-display scenarios in a museum setting and found that visitors reported a much higher level of engagement with the virtual display when it was presented alongside a corresponding exhibit of the real object. More recently, The PURE-FORM project (Bergamasco et al. 2002), in collaboration with several European museums, tackled subjects of greater complexity. Employing 3D laser scanning to create high-resolution 3D models of figurative sculpture, the project compiled a repository of haptically accessible models.

Simulation Training for Conservation

In order to achieve adequate competence in treating delicate and irreplaceable works of art, students being trained in conservation techniques must accumulate many hours of experience in a variety of related manual tasks. They must also become familiar with the behaviours of a range of materials. Haptics, combined with visual computer interaction, offers a means of creating a simulation training system for conservators.

Simulated conservation operations can be performed without risk to the artefact while skills are being built. Additionally, training can be accelerated through aural or visual performance feedback, which reinforces appropriate techniques and alerts to inappropriate actions such as use of excessive force. Simulation software can also track progress by compiling statistical data on student performance that can be periodically reviewed by the tutor.

A typical, yet significant problem in preserving works of art on paper is the removal of aged and degraded backing material adhered to the reverse of original examples. This challenging conservation task was the focus for the study (Figure 16.3). Fragile and delicate watercolours or prints can be damaged by the presence of poor-quality, often highly acidic paper or board backings. Moisture or solvent-based treatments,

Figure 16.3 A complex backing removal from the reverse of an eighteenth-century print, in progress.

such as soaking or steam humidification, can be effective for backing removal, but may not be feasible due to the sensitivity of the original object. The use of hand tools such as scalpels and spatulas often provides the only viable means of detaching these backings. Mechanical removal, although slow and exacting, allows greater degrees of precision and damage prevention.

The length of a typical conservation course is finite; however, developing acumen in the necessary range of diverse manual skills requires a considerable amount of time. This education process is also risky because students typically hone their techniques on genuine works of art. Simulation training may help mitigate the challenges associated with such instruction by allowing students to acquire and practice critical manual skills virtually, before applying them on real objects. Additionally, there is real hope that simulation training might facilitate a reduction in the amount of time usually required by conservation students to master the difficult process of removing backings.

In the simulation prototype, the physical characteristics and dynamic properties of paper-based art—and their backings—are modelled according to values from existing conservation research and paper-industry standards (Mark 1993). The entire process is conducted in conjunction with empirical evaluation carried out by experienced conservators, and the simulation affords the possibility to adjust parameters for properties such as stiffness, friction, texture, relief, and recognised deformation characteristics. Future versions will include a greater range of variable physical effects, including material type and the relative humidity of the environment.

Haptic simulation is already used in medical training, and evaluation of skill acquisition in surgical simulations has yielded positive results (Gorman 1998). Haptic tasks, however, are highly individualised. Therefore, data obtained from an application such as surgery cannot be used to validate the haptic training conducted in a dissimilar field such as art conservation. As a result, a programme of field testing was conducted to determine whether skill development actually occurred among a group of fifteen novice conservation students.

The group used the simulator for short periods of time over a four-week period and participated in a sequence of performance tests. Interaction data, including force exerted, hand orientation, and the degree of contact, were collected by the simulation software—via the haptic device—during each test. The objective measurement of dexterity was problematic in the absence of any established standards. In this case, three key skill factors were identified, in consultation with conservation practitioners, as assessment criteria for the tests: the maximum force exerted, the tool orientation, and instances of undesirable contact with the fabric of the original artefact. These skills corresponded to the essential elements of real-world backing removal: applied force and angle of incidence of the scalpel blade. The level of force applied to the backing represents a significant factor because too little force will produce a negligible effect and too great a force could result in undesirable damage.

The angle of incidence of the scalpel to the object plane must be kept low in order to remove shallow amounts of backing material gradually. A higher angle of incidence increases the risk of penetrating the reverse side of the original paper with the blade. Any contact, however slight, between the scalpel and the original paper during removal of the backing material can potentially cause damage.

In tests, each instance of contact with the virtual backing and paper was recorded, as were the force values and angle of incidence relative to the haptic device. These data allowed the calculation of an overall score for each subject tested. A baseline score was derived from the first set of tests, while the data from subsequent tests were interpreted comparatively to evaluate whether skill improvement was taking place.

In the test group, two novice student types appeared to emerge: the 'tentative' and the 'over-confident'. Typically, for the 'tentative', the peak force score began low and increased in significant increments for the first three sessions before it levelled off. For the 'over-confident', the force and damage contact scores started at a high value and decreased steadily towards a more moderate result by the third session. The best performers had higher average force values with low contact damage frequency. The angle-of-incidence data was found to vary in relation to the other performance indicators. Interpretation of this factor was found to be of limited value to the test, probably because of the physical restrictions of the haptic device when compared to a fully mobile hand tool. Of particular note, however, was that these test results suggested that skill improvement occurred in the majority of both subject types, thus confirming the viability of simulation training for this and possibly other haptic tasks in conservation.

Future Directions for Haptic Interaction

Single-point haptic interaction provides a surprisingly convincing simulation experience and can be of significant value in many applications. There are, however, some considerations that must be made when adopting the technology. The range of perceptual information that such a device can deliver is much more restricted than that of normal human haptic exploration. Pinching and grasping actions, for example, are impossible. Touch-based information acquisition relative to scale and contour is also limited (Wall and Brewster 2004). In addition, it is important to note that other forms of somatic sensory information normally gathered via the skin, including thermal properties and fine surface texture, are completely lacking in currently available technologies.

The visual component of a virtual interaction environment provides essential cues that allow users to accommodate the perceptual deficiencies of single-point haptic interaction. Unfortunately, such cues are not always available. Blind or partially sighted users, for example, experience extreme difficulty navigating the virtual space with only a single point of spatial reference. Motivated by the need to more closely approximate natural human interaction, researchers are pursuing improvements to haptics (e.g. multi-fingered haptic devices).

Psychophysical research has concluded that a two- and, ideally, three-fingered haptic grasp provides feedback that is much closer to real-world interaction and allows a more natural orientation of the hand (McKnight et al. 2004). A triple-finger PHANToM-based haptic system, developed at the University of Reading (Wall & Harwin 2001), is presently being evaluated for its usability. Significantly, it has been suggested that three-finger interaction is optimal for the acquisition of haptic information: four or five haptic points do not necessarily provide additional perceptual benefits in a one-handed scenario. Jansson and Monaci (2006, 243–49) suggest that, for object identification, 'providing spatially distributed information at the contact areas is more important than increasing the number of areas'.

An obvious and significant physiological factor in haptic perception is that humans use both hands in real-world interaction. We instinctively use our own bodies to their fullest potential as frames of reference in our exploration of the world. In practice, the non-dominant hand usually holds an object, thus obtaining a static frame of spatial reference, whilst the dominant hand explores. This deeply embedded behaviour, known as 'egocentric reference' (Luyat et al. 2001, 542), is clearly manifest in haptic exploration.

The development of bi-manual haptic interaction systems remains an unresolved challenge in haptic technological research. However, specialist bi-manual device arrangements for simulations including laparoscopic surgical investigations (Basdogan et al. 2001) and robotic telepresence (Buss et al. 2006) have been successfully developed. Universal device designs such as the SPIDAR G&G (Murayama et al. 2004) are promising, but still offer only one point of haptic feedback per hand.

There is a considerable amount of activity focused on computer-interaction design and ergonomics research with an eye towards developing alternatives to the standard mouse and keyboard interface. Gesture interaction via hand signing and specialist gesture syntax (Barker et al. 2007) is one development. Recent advances in computer vision have finally enabled remote operation. In fact, communicating with a computer is no longer dependent on contact with, or proximity to, the physical device. Gesture interaction offers exciting potential and may provide a hybrid solution to bi-manual control. This feature could be unobtrusively integrated alongside haptic devices, with a minimum of additional processing demands and hardware components.

Much has already been achieved with haptic technology. Demonstrably, haptic interaction is best implemented where it can provide the greatest perceptual value. In simple point-and-click tasks, for example, extraneous haptic feedback would not benefit the user. As a result, haptic technology probably will not displace conventional computer interaction. Rather, it is likely that haptics will continue to be focused on specialist applications where the technology offers desirable perceptual enhancement or cognitive performance benefits.

The emerging reality is that current needs for sophisticated and highly authentic haptic interaction—capabilities that match the realism of contemporary visual display technology—far outstrip the capabilities of available technology. However, when breakthroughs in the design and features of device technology are achieved, they will doubtlessly stimulate newer and more exciting advances in haptic applications.

References

3D Labs Inc., OpenGL Shading Language [online]. [http://developer.3dlabs.com/openGL2/index.htm] (Accessed 15.01.07)

Barker, L., Geary, A., Harrison, J.P. 2007. Towards an ergonomic gestural interface for computers. *Proceedings, Ergonomics Society Conference*, Nottingham University, UK.

Basdogan, C., Ho, C., Srinivasan, M.A. 2001. Virtual environments for medical training: Graphical and haptic simulation of common bile duct exploration. *IEEE Transactions on Mechatronics* 6(3): 269–85.

Bergamasco, M., Frisoli, A., Barbagli, F. 2002. Haptics technologies and cultural heritage applications. *Proceedings Computer Animation*, 25–32.

Brewster, S.A. 2001. The impact of haptic 'touching' technology on cultural applications. *Proceedings EVA Scotland*, 1–14.

Buss, M., Kuschel, K., Lee, K., Peer, A., Ueberle, M., Stanczyk, B. 2006. High-fidelity telepresence systems: Design, control, and evaluation. *Proceedings, Joint International COE/HAM–SFB453 Workshop on Human Adaptive Mechatronics and High-Fidelity Telepresence*, Tokyo, 57–62.

Geary, A., Coldwell, M., and Rashan, A. 2006. VHIP: A prototype haptic environment for fine art printmakers. *Proceedings Eurohaptics*, 639–41.

Goldberg, S. B., Bekey, G.A., Akatsuka, Y. 1998. DIGIMUSE: Interactive remote viewing of three-dimensional art objects. *Telemanipulator and Telepresence Technologies V*, (3524–26). Proceedings, SPIE.

Gorman, P., Lieser, J., Murray, W., Haluck, R., Krummel, T. 1998. Assessment and validation of a force feedback virtual reality based surgical simulator. *Proceedings, Third PHANToM Users' Group Workshop*, Cambridge, Massachusetts, 27–29.

Jansson, G., Monaci, L. 2006. Identification of real objects under conditions similar to those in haptic displays: Providing spatially distributed information at the contact areas is more important than increasing the number of areas. *Virtual Reality* 9(3): 243–49.

Lee, S., Sukhatme G., Kim, G. J., Park, C. 2006. Haptic teleoperation of a mobile robot: A user study. *Presence: Teleoperation Virtual Environments*, 14(3): 345–65.

Luyat, M., Gentaz, E., Corte, T.R., Guerraz, M. 2001.Reference frames and haptic perception of orientation: Body and head tilt effects on the oblique effect. *Perceptual Psychophysics* 63(3): 541–54.

Mark, R.E. (ed.). 1993. *Handbook of Physical and Mechanical Testing of Paper and Paperboard* 1 & 2. New York: Marcel Dekker.

Massie, T.H., Salisbury, J.K. 1994. The PHANTOM Haptic interface: A device for probing virtual objects. *Symposium on haptic interfaces for virtual environment and teleoperator systems. Proceedings, ASME Winter Annual Meeting*, Chicago, 295–302.

McKnight, S., Melder, N., Barrow, A.L., Harwin, W.S., Wann, J.P. 2004. Psychophysical size discrimination using multi-fingered haptic interfaces *Proceedings of EuroHaptics 2004*, Munich, 274-81.

Murayama, J., Bougrila, L., Luo, Y.L., Akahane, K., Hasegawa, S., Hirsbrunner, B., Sato, M. 2004. SPIDAR G&G: A new two-handed haptic interface for bimanual VR interaction. *Proceedings of EuroHaptics 2004*, Munich, 138–46.

Reachin Technologies AB [online]. *History*. [http://www.reachin.se/companyinfo/history/] (Accessed 15.01.07)

Scali, S., Wright, M., Shillito, A.M. 2003. 3D modelling is not for WIMPs. *Proceedings, Tenth International Conference on Human-Computer Interaction*, Crete, 701–05.

SensAble Technologies Inc. [online]. PHANTOM Omni Haptic Device. [http://www.sensable.com/haptic-phantom-omni.htm] (Accessed 15.01.07)

SensAble Technologies Inc. [online]. *SensAble Technologies Announces FreeForm Concept Version 1.0 with PHANToM Omni*. [http://www.sensable.com/pr_20031107b/news-archive-detail.htm] (Accessed 15.01.07)

SenseGraphics AB [online]. Immersive Workbench. [http://www.sensegraphics.com/products.php] (Accessed 15.01.07)

Wall, S., Brewster, S. 2004. Providing external memory aids in haptic visualisations for blind computer users. *Proceedings, Fifth International Conference on Disability, Virtual Reality & Associated Technology*, University of Reading, UK, 151–64.

Wall, S.A., Harwin, W.S. 2001. Design of a multiple contact point haptic interface. *Proceedings of Eurohaptics 2001*, University of Birmingham, UK, 146–48.

Worden, L. 2006, November. No small change at the mint. *COINage Magazine*.

INDEX

ABOUT THE CONTRIBUTORS

Fiona Candlin is Lecturer in Museum Studies at Birkbeck College and The British Museum, where she is course director for the World Arts and Artefacts and Collections programmes. A Leverhulme Fellowship enabled her to develop a cross disciplinary analysis of touch in relation to museums, art history, and audiences.

Julia Cassim is Senior Research Fellow at the Royal College of Art Helen Hamlyn Centre. Her research focuses on inclusive design knowledge transfer mechanisms in partnership with disabled people. She is Visiting Professor at Kyushu University, Japan, where she was arts columnist for *The Japan Times* and founded Access Vision.

Jan Geisbusch is a doctoral student in the Department of Anthropology at University College London. His research focuses on popular religion, the cult of saints and its material aspects, in particular within the Roman Catholic Church. For his thesis he has recently carried out fieldwork in Rome and through eBay.

Angela Geary is Reader in Visual Interpretation of Cultural Heritage and directs SCIRIA at University of the Arts London. Her research interests include multisensory interaction and the development of accessible 3D computer visualisation techniques for cultural heritage. Her consultation clients include the National Trust and Historic Royal Palaces.

Mark Geller holds a BA from Princeton and a PhD from Brandeis. He is currently Professor of Semitic Languages at University College London.

He holds research fellowships at the Alexander von Humboldt-Stiftung, the Netherlands Institute of Advanced Study, National Endowment for the Humanities (USA), and the Wellcome Trust.

Christos Giachritsis took a degree in sociology from Panteion University in Athens, then moved to Birmingham, completing a PhD on vision in 2000, and obtaining a BSc in mathematics from the Open University. He is currently Haptics Researcher in a virtual reality project at Birmingham that is funded by the European Commission.

Claire Jacques took an MA in museum studies at Leicester in 1998, then became a Collections Manager for Lincolnshire Heritage Services. In 2002 she moved into the education and access field in museums and galleries. She is now the Community Engagement Manager for Lincolnshire County Council Culture and Adult Education.

Marie Jefsioutine is Faculty Research Fellow at Birmingham Institute of Art and Design, University of Central England, Birmingham, researching user-centred design and design research methods. Having worked in multimedia design for many years at the Open University and Goldsmith's College, she has particular interests in design, e-learning and museum interactives.

Jessica Johnson, Senior Objects Conservator, National Museum of the American Indian, received an MA in anthropology from the University of Arizona, in 1986 and a BSc in conservation from the Institute of Archaeology, University College London, 1990. Current research involves community consultation in conservation and identification of pesticides on museum collections.

Sharareh Khayami is the founder and director of BlindArt. Sheri is visually impaired and has always been a patron of the arts, supporting young artists through commissions. Through exhibitions of **Sense &** Sensuality and the BlindArt Permanent Collection, Sheri promotes touching art to both the arts sector and general public.

Andrew Lamb has worked with historical musical instruments since 1986. He studied musical instrument conservation at the Royal College of Art and the Victoria and Albert Museum, then worked with a number of music collections before becoming conservator at the Bate Collection of Musical Instruments, Faculty of Music, Oxford.

Sally MacDonald is Director of UCL Museums and Collections. She has worked in museums for over 20 years, leading museums of archaeology, decorative arts, and social history, and winning awards for innovation and achievement. She has been involved in several interdisciplinary projects exploring ideas related to touch and handling.

David Prytherch is a Research Fellow in Haptics at User-lab, Birmingham Institute of Art and Design, University of Central England, Birmingham. Research interests include haptic perception and skill development in the arts and perceptual factors in experience satisfaction and process motivation in the development of human–computer interface systems for creativity.

Elizabeth Pye holds an MA in archaeology and Diploma in conservation, and is Senior Lecturer at UCL Institute of Archaeology. She leads the conservation team for the international archaeological project at Çatalhöyük, Turkey, and has particular interests in heritage and conservation in Africa and in issues of access to museum collections.

Roberta Roberts graduated in computer science and psychology at Birmingham in 1996. After working on website development for the Health Service, she took an MRes in cognitive sciences followed by a PhD on touch in psychology at Birmingham, where since 2005 she has held a postdoctoral research fellowship in psychology.

Michael Rowlands is Professor of Anthropology at UCL. His research interests are in material culture, cultural heritage, and long-term change. Recent publications include *Social Transformations in Archaeology* (with Kristian Kristiansen), *Handbook of Material Culture* (with Chris Tilley et al.) and *Heritage and Memory in Africa* (with Ferdinand de Jong).

Charles Spence is head of the Crossmodal Research Laboratory, Department of Experimental Psychology, Oxford University. For the last ten years, he has been University Lecturer in Experimental Psychology at Oxford. His research focuses on understanding the senses and has major implications for the design of everything we use daily.

Emily Tabassi is the Learning and Access Officer for Nottingham Museums. A former primary-school teacher, she has a degree in live and performance art and an MA in museums and heritage management. She began her museum career in a contemporary art gallery and as a freelance museum educator.

Tara Trewinnard-Boyle is the Learning and Access Assistant for Nottingham Museums. She has a degree in archaeology and will complete her MA in museum studies in 2008. A former Royal Air Force Officer, she began her museum career in 2004 as project officer on the redevelopment of an archaeology gallery.

Alan Wing took his undergraduate psychology degree at Edinburgh, PhD at McMaster University, and, after a postdoctoral fellowship at Bell Labs, New Jersey, joined the MRC Applied Psychology Unit in Cambridge. In 1997 he was awarded a chair in Human Movement at Birmingham, becoming Director of Research for Psychology in 2001.

Printed in the United States
by Baker & Taylor Publisher Services